MW00358618

DISCARD

THIS IS YOUR **PASSBOOK®** FOR ...

GENERAL APTITUDE TEST (BATTERY)

NLC®

NATIONAL LEARNING CORPORATION®
passbooks.com

PASSBOOK® SERIES

THE *PASSBOOK® SERIES* has been created to prepare applicants and candidates for the ultimate academic battlefield – the examination room.

At some time in our lives, each and every one of us may be required to take an examination – for validation, matriculation, admission, qualification, registration, certification, or licensure.

Based on the assumption that every applicant or candidate has met the basic formal educational standards, has taken the required number of courses, and read the necessary texts, the *PASSBOOK® SERIES* furnishes the one special preparation which may assure passing with confidence, instead of failing with insecurity. Examination questions – together with answers – are furnished as the basic vehicle for study so that the mysteries of the examination and its compounding difficulties may be eliminated or diminished by a sure method.

This book is meant to help you pass your examination provided that you qualify and are serious in your objective.

The entire field is reviewed through the huge store of content information which is succinctly presented through a provocative and challenging approach – the question-and-answer method.

A climate of success is established by furnishing the correct answers at the end of each test.

You soon learn to recognize types of questions, forms of questions, and patterns of questioning. You may even begin to anticipate expected outcomes.

You perceive that many questions are repeated or adapted so that you can gain acute insights, which may enable you to score many sure points.

You learn how to confront new questions, or types of questions, and to attack them confidently and work out the correct answers.

You note objectives and emphases, and recognize pitfalls and dangers, so that you may make positive educational adjustments.

Moreover, you are kept fully informed in relation to new concepts, methods, practices, and directions in the field.

You discover that you arre actually taking the examination all the time: you are preparing for the examination by "taking" an examination, not by reading extraneous and/or supererogatory textbooks.

In short, this PASSBOOK®, used directedly, should be an important factor in helping you to pass your test.

SAMPLE QUESTIONS

It is important that all candidates study the instructions and questions on this form before the day of the examination. No samples will be provided in the examination room except for the abstract reasoning questions.

Each question has five suggested answers lettered A, B, C, D, and E. Decide which one is the best answer to the question. On the Sample Answer Sheet, find the answer space numbered the same as the question and darken completely the box lettered the same as the best suggested answer. Then compare your answers with the answers given in the Correct Answers to Sample Questions. Use the blank spaces on this sheet as scratch paper. During the examination, use the blank spaces in the test booklet as scratch paper.

Sample Questions 1 through 4—*Verbal Abilities*

1. MANDATORY means most nearly
   A) basic
   B) obligatory
   C) discretionary
   D) discriminatory
   E) advisory

2. SURVEILLANCE means most nearly
   A) continued confinement
   B) indefinite parole
   C) constant protection
   D) unwarranted suspicion
   E) close supervision

3. (*Reading*) "Whenever two groups of people whose interests at the moment conflict meet to discuss a solution of that conflict, there is laid the basis for an interchange of facts and ideas which increases the total range of knowledge of both parties and tends to break down the barrier which their restricted field of information has helped to create."

   Select the alternative that is best supported by the quotation. Conflicts between two parties may be brought closer to a settlement through
   A) frank acknowledgment of error
   B) the exchange of accusations
   C) gaining a wider knowledge of facts
   D) submitting the dispute to an impartial judge
   E) limiting discussion to plans acceptable to both groups

4. (*Reading*) "One of the primary steps in the development of management in any enterprise is proper organization. After the business has been conceived and the broad policies that are to be pursued have been established, before any operating methods may be devised, at least a skeleton organization must be developed."

   Select the alternative that is best supported by the quotation. In industry, some kind of organization is necessary in order that
   A) the type of enterprise may be decided upon
   B) policies may be established
   C) routine work may be planned
   D) capital may be invested
   E) a manager may be selected

Sample Questions 5 through 9—*Abstract Reasoning*

In each of these questions, look at the symbols in the first two boxes. Something about the three symbols in the first box makes them alike; something about the two symbols in the other box with the question mark makes them alike. Look for some characteristic that is common to all symbols in the same box, yet makes them different from the symbols in the other box. Among the five answer choices, find the symbol that can best be substituted for the question mark, because it is *like* the symbols in the second box, and, *for the same reason*, different from those in the first box.

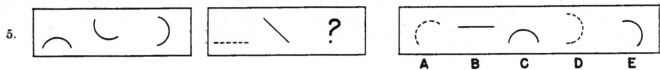

In question 5, all the symbols in the first box are curved lines. The second box has two lines, one dotted and one solid. Their *likeness* to each other consists in their straightness; and this straightness makes them *different* from the curves in the other box. The answer must be the *only* one of the five lettered choices that is a straight line, either dotted or solid. Now do questions 6 through 9.

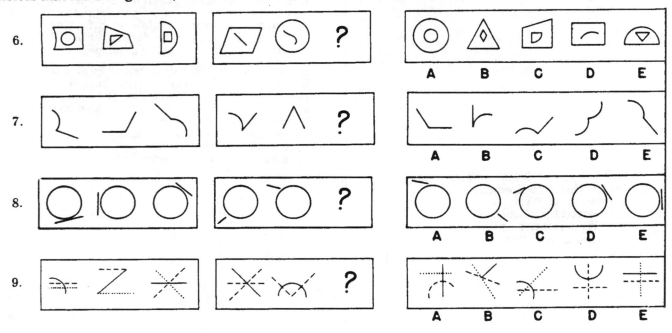

NOTE.—There is not supposed to be a *series* or progression in these symbol questions. If you look for a progression in the first box and try to find the missing figure to fill out a similar progression in the second box, you will be wasting time. For example, look at question 5. A competitor who saw that both boxes had a horizontal figure followed by an oblique one might try to find a vertical figure to match the last one in the first box. If he chose D he would be missing the real point of the question. Remember, look for a *likeness* within each box and a *difference* between the two boxes.

SAMPLE ANSWER SHEET						CORRECT ANSWERS TO SAMPLE QUESTIONS				
	A	B	C	D	E	A	B	C	D	E
5	☐	☐	☐	☐	☐	☐	▮	☐	☐	☐
6	☐	☐	☐	☐	☐	☐	☐	☐	▮	☐
7	☐	☐	☐	☐	☐	☐	▮	☐	☐	☐
8	☐	☐	☐	☐	☐	▮	☐	☐	☐	☐
9	☐	☐	☐	☐	☐	☐	☐	☐	▮	☐

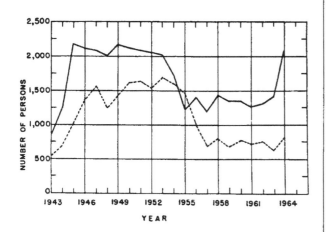

POPULATION MOVEMENT TO AND FROM COUNTY X
1943 TO 1964

MOVING TO COUNTY ----------
MOVING FROM COUNTY ————

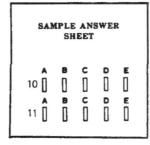

SAMPLE ANSWER
SHEET

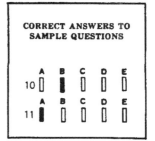

CORRECT ANSWERS TO
SAMPLE QUESTIONS

10. The graph above indicates that, with respect to County X, migratory activities during the period from 1943 to 1964 tended mostly to result in
A) population gains
B) population losses
C) gradual stabilization of population
D) irregular fluctuations in population without consistent direction
E) cycles of alternating losses and gains in population which tended to balance each other

11. According to the table below, which industry division showed the greatest percentage increase from 1945 to 1960?
A) Contract Construction
B) Manufacturing
C) Trade
D) Service
E) Government

EMPLOYEES IN NONAGRICULTURAL ESTABLISHMENTS BY INDUSTRY, 1940–1960

(In thousands)

Industry Division	1940	1945	1950	1955	1960
Mining	916	826	901	792	712
Contract Construction	1,294	1,132	2,333	2,802	2,885
Manufacturing	10,870	15,302	15,241	16,882	16,796
Transportation and Public Utilities	3,013	3,872	4,034	4,141	4,004
Trade	6,940	7,522	9,386	10,535	11,391
Finance	1,419	1,394	1,919	2,335	2,669
Service	3,477	4,055	5,382	6,274	7,392
Government	4,192	5,967	6,026	6,914	8,520

HOW TO TAKE A TEST

You have studied long, hard and conscientiously.

With your official admission card in hand, and your heart pounding, you have been admitted to the examination room.

You note that there are several hundred other applicants in the examination room waiting to take the same test.

They all appear to be equally well prepared.

You know that nothing but your best effort will suffice. The "moment of truth" is at hand: you now have to demonstrate objectively, in writing, your knowledge of content and your understanding of subject matter.

You are fighting the most important battle of your life—to pass and/or score high on an examination which will determine your career and provide the economic basis for your livelihood.

What extra, special things should you know and should you do in taking the examination?

I. YOU MUST PASS AN EXAMINATION

A. WHAT EVERY CANDIDATE SHOULD KNOW
Examination applicants often ask us for help in preparing for the written test. What can I study in advance? What kinds of questions will be asked? How will the test be given? How will the papers be graded?

B. HOW ARE EXAMS DEVELOPED?
Examinations are carefully written by trained technicians who are specialists in the field known as "psychological measurement," in consultation with recognized authorities in the field of work that the test will cover. These experts recommend the subject matter areas or skills to be tested; only those knowledges or skills important to your success on the job are included. The most reliable books and source materials available are used as references. Together, the experts and technicians judge the difficulty level of the questions.

Test technicians know how to phrase questions so that the problem is clearly stated. Their ethics do not permit "trick" or "catch" questions. Questions may have been tried out on sample groups, or subjected to statistical analysis, to determine their usefulness.

Written tests are often used in combination with performance tests, ratings of training and experience, and oral interviews. All of these measures combine to form the best-known means of finding the right person for the right job.

II. HOW TO PASS THE WRITTEN TEST

A. BASIC STEPS

1) Study the announcement

How, then, can you know what subjects to study? Our best answer is: "Learn as much as possible about the class of positions for which you've applied." The exam will test the knowledge, skills and abilities needed to do the work.

Your most valuable source of information about the position you want is the official exam announcement. This announcement lists the training and experience qualifications. Check these standards and apply only if you come reasonably close to meeting them. Many jurisdictions preview the written test in the exam announcement by including a section called "Knowledge and Abilities Required," "Scope of the Examination," or some similar heading. Here you will find out specifically what fields will be tested.

2) Choose appropriate study materials

If the position for which you are applying is technical or advanced, you will read more advanced, specialized material. If you are already familiar with the basic principles of your field, elementary textbooks would waste your time. Concentrate on advanced textbooks and technical periodicals. Think through the concepts and review difficult problems in your field.

These are all general sources. You can get more ideas on your own initiative, following these leads. For example, training manuals and publications of the government agency which employs workers in your field can be useful, particularly for technical and professional positions. A letter or visit to the government department involved may result in more specific study suggestions, and certainly will provide you with a more definite idea of the exact nature of the position you are seeking.

3) Study this book!

III. KINDS OF TESTS

Tests are used for purposes other than measuring knowledge and ability to perform specified duties. For some positions, it is equally important to test ability to make adjustments to new situations or to profit from training. In others, basic mental abilities not dependent on information are essential. Questions which test these things may not appear as pertinent to the duties of the position as those which test for knowledge and information. Yet they are often highly important parts of a fair examination. For very general questions, it is almost impossible to help you direct your study efforts. What we can do is to point out some of the more common of these general abilities needed in public service positions and describe some typical questions.

1) General information

Broad, general information has been found useful for predicting job success in some kinds of work. This is tested in a variety of ways, from vocabulary lists to questions about current events. Basic background in some field of work, such as sociology or economics, may be sampled in a group of questions. Often these are principles which have become familiar to most persons through exposure rather than through formal training. It is difficult to advise you how to study for these questions; being alert to the world around you is our best suggestion.

2) Verbal ability

An example of an ability needed in many positions is verbal or language ability. Verbal ability is, in brief, the ability to use and understand words. Vocabulary and grammar tests are typical measures of this ability. Reading comprehension or paragraph interpretation questions are common in many kinds of civil service tests. You are given a paragraph of written material and asked to find its central meaning.

IV. KINDS OF QUESTIONS

1. Multiple-choice Questions

Most popular of the short-answer questions is the "multiple choice" or "best answer" question. It can be used, for example, to test for factual knowledge, ability to solve problems or judgment in meeting situations found at work.

A multiple-choice question is normally one of three types:
- It can begin with an incomplete statement followed by several possible endings. You are to find the one ending which *best* completes the statement, although some of the others may not be entirely wrong.
- It can also be a complete statement in the form of a question which is answered by choosing one of the statements listed.
- It can be in the form of a problem – again you select the best answer.

Here is an example of a multiple-choice question with a discussion which should give you some clues as to the method for choosing the right answer:

When an employee has a complaint about his assignment, the action which will *best* help him overcome his difficulty is to
A. discuss his difficulty with his coworkers
B. take the problem to the head of the organization
C. take the problem to the person who gave him the assignment
D. say nothing to anyone about his complaint

In answering this question, you should study each of the choices to find which is best. Consider choice "A" – Certainly an employee may discuss his complaint with fellow employees, but no change or improvement can result, and the complaint remains unresolved. Choice "B" is a poor choice since the head of the organization probably does not know what assignment you have been given, and taking your problem to him is known as "going over the head" of the supervisor. The supervisor, or person who made the assignment, is the person who can clarify it or correct any injustice. Choice "C" is, therefore, correct. To say nothing, as in choice "D," is unwise. Supervisors have and interest in knowing the problems employees are facing, and the employee is seeking a solution to his problem.

2. True/False

3. Matching Questions
Matching an answer from a column of choices within another column.

V. RECORDING YOUR ANSWERS

Computer terminals are used more and more today for many different kinds of exams.
For an examination with very few applicants, you may be told to record your answers in the test booklet itself. Separate answer sheets are much more common. If this separate answer sheet is to be scored by machine – and this is often the case – it is highly important that you mark your answers correctly in order to get credit.

VI. BEFORE THE TEST

YOUR PHYSICAL CONDITION IS IMPORTANT
If you are not well, you can't do your best work on tests. If you are half asleep, you can't do your best either. Here are some tips:

1) Get about the same amount of sleep you usually get. Don't stay up all night before the test, either partying or worrying—DON'T DO IT!
2) If you wear glasses, be sure to wear them when you go to take the test. This goes for hearing aids, too.
3) If you have any physical problems that may keep you from doing your best, be sure to tell the person giving the test. If you are sick or in poor health, you relay cannot do your best on any test. You can always come back and take the test some other time.

Common sense will help you find procedures to follow to get ready for an examination. Too many of us, however, overlook these sensible measures. Indeed, nervousness and fatigue have been found to be the most serious reasons why applicants fail to do their best on civil service tests. Here is a list of reminders:

• Begin your preparation early – Don't wait until the last minute to go scurrying around for books and materials or to find out what the position is all about.
• Prepare continuously – An hour a night for a week is better than an all-night cram session. This has been definitely established. What is more, a night a week for a month will return better dividends than crowding your study into a shorter period of time.
• Locate the place of the exam – You have been sent a notice telling you when and where to report for the examination. If the location is in a different town or otherwise unfamiliar to you, it would be well to inquire the best route and learn something about the building.
• Relax the night before the test – Allow your mind to rest. Do not study at all that night. Plan some mild recreation or diversion; then go to bed early and get a good night's sleep.
• Get up early enough to make a leisurely trip to the place for the test – This way unforeseen events, traffic snarls, unfamiliar buildings, etc. will not upset you.

- Dress comfortably – A written test is not a fashion show. You will be known by number and not by name, so wear something comfortable.
- Leave excess paraphernalia at home – Shopping bags and odd bundles will get in your way. You need bring only the items mentioned in the official notice you received; usually everything you need is provided. Do not bring reference books to the exam. They will only confuse those last minutes and be taken away from you when in the test room.
- Arrive somewhat ahead of time – If because of transportation schedules you must get there very early, bring a newspaper or magazine to take your mind off yourself while waiting.
- Locate the examination room – When you have found the proper room, you will be directed to the seat or part of the room where you will sit. Sometimes you are given a sheet of instructions to read while you are waiting. Do not fill out any forms until you are told to do so; just read them and be prepared.
- Relax and prepare to listen to the instructions
- If you have any physical problem that may keep you from doing your best, be sure to tell the test administrator. If you are sick or in poor health, you really cannot do your best on the exam. You can come back and take the test some other time.

VII. AT THE TEST

The day of the test is here and you have the test booklet in your hand. The temptation to get going is very strong. Caution! There is more to success than knowing the right answers. You must know how to identify your papers and understand variations in the type of short-answer question used in this particular examination. Follow these suggestions for maximum results from your efforts:

1) Cooperate with the monitor
The test administrator has a duty to create a situation in which you can be as much at ease as possible. He will give instructions, tell you when to begin, check to see that you are marking your answer sheet correctly, and so on. He is not there to guard you, although he will see that your competitors do not take unfair advantage. He wants to help you do your best.

2) Listen to all instructions
Don't jump the gun! Wait until you understand all directions. In most civil service tests you get more time than you need to answer the questions. So don't be in a hurry. Read each word of instructions until you clearly understand the meaning. Study the examples, listen to all announcements and follow directions. Ask questions if you do not understand what to do.

3) Identify your papers
Civil service exams are usually identified by number only. You will be assigned a number; you must not put your name on your test papers. Be sure to copy your number correctly. Since more than one exam may be given, copy your exact examination title.

4) Plan your time
Unless you are told that a test is a "speed" or "rate of work" test, speed itself is usually not important. Time enough to answer all the questions will be provided, but this

does not mean that you have all day. An overall time limit has been set. Divide the total time (in minutes) by the number of questions to determine the approximate time you have for each question.

5) Do not linger over difficult questions

If you come across a difficult question, mark it with a paper clip (useful to have along) and come back to it when you have been through the booklet. One caution if you do this – be sure to skip a number on your answer sheet as well. Check often to be sure that you have not lost your place and that you are marking in the row numbered the same as the question you are answering.

6) Read the questions

Be sure you know what the question asks! Many capable people are unsuccessful because they failed to *read* the questions correctly.

7) Answer all questions

Unless you have been instructed that a penalty will be deducted for incorrect answers, it is better to guess than to omit a question.

8) Speed tests

It is often better NOT to guess on speed tests. It has been found that on timed tests people are tempted to spend the last few seconds before time is called in marking answers at random – without even reading them – in the hope of picking up a few extra points. To discourage this practice, the instructions may warn you that your score will be "corrected" for guessing. That is, a penalty will be applied. The incorrect answers will be deducted from the correct ones, or some other penalty formula will be used.

9) Review your answers

If you finish before time is called, go back to the questions you guessed or omitted to give them further thought. Review other answers if you have time.

10) Return your test materials

If you are ready to leave before others have finished or time is called, take ALL your materials to the monitor and leave quietly. Never take any test material with you. The monitor can discover whose papers are not complete, and taking a test booklet may be grounds for disqualification.

VIII. EXAMINATION TECHNIQUES

1) Read the general instructions carefully. These are usually printed on the first page of the exam booklet. As a rule, these instructions refer to the timing of the examination; the fact that you should not start work until the signal and must stop work at a signal, etc. If there are any *special* instructions, such as a choice of questions to be answered, make sure that you note this instruction carefully.

2) When you are ready to start work on the examination, that is as soon as the signal has been given, read the instructions to each question booklet, underline any key words or phrases, such as *least, best, outline, describe*

and the like. In this way you will tend to answer as requested rather than discover on reviewing your paper that you *listed without describing*, that you selected the *worst* choice rather than the *best* choice, etc.

3) If the examination is of the objective or multiple-choice type – that is, each question will also give a series of possible answers: A, B, C or D, and you are called upon to select the best answer and write the letter next to that answer on your answer paper – it is advisable to start answering each question in turn. There may be anywhere from 50 to 100 such questions in the three or four hours allotted and you can see how much time would be taken if you read through all the questions before beginning to answer any. Furthermore, if you come across a question or group of questions which you know would be difficult to answer, it would undoubtedly affect your handling of all the other questions.

4) If the examination is of the essay type and contains but a few questions, it is a moot point as to whether you should read all the questions before starting to answer any one. Of course, if you are given a choice – say five out of seven and the like – then it is essential to read all the questions so you can eliminate the two that are most difficult. If, however, you are asked to answer all the questions, there may be danger in trying to answer the easiest one first because you may find that you will spend too much time on it. The best technique is to answer the first question, then proceed to the second, etc.

5) Time your answers. Before the exam begins, write down the time it started, then add the time allowed for the examination and write down the time it must be completed, then divide the time available somewhat as follows:
   - If 3-1/2 hours are allowed, that would be 210 minutes. If you have 80 objective-type questions, that would be an average of 2-1/2 minutes per question. Allow yourself no more than 2 minutes per question, or a total of 160 minutes, which will permit about 50 minutes to review.
   - If for the time allotment of 210 minutes there are 7 essay questions to answer, that would average about 30 minutes a question. Give yourself only 25 minutes per question so that you have about 35 minutes to review.

6) The most important instruction is to *read each question* and make sure you know what is wanted. The second most important instruction is to *time yourself properly* so that you answer every question. The third most important instruction is to *answer every question*. Guess if you have to but include something for each question. Remember that you will receive no credit for a blank and will probably receive some credit if you write something in answer to an essay question. If you guess a letter – say "B" for a multiple-choice question – you may have guessed right. If you leave a blank as an answer to a multiple-choice question, the examiners may respect your feelings but it will not add a point to your score. Some exams may penalize you for wrong answers, so in such cases *only*, you may not want to guess unless you have some basis for your answer.

7) Suggestions
   a. Objective-type questions
      1. Examine the question booklet for proper sequence of pages and questions
      2. Read all instructions carefully
      3. Skip any question which seems too difficult; return to it after all other questions have been answered
      4. Apportion your time properly; do not spend too much time on any single question or group of questions
      5. Note and underline key words – *all, most, fewest, least, best, worst, same, opposite,* etc.
      6. Pay particular attention to negatives
      7. Note unusual option, e.g., unduly long, short, complex, different or similar in content to the body of the question
      8. Observe the use of "hedging" words – *probably, may, most likely,* etc.
      9. Make sure that your answer is put next to the same number as the question
      10. Do not second-guess unless you have good reason to believe the second answer is definitely more correct
      11. Cross out original answer if you decide another answer is more accurate; do not erase until you are ready to hand your paper in
      12. Answer all questions; guess unless instructed otherwise
      13. Leave time for review

   b. Essay questions
      1. Read each question carefully
      2. Determine exactly what is wanted. Underline key words or phrases.
      3. Decide on outline or paragraph answer
      4. Include many different points and elements unless asked to develop any one or two points or elements
      5. Show impartiality by giving pros and cons unless directed to select one side only
      6. Make and write down any assumptions you find necessary to answer the questions
      7. Watch your English, grammar, punctuation and choice of words
      8. Time your answers; don't crowd material

8) Answering the essay question

Most essay questions can be answered by framing the specific response around several key words or ideas. Here are a few such key words or ideas:

M's: manpower, materials, methods, money, management
P's: purpose, program, policy, plan, procedure, practice, problems, pitfalls, personnel, public relations
a. Six basic steps in handling problems:
      1. Preliminary plan and background development
      2. Collect information, data and facts
      3. Analyze and interpret information, data and facts
      4. Analyze and develop solutions as well as make recommendations

5. Prepare report and sell recommendations
6. Install recommendations and follow up effectiveness

b. Pitfalls to avoid
1. *Taking things for granted* – A statement of the situation does not necessarily imply that each of the elements is necessarily true; for example, a complaint may be invalid and biased so that all that can be taken for granted is that a complaint has been registered
2. *Considering only one side of a situation* – Wherever possible, indicate several alternatives and then point out the reasons you selected the best one
3. *Failing to indicate follow up* – Whenever your answer indicates action on your part, make certain that you will take proper follow-up action to see how successful your recommendations, procedures or actions turn out to be
4. *Taking too long in answering any single question* – Remember to time your answers properly

EXAMINATION SECTION

EXAMINATION SECTION
COMMENTARY

This section illustrates the different types of questions in a written test of general aptitude and competency. These questions are similar to actual questions in difficulty, content, and form. Competitors should carefully study every question so that they are prepared for questions of the same type in the examination. Some difficult questions are included in this section and competitors should not be discouraged if they miss some of them. No applicant is expected to answer all questions correctly on the written test.

The written test consists of several sections which measure the abilities that are considered essential in carrying out the duties of the positions filled through this examination.

QUESTIONS AND ANSWERS
EXPLANATION OF ANSWERS

DIRECTIONS: Each question or incorrect answer is followed by several suggested answers or completions. Select the one that BEST answers the question or completes the statement.

Question-type 1
Many jobs require the ability to analyze, understand, and interpret written material of varying levels of complexity and to retain the content for at least a limited period of time. Question-type 1 is primarily designed to test these comprehension and retention abilities. The following questions, therefore, require competitors to understand a given paragraph and to select an answer based on their comprehension of the conceptual content of the paragraph. The right answer is either
(1) a repetition, formulated in different terminology, of the main concept or concepts found in the paragraph, or
(2) a conclusion whose inherence in the content of the paragraph is such that it is equivalent to a restatement

1. Through advertising, manufacturers exercise a high degree of control over consumers' desires. However, the manufacturer assumes enormous risks in attempting to predict what consumers will want and in producing goods in quantity and distributing them in advance of final selection by the consumers.
The paragraph best supports the statement that manufacturers
   A. can eliminate the risk of overproduction by advertising
   B. completely control buyers' needs and desires
   C. must depend upon the final consumers for the success of their undertakings
   D. distribute goods directly to the consumers
   E. can predict with great accuracy the success of any product they put on the market

The conclusion derived by the correct alternative, C, is inherent in the content of the paragraph; although it acknowledges that advertising plays an important role in determining consumers' desires, it affirms that final selection rests with the consumers and that manufacturers therefore take *enormous* risks in attempting to predict final selection. Alternative B contradicts the opening sentence of the paragraph which refers only to a "high degree of control." Alternatives A and E likewise affirm the opposite of what the paragraph postulates, i.e., that the manufacturer's predictions entail enormous risks. Alternative D is almost irrelevant to the paragraph since distribution techniques have not been considered.

2. The function of business is to increase the wealth of the country and the value and happiness of life. It does this by supplying the material needs of men and women. When the nation's business is successfully carried on, it renders public service of the highest value.

The paragraph best supports the statement that

A. all businesses which render public service are successful
B. human happiness is enhanced only by the increase of material wants
C. the value of life is increased only by the increase of wealth
D. the material needs of men and women are supplied by well-conducted business
E. business is the only field of activity which increases happiness

The correct alternative, D, restates the main idea in the original paragraph that business increases the value and happiness of life by supplying the material needs of men and women. Alternative A derives its conclusion incorrectly, i.e., the proposition that all successful businesses render public service, cannot be logically reversed to "all businesses which render public service are successful." Alternatives B and C assume an equation between happiness and wealth which is not supported by the content of the paragraph. Alternative E like wise equates happiness with business endeavors or their products, which the content of the paragraph does not warrant.

3. Honest people in one nation find it difficult to understand the viewpoints of honest people in another. Foreign ministries and their ministers exist for the purpose of explaining the viewpoints of one nation in terms under-stood by the ministries of another. Some of their most important work lies in this direction.

The paragraph best supports the statement that

A. people of different nations may not consider matters in the same light
B. it is unusual for many people to share similar ideas
C. suspicion prevents understanding be-tween nations
D. the chief work of foreign ministries is to guide relations between nations united by a common cause
E. the people of one nation must sympathize with the viewpoints of the people of other nations

The conclusion derived by the correct alternative, A, is inherent in the content of the paragraph; if honest people in one nation find it diffcult to understand the viewpoints of honest people in another, it is because they often see matters in different lights. Alternatives B, C and D find little or no support in the paragraph: B is concerned with "many people" whereas the paragraph refers to people of different nations; C assumes that nations are suspicious of each other and that suspicion prevents understanding; D contradicts the main idea expressed by the paragraph since foreign ministries should work towards mutual understanding between nations having discrepant viewpoints whether or not they have a common cause. Alternative E sets forth an ethical command which to an extent stems from the content of the paragraph but which is not completely warranted by it as is the conclusion of alternative A.

4. Education should not stop when the individual has been prepared to make a livelihood and to live in modern society. Living would be mere existence were there no appreciation and enjoyment of the riches of art, literature and science.

The paragraph best supports the statement that true education

A. is focused on the routine problems of life
B. prepares one for a full enjoyment of life
C. deals chiefly with art, literature and science

D. is not possible for one who does not enjoy scientific literature

E. disregards practical ends

The correct alternative, B, restates the main idea presented in the paragraph that living is mere existence for those individuals who lack the enjoyment of art, literature and science. Alternative A directly contradicts this main idea, and alternatives C and E also contradict the paragraph which acknowledges that education should prepare the individual to make a livelihood although it shouldn't stop there. Alternative D goes beyond the paragraph in that it affirms that each individual *must* enjoy scientific literature whereas the original statement simply suggests that life in general would be limited if the riches of science, art and literature were not available for appreciation and enjoyment.

Question-type II

Many jobs require the use of clear and succinct verbal and written expression. Basic vocabulary limitations impede the precise correspondence of words and concepts and thus hinder effective language communication. Accordingly, the following questions present a key word and five suggested answers. The competitor's task is to find the suggested answer that is closest in meaning to the key word. The wrong alternatives may have a more or less valid connection with the key word. In some cases, therefore, the right choice differs from a wrong choice only in the degree to which its meaning comes close to that of the key word.

1. *Subsume* means most nearly
    A. understate
    B. absorb
    C. include
    D. belong
    E. cover

To *subsume* means to include within a larger class or order (alternative C). Alternative A is unrelated in meaning. Alternatives D and E are somewhat related since an element included in a group or class can be said to belong to it and to be covered by it. To a degree, likewise, it may be said that an element included in a group or class is absorbed (alternative B) by the group or class, although strictly speaking, a subsumed element partially preserves its individual identity whereas an absorbed element does not.

2. *Notorious* means most nearly
    A. condemned
    B. unpleasant
    C. vexatious
    D. pretentious
    E. well-known

Notorious means being or constituting something commonly known. Thus alternative E is almost synonymous in meaning. Alternatives B, C and D are unrelated in meaning, since a notorious individual may or may not be unpleasant, vexatious or pretentious. Alternative A hinges on a secondary nuance of the word notorious: being widely and unfavorably known. However, being unfavorably well-known does not necessarily imply being condemned.

3. *Novices* means most nearly
    A. volunteers
    B. experts
    C. trainers
    D. beginners
    E. amateurs

Novice designates one who has no training or experience in a specific field or activity and is hence a beginner (alternative D). An expert (alternative B) is therefore the exact opposite. A trainer (alternative C) may or may not be an expert but must certainly have a certain amount of knowledge. Volunteers (alternative A) are in most cases not novices since they usually volunteer for something they are knowledgeable in. An amateur (alternative E) is one who engages in a particular pursuit, study or science as a pastime rather than as a profession. Thus an amateur may be a novice in the initial stages of formal training, but more often than not will be an expert who has acquired expertise in a particular field through the consistent pursuit of a pastime or pleasure.

4. To *succumb* means most nearly
    A. to aid
    B. to oppose
    C. to yield
    D. to check
    E. to be discouraged

To *succumb* is to cease to resist or contend before a superior or overpowering force or desire, hence to yield (alternative C). Alternative B expresses the stage prior to succumbing. Alternative A is not related except perhaps accidentally—an individual who succumbs may involuntarily serve the purpose of the overpowering force. Alternative D is unrelated in meaning, and alternative E is related only vaguely in the sense that the succumbing party may be susceptible to discouragement.

Question-type III
The ability to discover the underlying relations or analogies existing among specific data is important in many jobs where solving problems involves the formation and testing of hypotheses. The questions in this section test this ability. Each question consists of a series of letters arranged in a definite pattern. The competitor must discover what the pattern is and decide which alternative gives the next letter in the series.

1. b c d b c e b c f b c g

 A) b B) c C) h D) i E) e
The answer is A. The sequence maintains two letters (b c) in the same order while the third letter is in consecutive alphabetical order (d e f g). The pattern b c g has been completed and the next letter should begin the pattern b c h.

2. b c c c d e e e f g g g h i i

 A) g B) h C) i D) j E) f
The answer is C. The pattern consists of letters written in alphabetical order with every second letter repeated three times. Since the last letter in the sequence, the i, is only repeated twice, it should be repeated a third time.

3. b n c d n e f g n h i j k

 A) n B) l C) m D) i E) j
The answer is A. The sequence consists of a fixed letter (n) placed after consecutive letter periods. These periods acquire an additional

letter each time and begin with the letter which alphabetically follows the last letter in the preceding period, i.e., *bn cdn efgn hijk*. The letter n must therefore be placed after the last period.

4. b c d b e f g e h i j h k l m

 A) k B) h C) l D) n E) o
The answer is A. The series is an alphabetical progression of four-letter sequences where each fourth letter repeats the first letter of each sequence: *bcdb efge hijh klmk*.

Question-type IV
As in the previous section the questions in this section measure the ability to discover the underlying relations or analogies existing among specific data. Each question consists of two sets of symbols where a common characteristic exists among the symbols in each set and where an analogy is maintained between the two sets of symbols. The competitor must discover which alternative gives the symbol that simultaneously preserves the characteristic common to the symbols in the second set and the analogy with the symbols in the first set.

1.

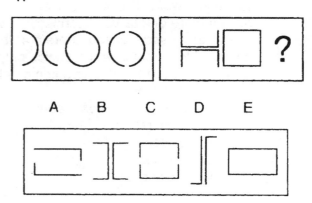

The answer is C. An analogy is established here between a circle and a square. Therefore a circle split into two halves is the same as a square split into two halves.

2.

 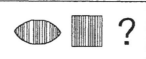

A   B   C   D   E

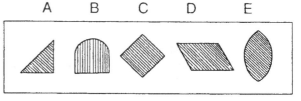

The answer is B. In this case the form of the symbols is irrelevant. The critical feature is found in the lines included within the symbols. The lines in the first three symbols are all slanted lines. The lines in the second two symbols are all vertical lines. Of the five alternatives, symbol B is the only one with vertical lines.

3.

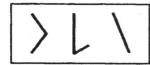 

A   B   C   D   E

The answer is E. The symbols in the first box are made up of straight lines. The symbols in the second box are made up of curved lines. The symbol in alternative E is the only one that preserves the pattern.

4.

A   B   C   D   E

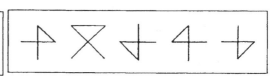

The answer is O. The first three symbols are identical except for their orientation the orientation of the second symbol is a 90 rotation of the first symbol. Likewise the third symbol is a 90° rotation of the second symbol. The symbols in the second box follow the same 90 rotation pattern. Alternative O is the only one that preserves the pattern.

Question-type V

The development of plans, systems and procedures is an essential function of many jobs. This function entails the ability to analyze given facts and discover their implications, as well as the ability to reason from general principles to the implications of these principles in specific situations. Question-type V tests these analytical abilities. Accordingly, each of the following questions consists of a statement which is to be accepted as true and should not be questioned for the purpose of this test. Following the statement are five alternatives. The correct alternative MUST derive from the information given in the original statement without drawing on additional information. By contrast, the four incorrect alternatives rest, to varying degrees, on the admission of new information.

1. No substantial alterations in the age structure took place between 2000-10 and life expectancy remained the same. A slight drop, nonetheless (from 38 to 37 percent), is noted in the proportion of the population 20 years of age and younger.
    Therefore, between 2000-10
    A. the proportion of the productive-age population increased
    B. there was a slight decrease in fertility rates
    C. there was a decrease in emigration
    D. there was a slight increase in infant mortality

E. production remained substantially the same

The correct alternative, A, follows from the data that there was a slight drop in the proportion of the population under 20 years of age and that life expectancy remained the same. Alternatives B and D are possible explanations of the slight decrease in the proportion of the younger population but do not derive from the original statement and would require additional evidence. Alternative C would likewise require additional information and would seem to apply more as a partial and possible explanation of a decrease in the productive-age population. Alternative E in no way derives from the given data since many factors affect production besides the age structure of the population.

2. A robot can take a walk in order to mail a letter; it can play chess, build other machines and generally exhibit rule-governed behavior. A robot can kill a person but, unlike a person, it cannot be ashamed. It can be annoying but not annoyed. It can *perhaps* exhibit behavior *as if* it were ashamed or annoyed.

   A. Robots are capable of thought.
   B. Robots can do things that people do but cannot be what people are.
   C. Robots and people are outwardly the same.
   D. Robots can make conscious decisions but have no moral consciousness.
   E. Robots never exhibit their inner thoughts and realities.

The correct alternative, B, derives its conclusion from the joint consideration of the actions enumerated in the original statement as actions that a robot can perform—mailing a letter, playing chess, killing a person—and the conscious states that are enumerated as impossible in a robot, i.e., being ashamed or annoyed. Furthermore, the last sentence in the original statement contrasts outward behaviors with the actual conscious states they represent. Alternative A rests on the assumption that thought can be equated with exhibited behavior and not with inner con-

sciousness. Alternative C assumes not only that all exhibited behavior is the same but that the outward *appearance* of a robot and a person is the same. Alternative D correctly derives a section of its conclusion—the lack of moral consciousness—from the stated fact that a robot cannot be ashamed, but assumes that a robot can kill a person after making a *conscious* decision, which contradicts the original statement. Alternative E likewise affirms, in contradiction of the original statement, that robots have inner consciousness.

3. The Thirty Years' War, 1618 to 1648, established the principle of religious toleration among the German states, but it also reduced the German population by at least one-third, and much of the cultivated land became wilderness.

   Therefore, the Thirty Years' War
   A. altered the geographical boundaries of the German states
   B. was generally beneficial to the German states
   C. was fought on German soil
   D. established a large number of religions within the German states
   E. caused the German population to become widely scattered

The correct alternative, C, derives its conclusion from the given facts that the German population was reduced by one-third and much of the cultivated land became wilderness. Alternative A, on the other hand, assumes the establishment of new borders from the extraneous information that borders are usually changed by wars. Alternative B derives its conclusion from the assumption that religious tolerance creates a surrounding influence beneficial to all aspects of national life. Alternative D assumes an equation between religious tolerance and religious pluralism, and alternative E likewise assumes an equation between the reduction of the population and the scattering of the population.

4. Though easy to learn, backgammon is a surprisingly subtle and complex game to play very well. It is a game that calls for mastery of the laws of probability and the

ability to weigh and undertake frequent shifts in strategy.

Therefore, a necessary quality for playing backgammon very well is

   A. the ability to deceive the opponent

   B. a willingness to take calculated risks

   C. a high degree of manual dexterity

   D. the ability to make quick decisions

   E. a mastery of advanced mathematics

The correct alternative, B, derives its conclusion from the given fact that the game is based on decisions of probability. Thus the player must take calculated risks. The four incorrect alternatives, on the other hand, rest on assumptions that, to varying degrees, go beyond the original statement. Alternative E, for example, assumes that a mastery of the laws of probability entails a more generic mastery of advanced mathematics. Alternative D assumes that frequent shifts in strategy cannot be carried out slowly.

Question-type VI

Many jobs require the ability to understand and utilize information presented in chart or table form. The following questions require competitors to deduce the missing values in a table of figures from the information in the rest of the table.

TABLE 1: GENERAL REVENUE OF STATE AND LOCAL GOVERNMENTS-STATES:
2000 Hypothetical data

STATE	Total amount (mil.do.)	REVENUE PER CAPITA [1] (dollars)						REVENUE (dollars) PER $1,000 OF PERSONAL INCOME IN CALENDAR YEAR 1999				
		Total	From Federal Government	From own sources;			Charges and miscellaneos	Total	From Federal Government	From own sources		Charges and miscellaneos
				Taxes								
				All taxes	Property tax	Other				Total	Taxes	
Ala 1,722		I	131	258	39	219	110	190	50	140	98	42
Alaska........1,259	4,168	358	417	102	315	3,393	1,001	86	915	II	815	
Ariz 1,172	662	121	426	166	260	115	206	38	168	132	36	
Ark 871	453	115	252	65	187	86	176	45	131	98	33	
Calif 17,028	853	164	559	262	297	130	204	39	165	134	31	
Colo 1,474	666	III	419	179	240	123	194	36	158	122	36	
Conn..........1,970	649	85	484	238	246	80	144	19	125	107	18	
Del 379	692	88	450	84	366	154	172	22	150	112	38	
D.C.................. IV	953	359	517	169	348	77	192	72	120	104	16	
Fla..............3,576	528	69	347	118	229	112	160	21	139	105	34	

[1]Based on resident population

1. What is the value of I?
   A. 800
   B. 600
   C. 499
   D. 757
   E. None of these, or cannot be calculated from data provided

The answer is C. The figure represents the total Revenue per Capita which is obtained by adding the three major columns therein: Charges and miscellaneous, All taxes and Federal Government: 110 + 258 + 131 = 499. Alternative D represents an erroneous double addition of the Property tax and Other subcolumns, the amounts corresponding to which were already included in the All taxes column. Alternatives A and B are irrelevant values.

2. What is the value of II?
   A. 392
   B. 828
   C. 100
   D. 1814
   E. None of these, or cannot be calculated from data provided

The answer is C. It is obtained by subtracting Charges and miscellaneous from the Total Revenue from own sources: 915 - 815 = 100. Alternatives A, B and D are irrelevant values.

3. What is the value of III?
   A. 124
   B. 141
   C. 176
   D. 203
   E. None of these, or cannot be calculated from data provided

The answer is A. It is obtained by adding the two major columns for which values are given in the Revenue per Capita subdivision, All taxes and Charges and miscellaneous, and subtracting the result from the total Revenue per Capita: 419 + 123 = 542; 666 - 542 = 124. Alternatives B, C and D are irrelevant values.

4. What is the value of IV?
   A. 725
   B. 687
   C. 710
   D. 1144
   E. None of these, or cannot be calculated from data provided

The answer is E. The Total General Revenue cannot be calculated, since the total population figure is missing. This figure should be multiplied by the Per Capita Income to obtain the Total Revenue. Alternative D erroneously adds the totals for Revenue per Capita and Revenue per $1,000 of Personal Income: 192 + 953 = 1145. Alternatives A, B and C are irrelevant values.

Question-type VII

Many jobs require employees to perform or check arithmetic operations involving fractions, percentages, etc. and to solve quanti-tative problems of varying complexity, where the approach to be utilized is not specified. The questions in this section test these abilities. Although the arithmetical processes involved are simple, the figuring should of course be done with care.

1. 113 17/52 - 33 5/13 =
   A. 79 49/52
   B. 80 3/52
   C. 80 12/52
   D. 80 49/52
   E. None of these

The answer is A. First of all fractions are reduced to a common denominator. Additionally, since the fraction being subtracted is larger than the one it is to be subtracted from, a unit must be taken from the whole number, 113, reducing it ito 112. The borrowed unit is converted into fraction form and added to 17/52, i.e., 52/52 + 17/52 = 69/52. The subtraction is then carried out: 112 69/52 - 33 20/52 = 79 49/52.

2. $\dfrac{16 \times 17}{(57 + 79)4} =$
   A. .50
   B. .72
   C. 1.9
   D. 8.0
   E. None of these

The answer is A. The numbers in parentheses are added, 57 + 79 = 136 and 136 is then broken into 17 x 2 x 4. Common factors are eliminated:

$$\frac{16 \times 17}{(57+79)4} = \frac{16 \times 17}{(136)4} = \frac{16 \times 17}{(17 \times 2 \times 4)4} =$$

$$\frac{16 \times 17}{17 \times 2 \times 4 \times 4} = \frac{1}{2} = .50$$

3. 221 1/19 x 10 11/35 =
   A. 80.3
   B. 2510.0
   C. 2510.1
   D. 2280
   E. None of these

The answer is D. Whole numbers are reduced to fractions:

$\frac{4200}{19} \times \frac{361}{35}$. Fractions are broken into their component factors and common factors are eliminated: $\frac{7 \times 6 \times 100}{19} \times \frac{19 \times 19}{7 \times 5} =$

$\frac{7 \times 6 \times 5 \times 20 \times 19 \times 19}{19 \times 7 \times 5} =$

$6 \times 20 \times 19 = 2280$.

4. $\frac{(418 + 56 - 8)313}{77 + (50 + 9)7 - 24} =$
   A. - 12378
   B. 310
   C. 313
   D. 1246.649
   E. None of these

The answer is C.

$\frac{(466)(313)}{77 + (59)7 - 24} = \frac{(466)(313)}{77 + 413 - 24} =$

$\frac{(466)(313)}{490 - 24} = \frac{(466)(313)}{466}$

Common factors are eliminated and the result is 313.

5. An office supply store buys 100 reams of special quality paper for $400. If 1 ream = 500 sheets of paper, how much must the store receive per 100 sheets to obtain a 20% gain on its cost?
   A. 83¢
   B. 85¢
   C. 96¢
   D. 98¢
   E. None of these

The answer is C. Since 1 ream = 500 sheets, 100 reams = 50000 sheets. To discover the cost of 100 sheets we set up a proportion:

$\frac{50000}{100} = \frac{400}{X}$; $50000X = 40000$; $X = \frac{40000}{50000} =$ 0.80. The cost of 100 sheets is 80¢. To discover the amount that the store must receive per 100 sheets to obtain a 20% gain on the 80¢ cost, we find what 20% of 80¢ is and add the result: $80 + (0.20)(80) = 80 + 16 = 96¢$.

6. A vase is packed in a carton with a 10" diameter and is surrounded by packing 2" thick at the mouth. If the diameter of the base is 1/2 the diameter of the mouth, what is the diameter of the base?
   A. 3"
   B. 4"
   C. 6"
   D. 8"
   E. None of these

The answer is A. Since the vase is surrounded by packing 2" thick at the mouth and the diameter of the carton is 10", we subtract: 10 - (2 + 2) = 10 - 4 = 6" which is the diameter of the mouth. Since the diameter of the base is 1/2 the diameter of the mouth: 1/2(6)=3".

7. Seventy 58" x 34" desks must be stored in a warehouse. If as many desks as possible are stored on the floor of a 15' x 25' room, how many desks will still require storage?
   A. 46
   B. 25
   C. 45
   D. 43
   E. None of these

The answer is C. First of all, the feet are reduced to inches: 15 x 12 = 180 and 25 x 12 = 300. Next we determine how many times the length of a desk fits into the length of the room and how many times the width of a desk fits into the width of the room:

$\frac{180}{34} = 5\frac{10}{34}$ and $\frac{300}{58} = 5\frac{10}{58}$ We then multiply the whole numbers, which means multiplying the number of desks per row by the number of rows: 5 x 5 = 25. Since 25 desks fit in the room, 45 desks will still require storage (70 - 25 = 45).

Alternative D is obtained by multiplying the width and length of the room and the width and length of a desk and dividing the total storage area by the total area of a desk: 180 x 300 = 54000 and 58 x 34 = 1972; 54000 ÷

$1972 = 27\frac{189}{493}$.

Since 70 - 27 = 43, more desks would fit in the same area. However, this solution is incorrect because it does not take into account that the storage space cannot be filled *completely* with desks. The shape of the desks is not adjustable to the shape of the room and there would always be unfilled spaces. Alternative A is obtained by determining how many times the width of a desk fits into the length of the room and the length of a desk fits into the width of the room:

$$\frac{300}{34} = 8\frac{14}{17} \text{ and } \frac{180}{58} = 3\frac{3}{29} \ .$$

The multiplication of the whole numbers yields 24, and 70 - 24 = 46. One more desk actually fits into the storage area if we follow the process used to obtain the correct answer, alternative C.

8. A mechanic repairs 16 cars per 8-hour day. Another mechanic in the same shop repairs 1 1/2 times this number in 3/4 the time. Theoretically, how long will it take to repair 16 cars in the shop?
    A. 2 2/3 hours
    B. 2 9/10 hours
    C. 3 hours
    D. 21/2 hours
    E. None of these

The answer is A. For the second mechanic we obtain 1 1/2 of 16 cars: 3/2 x 16 = 24 and 3/4 of 8 hours: 3/4 x 8 = 6 hours. The second mechanic therefore repairs 24 cars per 6-hour day. Secondly we determine how many cars each mechanic repairs per hour-the first mechanic: 2 cars/hr. and the second mechanic 4 cars/hr. Therefore 6 cars are repaired every hour if both outputs are added. Lastly we determine how many hours are required to repair 16 cars: we divide the 16 cars by the 6 cars/hr. which yields 2 2/3 hrs.

Question-type VIII
Many jobs require the ability to solve a presented problem when all the necessary facts to solve the problem are not given. Solution to the problem involves making some reasonable assumptions or anticipating what the most likely of several possible occurrences might be. This ability becomes especially important when decisions must be reached based on incomplete evidence. Accordingly, the questions in this section require competitors to select the best or most reasonable answer from five alternatives. In order to do so, competitors are required to use general knowledge not included in the original statement. Since the correct alternative consists of the best or most reasonable answer, it is essential to keep in mind that some alternatives may be plausible, although not as plausible as the correct alternative.

1. The development of a country's water power is advocated as a means of conserving natural resources CHIEFLY because such a hydroelectric policy would tend to
    A. stimulate the growth of industries in hitherto isolated regions
    B. encourage the substitution of machinery for hand labor
    C. provide a larger market for coal
    D. make cheap electricity available in rural areas
    E. lessen the use of irreplaceable fuel materials

Of the five alternatives, the correct alternative, E, derives from the fundamental or most essential reason for the endorsement of a hydroelectric policy, i.e., water is not a depletable energy resource. Alternatives A and D are plausible but are not as determinative as E. Alternative C is easily discarded since coal would have a larger market in the absence of hydroelectric power. Alternative B is also easily discarded since hydroelectric energy would increase the availability of both the fuel and/or electricity needed to run machinery.

2. Complaints by the owners of large cars that they cannot see an already-parked small car in a parking lot until they have begun to pull into a space, are BEST justified if
    A. there are few empty parking spaces in the lot
    B. the small car has been parked for a long time
    C. the owners of large cars have poor vision
    D. there is a designated parking area for small cars
    E. there are few other small cars in the lot

The correct alternative, D, hinges on the fact that strict *justification* for a complaint is more firmly rooted in legality than in individual situations or attitudes. Thus, for example, the owner of a large car who happens to find few empty parking spaces in a lot (alternative A), or who knows or assumes that a small car has been parked in a certain space for a long time (alternative B), can justify his or her annoyance only on the subjective level. On the other hand if a small car is parked in a space designated for large cars, the individual's annoyance and complaint acquire objective and formal justification.

3. A country that is newly settled usually produces very little art, music or literature. The MOST REASONABLE explanation of this fact is that
   A. its people have had few experiences to draw on
   B. there is little use for such work
   C. suitable materials for such work must be imported
   D. the physical development of the country absorbs most of the interest and energy of the people
   E. there is as yet no governmental encouragement of the arts

The correct alternative, D, presents the most basic explanation for the lack of artistic production in a newly-settled country. The development of a newly-settled country necessitates the undivided attention of its people, and manpower is thus basically unavailable for the production of art, music or literature. Alternative A is implausible since newly-settled people have many experiences which are eventually represented in the art, music and literature of later generations. Alternatives B, C and E make assumptions about conditions necessary for the production of art, music and literature which are only partially valid. Alternative B incorrectly assumes that art is always produced for utilitarian purposes. Alternative C partially applies to art and music but not at all to literature. Alternative E is only partially plausible. The government of a newly-settled country is likely to encourage the production of goods rather than the production of art, music or literature.

However, artistic production can occur without governmental encouragement,

4. The CHIEF reason why every society has certain words and concepts that are never precisely translated into the language of another society is that
   A. the art of good translation is as yet not sufficiently developed
   B. there is too great a disparity between the intellectual levels attained by different societies
   C. every society possesses cultural elements which are unique to itself
   D. words and concepts never express the true nature of a society
   E. every society has some ideas which it does not wish to share with other societies

The correct alternative, C, is the most basic reason why certain concepts are never precisely translated. Languages express the sociopolitical contexts in which they are spoken and are bound to have expressions that are unique to these contexts. Alternative A fails to distinguish between the qualitative and the quantitative. Whereas the art of good translation appears to be as yet not sufficiently widespread, it is indeed available. Furthermore its total unavailability would still constitute a secondary explanation, over and against alternative C, for the impossibility of the precise translation of certain words. Alternative B rests on the assumption that *all* existing societies are substantially disparate in their level of development, which is known not to be the case. Alternative D assumes the truth of the postulate expounded by some philosophical theories that words and concepts have no referential value. Alternative E presents a farfetched ethical judgment whose plausibility rests on the assumption that social groups are secretive and that the function of language is to exclude communication beyond the social group.

Question-type IX

As in the previous section the questions in this section measure the ability to solve a problem when all the facts relevant to its solution are not given. More specifically, many jobs require the employee to discover connections between events sometimes apparently unrelated. In order to do this the employee will find it necessary to correctly infer that unspecified events have probably occurred or are likely to occur. This ability becomes especially important when action must be taken on incomplete information. Accordingly, these questions require competitors to choose among five suggested alternatives, each of which presents a different sequential arrangement of five events. Competitors must choose the MOST logical of the five suggested sequences. In order to do so, they MAY be required to draw on general knowledge to infer missing concepts or events that are essential to sequencing the five given events. Competitors should be careful to infer only what is essential to the sequence. The plausibility of the wrong alternatives will always require the inclusion of unlikely events or of additional chains of events which are NOT essential to sequencing the five given events.

1. 1. a body was found in the woods
   2. a man proclaimed innocence
   3. the owner of a gun was located
   4. a gun was traced
   5. the owner of a gun was questioned
   A. 4-3-5-2-1   D. 1-3-5-2-4
   B. 2-1-4-3-5   E. 1-2-4-3-5
   C. 1-4-3-5-2

The correct alternative, C, interrelates the events in the simplest and most logical sequence: if a body is found (1), it is probable that a weapon will be found and traced (4), that its owner will then be located (3) and questioned (5) and that he will proclaim his innocence (2). The plausibility of alternatives A and B rests on a more involved and less logical sequence because it requires the inclusion of an additional chain of events in order to make the discovery of a body (1) follow from a proclamation of innocence (2). The plausibility of alternative D likewise requires the inclusion of an additional chain

of events to explain why a man would be located and questioned before the gun was traced. Sequence E rests on the assumption that the owner of the gun and the man proclaiming innocence are two persons. In this case the man proclaiming innocence loses his relation to the other events and becomes superfluous unless additional events are included.

2. 1. a man was in a hunting accident
   2. a man fell down a flight of steps
   3. a man lost his vision in one eye
   4. a man broke his leg
   5. a man had to walk with a cane
   A. 2-4-5-1-3   D. 1-3-5-2-4
   B. 4-5-1-3-2   E. 1-3-2-4-5
   C. 3-1-4-5-2

The correct alternative, E, provides the most likely causal relationship for the five events. Accidents with weapons such as those used when hunting (1) can result in a loss of vision (3). One-eyed vision impedes depth perception and could result in a fall down a flight of steps (2) causing a broken leg (4) and necessitating the use of a cane (5). Alternatives A and B are less plausible because they establish a causal relationship between walking with a cane and having the type of hunting accident that results in loss of vision. In addition, it is less likely that a man with a broken leg would go hunting than that a man with impaired vision would have to go up or down steps. Alternative D is less plausible than E because a broken leg rather than impaired vision is likely to necessitate the use of a cane. Alternative C is less plausible than E because it is likely that a loss of vision will follow rather than precede a hunting accident. Also, a broken leg is more likely to result from a fall than from a hunting accident.

3. 1. a man is offered a new job
   2. a woman is offered a new job
   3. a man works as a waiter
   4. a woman works as a waitress
   5. a woman gives notice
   A. 4-2-5-3-1   D. 3-1-4-2-5
   B. 4-2-5-1-3   E. 4-3-2-5-1
   C. 2-4-5-3-1

The correct alternative, B, provides the best temporal sequence for the five events by establishing a causal relationship where the three events concerning the woman trigger the two events concerning the man. A woman works as a waitress (4); she is offered a new job (2); gives notice to her employer (5); who offers her job to a man (1); who begins work as a waiter (3) when the woman leaves. The other four alternatives describe plausible situations but do not establish a causal relationship between the two sets of events. Thus if the new job that is offered to the man is not the one vacated by the woman, there is no way to determine whether a woman works as a waitress (4) before a man works as a waiter (3) or vice versa unless additional events are included.

4.   1.   a train left the station late
     2.   a man was late for work
     3.   a man lost his job
     4.   many people complained because the train was late
     5.   there was a traffic jam

   A.   5-2-1-4-3   D.   1-5-4-2-3
   B.   5-1-4-2-3   E.   2-1-4-5-3
   C.   5-1-2-4-3

The correct alternative, A, follows from the inference that the man who is late for work is essential to the departure of the train. This is the only assumption that leads to a logical and interrelated sequence for the five events. The other four alternatives do not really interrelate the events and become plausible only if numerous assumptions are made. In addition, the four alternatives sever the connection between the numerous complaints (4) and the lost job (3). Without this connection event 4 becomes superfluous.

———

EXAMINATION SECTION
TEST 1

DIRECTIONS: Each question or incomplete statement is followed by several suggested answers or completions. Select the one that BEST answers the question or completes the statement. *PRINT THE CORRECT ANSWER IN THE SPACE AT THE RIGHT.*

1. To learn a foreign LANGGWAYJ is tedious work.
   The word in capitals is misspelled. Write it correctly at the right.

   1._____

2. The APRENTIS learns a trade.
   The word in capitals is misspelled. Write it correctly at the right.

   2._____

3. The SOHRS of the stream is high in the hills.
   The word in capitals is misspelled. Write it correctly at the right.

   3._____

4. Animals often show great INTELIJENS.
   The word in capitals is misspelled. Write it correctly at the right.

   4._____

5. Our hotels AKOMODAYT many people.
   The word in capitals is misspelled. Write it correctly at the right.

   5._____

6. Who determines whether a Congressman who is considered undesirable shall be seated?

   6._____

   A. Congress   B. Supreme Court   C. President
   D. Cabinet   E. The people

7. *Aviation in the United States is accomplishing much. The total number of miles flown annually now amounts to move than the total for any other country in the world and is about equal to the combined mileage of Germany and France.*
   According to the above paragraph, which one of the following statements is TRUE?

   7._____

   A. The total number of miles flown annually in the United States is less than that of any other country.
   B. Germany leads in the number of miles flown annually.
   C. The United States surpasses every country in the world in the number of miles flown annually.
   D. Both Germany and France have greater air mileage than the United States.
   E. Because of the bigger size of the United States, our planes must fly farther than the planes in the rest of the countries combined.

8. DIG is to TRENCH as BUILD is to

   8._____

   A. excavator   B. wall   C. mine
   D. construct   E. replace

9. TIGER is to CAT as WOLF is to

   9._____

   A. snarl   B. dog   C. fur   D. wild   E. hunted

10. GENEROUS is to MISERLY as FRIENDLY is to   10._____

     A. surly   B. kind   C. stingy   D. weak   E. clever

11. EAST is to WEST as DOWN is to   11._____

     A. earth   B. up   C. out   D. sky   E. rise

12. CLOTHES are to FABRIC as HOUSE is to   12._____

     A. lot   B. shelter   C. wood
     D. residence   E. large

13. BOSTON is to SEASHORE as PITTSBURGH is to   13._____

     A. capitol   B. inland   C. smaller
     D. city .   E. agriculture

14. I wish to build a tank 5 feet long and 4 feet high that will hold 300 gallons.   14._____

What will the width of the tank be if $7\frac{1}{2}$ gallons equal 1 cubic foot?

15. By what number is 3/4 of the product of 12 x 5 multiplied to give 405?   15._____

16. *Specimen signatures of consignee and consignor are sent on Form 6006.*   16._____
What one word in the above sentence indicates the receiver?

17. CAUCASIAN is to WHITE MAN as MONGOLIAN is to   17._____

     A. Black   B. Indian   C. Moor
     D. Chinese   E. mountaineers

18. *There is many a slip between the cup and the lip.*   18._____
The above quotation means MOST NEARLY

     A. in life, as in wine, drink not to the dregs
     B. forget past troubles
     C. don't be too sure of the future
     D. a full cup spells prosperity
     E. a steady hand in all things is a necessity

19. *A new invention restores colors which were lost to some talking motion pictures when*   19._____
the sound track was introduced along the edge of the photographic film. By this new
development, a producer may 'turn on the moonlight' for love scenes or use all the tints
from blue to red in the gamut of human emotions.
Judging from the above paragraph, which one of the following statements is TRUE?

     A. Colors cannot be used with the talkies.
     B. Only red or blue can be used in motion pictures.
     C. A producer can now use all colors in talking films.
     D. Human emotions can be shown only with moonlight pictures.

20. LAUGHTER is to REJOICING as WEEPING is to   20._____

     A. punishment   B. parting   C. sorrow
     D. disappointment   E. disillusionment

21. IRON is to HEAVY as FEATHERS are to   21._____

    A. goose   B. gray   C. light   D. grown   E. metal

22. AGREE is the opposite of   22._____

    A. quarrel   B. deny   C. warn
    D. dislike   E. unpleasant

23. ABUNDANT is the opposite of   23._____

    A. plenty   B. bouncing   C. scarce
    D. low   E. rare

24. He played the part of the VILIN.   24._____
    The word in capitals is misspelled. Write it correctly at the right.

25. These parts are INTURCHAYNJUBUL.   25._____
    The word in capitals is misspelled. Write it correctly at the right.

KEY (CORRECT ANSWERS)

1. language		11. B	
2. apprentice		12. C	
3. source		13. B	
4. intelligence		14. 2 ft.	
5. accommodate		15. 9	
6. A		16. consignee	
7. C		17. D	
8. B		18. C	
9. B		19. C	
10. A		20. C	

21. C
22. A
23. C
24. villain
25. interchangeable

TEST 2

DIRECTIONS: Each question or incomplete statement is followed by several suggested answers or completions. Select the one that BEST answers the question or completes the statement. *PRINT THE CORRECT ANSWER IN THE SPACE AT THE RIGHT.*

1. Extreme heat will LIKWIFY.
   The word in capitals is misspelled. Write it correctly at the right.

   1.____

2. It was his birthday ANIVURSAREE.
   The word in capitals is misspelled. Write it correctly at the right.

   2.____

3. The kittens were FROLIKING in the grass.
   The word in capitals is misspelled. Write it correctly at the right.

   3.____

4. C is to CC as AB is to

   4.____

   A. ABC   B. AA   C. BB   D. AABB   E. AAB

5. RIVER is to AMAZON as LAKE is to

   5.____

   A. deep   B. Ohio   C. Superior
   D. island   E. Mississippi

6. Which one of the following answers may be applied to LAKE MICHIGAN but not to LAKE ERIE and LAKE ONTARIO?

   6.____

   A. Fresh water   B. Inland
   C. Navigable   D. St. Lawrence waterway
   E. Not adjacent to Canada

7. A tank can be filled through an intake pipe in 6 hours and emptied through an outlet pipe in 10 hours.
   If the tank is empty and both intake and outlet pipes are opened, how long will it take the tank to fill?

   7.____

8. A boy paid 36¢ for marbles. He lost three and then sold 1/3 of the remainder at cost for 90¢.
   How many marbles did he buy originally?

   8.____

9. Whenever there are urgent reasons for filling a vacancy *in any position in the competitive division and the director is unable to certify to the appointing officer, upon requisition by the latter, a list of persons eligible for appointment after a competitive examination, the appointing officer may nominate a person to the director for noncompetitive examination, and if such nominee is certified by the said director as qualified after such noncompetitive examination, he may be appointed provisionally to fill the vacancy only until a selection and appointment can be made after competitive examination, but no such appointment shall be continued for more than thirty days and successive appointments shall not be made.*
   The above paragraph states that

   9.____

   A. when no eligible register exists, appointments may be made to permanent positions by noncompetitive examinations of applicants

B. appointment is made only of the person nominated by the appointing officer
C. if an appointment continues for more than thirty days, it becomes permanent
D. permanent appointment can be made only after successful competitive examination
E. when an urgent need for filling a vacancy exists, it may be filled permanently without holding an examination

10. PHASES means   10._____

    A. varying aspects   B. sentences
    C. frightening   D. bluffing
    E. receptacle for flowers

11. AUGMENT means MOST NEARLY   11._____

    A. forecast   B. increase   C. drill
    D. hollow out   E. sell

12. CYNICAL means MOST NEARLY   12._____

    A. cone shaped   B. faithless   C. morose
    D. sneering   E. cutting

13. ALLEGES means MOST NEARLY   13._____

    A. suspects   B. studies   C. claims
    D. fears   E. denies

14. ACCOSTED means MOST NEARLY   14._____

    A. reviled   B. hated   C. liked
    D. addressed   E. deceived

15. ABSOLVED means MOST NEARLY   15._____

    A. acquitted   B. responsible   C. anointed
    D. discovered   E. vain

16. ABANDON means MOST NEARLY   16._____

    A. enthusiasm   B. skill   C. loss
    D. unrestraint   E. listlessness

17. APPREHENSIVE means MOST NEARLY   17._____

    A. angry   B. guilty   C. anxious
    D. generous   E. arrested

18. Two-thirds of a hay crop was sold. One-half of the remainder was used for fodder and 60 bales still remained unused.   18._____
How many bales were there in the entire crop?

19. A clerk threw off 1/3 of the mail sacks at A and 1/5 of the remainder at B. He then had 48 bags left.   19._____
How many were on the train when he started?

20. A man's salary was increased by 25%. He was then earning $175 a month.   20._____
What did he earn before the increase?

21. Street car tracks run PAIRULEL.
    The word in capitals is misspelled. Write it correctly at the right.

21._____

22. They went KANOOING on the river.
    The word in capitals is misspelled. Write it correctly at the right.

22._____

23. It is unwise to keep a VISHUS dog.
    The word in capitals is misspelled. Write it correctly at the right.

23._____

24. *That which comes through hard work is most appreciated.*
    The above quotation means MOST NEARLY

24._____

    A. easy riches lose their value
    B. easy come, easy go
    C. we appreciate that most which is hard to get
    D. hard work brings success

25. ALERTNESS is to SUCCESS as PROCRASTINATION is to

25._____

    A. idleness   B. failure   C. postponement
    D. leisure   E. uselessness

KEY (CORRECT ANSWERS)

1. liquefy	11. B
2. anniversary	12. D
3. frolicking	13. C
4. D	14. D
5. C	15. A
6. E	16. D
7. 15	17. C
8. 12	18. 360
9. D	19. 90
10. A	20. $140

21. parallel
22. canoeing
23. vicious
24. C
25. B

TEST 3

DIRECTIONS: Each question or incomplete statement is followed by several suggested answers or completions. Select the one that BEST answers the question or completes the statement. *PRINT THE CORRECT ANSWER IN THE SPACE AT THE RIGHT.*

1. A raise in pay allowed for this month and including the previous month is called

1.____

    A. delayed   B. postponed   C. revertible
    D. retroactive   E. past due

2. Which one of the following applies to LOCK and MAILBOX but not to STAMP?

2.____

    A. Canceled   B. Soiled
    C. Government property   D. Metal
    E. Gummed

3. INTEREST ON LOANS is to TIME as PARCEL POST RATES are to

3.____

    A. notes   B. weight   C. amount
    D. yearly   E. distance

4. To ATTEST is to

4.____

    A. heed   B. bear witness   C. make an oath
    D. try   E. question

5. F.O.B. is to FREIGHT SHIPMENT as C.O.D. is to

5.____

    A. charge account   B. store sales
    C. customers   D. package delivery
    E. purchases

6. *Blessed is he who has found his work.*
The above quotation means MOST NEARLY

6.____

    A. despatch is the soul of business
    B. thrice happy they who have an occupation
    C. drive your business, let not it drive you
    D. business neglected is business lost
    E. unoccupied is unprofitable

7. *The empty vessel makes the greatest sound.*
The above quotation means MOST NEARLY

7.____

    A. the dog that means to bite doesn't bark
    B. a boaster and a liar are cousins
    C. a deep stream flows silently
    D. aim above the mark to hit the mark
    E. the failure tells everyone how to run his business

8. *Hitch your wagon to a star.*
   The above quotation means MOST NEARLY

   A. a bird in the hand is worth two in the bush
   B. aim high and you will hit high
   C. as good do nothing as to no purpose
   D. your ability should determine your aim
   E. let nothing stop you

   8._____

9. *Little things are great to little men.*
   The above quotation means MOST NEARLY

   A. the elephant does not feel the flea bite
   B. little leaks sink great ships
   C. small minds are won by trifles
   D. drop by drop the tank is drained
   E. big oaks from little acorns grow

   9._____

10. *A pound of pluck is worth a ton of luck.*
    The above quotation means MOST NEARLY

    A. lucky men are as rare as white crows
    B. good luck is often bad luck
    C. diligence is the mother of good luck
    D. luck may carry a man across the brook if he will but leap
    E. courage overcomes more than luck

    10._____

11. To DISTRIBUTE is to

    A. agitate   B. collect   C. dispense
    D. derange   E. disintegrate

    11._____

12. A REMARKABLE occurrence is

    A. commonplace   B. extraordinary   C. needful
    D. uneventful   E. portentous

    12._____

13. WHALE is to LARGE as THUNDER is to

    A. lightning   B. injure   C. rain
    D. loud   E. distant

    13._____

14. *If you are shipping canned goods from Wisconsin to San Francisco, the goods can be put down in the San Francisco market cheaper if they are hauled east by train and then carried all the way around the coast by water. For the interstate commerce commission has so built its rate structure that it is cheaper for the Wisconsin farmer to go 4,000 miles out of his way than use the direct rail route west.*
    According to the above paragraph, which one of the following statements is TRUE?

    A. The Wisconsin farmer must go 4,000 miles out of his way to ship goods to the west coast.
    B. To ship the goods by water will save time.
    C. He can save money by shipping by the direct rail route west.
    D. In sending goods to the west coast, it is cheaper for him to send them 6,000 miles by water and rail than 2,000 miles by rail only

    14._____

15. *The Atlantic Ocean is noted for the Gulf Stream which passes northward from the Gulf of*   15._____
    Mexico, but which preserves its warmth until it reaches the British Isles. This is one of the
    reasons why England enjoys a warmer climate than Labrador, though both are in about
    the same latitude. The countries of southern Europe gain much of their warmth from the
    winds that blow across the Mediterranean Sea from the Sahara Desert.
    According to the above paragraph, which one of the following statements is TRUE?
    England is warmer than Labrador because

    A. the warm winds from the Sahara Desert reach England
    B. England is farther south than Labrador
    C. the Gulf Stream becomes cold before it reaches Labrador
    D. the Gulf Stream stays warm until it reaches England
    E. the Gulf of Mexico is directly across the ocean from England

16. *On the west coast, a campaign for a safe and sane Fourth of July was started, resulting*   16._____
    in laws that forbade the sale of fireworks in that section. The Fourth there is one of the
    quietest days of the year, the people expressing their patriotism in less harmful, though
    equally enjoyable, ways. In the east, where tradition is strong, there is no such law; but a
    tradition that brings in its wake the many tragedies that fireworks do is more honored in
    the breach than in the observance.
    According to the above paragraph, which one of the following statements is TRUE?
    The use of fireworks on the Fourth of July

    A. has been forbidden in all eastern states
    B. is traditional and so should not be prohibited
    C. is the only enjoyable way in which patriotism can be expressed
    D. is forbidden in certain western states
    E. causes very few accidents

17. A man was 69 years old on October 20th, 1992. Through 1992, in how many presidential   17._____
    elections could he have voted?

18. Two mechanics were repairing a motor, and one of the men, without knowing it, rubbed a   18._____
    smudge of grease on his face. When the job was completed, they looked at each other
    and the man with the clean face washed his face while the one with the dirty face did not.
    Which one of the following statements will explain this action?

    A. The man with the clean face wanted to impress his employer.
    B. They always washed their faces after completing a job.
    C. The man with the clean face thought his own face might be dirty.
    D. The man with the dirty face did not care about his appearance.
    E. The man with the dirty face was about to start another job.

19. *In withdrawing stamps, postal cards, stamped envelopes, and newspaper wrappers from*   19._____
    the reserve stock, postmaster should select the oldest on hand for sale to the public, pro-
    vided they are in perfect condition. This will lessen the chances for stock to become
    shopworn and damaged, and tend to keep it fresh. Damaged or soiled stamped paper or
    stamps should never be offered for sale to the public.
    According to the above paragraph, which one of the following statements is TRUE?

A. Postmasters should offer for sale only new, fresh stocks of stamps.
B. All old stock, regardless of condition, should be quickly sold.
C. Oldest stock, in perfect condition, should be sold first.
D. All old stock of stamps should be withdrawn and not offered for sale.
E. Imperfect stamps should be sold quickly before they become old.

20. *At the time of his Gettysburg Address, Lincoln himself had no knowledge of what the final result of the Civil War was to be. He knew that the great principles for which he had stood were the principles on which the war was being fought. He knew that his own firm resolution and deep patriotism had sent thousands to their deaths and that many thousands more might die. With his mind burdened with unthinkable responsibilities, he took his place on the still scarred battlefield and spoke not only to soldiers, but to the fathers and mothers of boys who might that very day be meeting death in distant battlefields. Judging entirely from the above quotation, which one of the following statements is TRUE?*   20._____

A. The Battle of Gettysburg was in progress when Lincoln made this Address.
B. Lincoln's patriotic principles were the underlying cause of the war.
C. Lincoln was in sympathy with the principles on which the war was being fought.
D. The Civil War had come to a close when Lincoln made his Gettysburg Address.
E. The fathers and mothers of the soldiers were present at the Battle of Gettysburg.

KEY (CORRECT ANSWERS)

1.	D	11.	C
2.	D	12.	B
3.	E	13.	D
4.	B	14.	D
5.	D	15.	D
6.	B	16.	D
7.	E	17.	13
8.	B	18.	C
9.	C	19.	C
10.	E	20.	C

GENERAL AND MENTAL ABILITY
COMMENTARY

No matter what the level of the examination tested for, be it for trainee or administrator, whether a specific substantive examination is drawn up *ad hoc* for the position announced or whether a brief, simple qualifying test is given, keen analysis of current testing practices reveals that the type of question indicative of general or mental ability or aptitude, or *intelligence,* is an inevitable component and/or element of most examinations.

In other words, the examiners assume that all candidates must possess, or show, a certain level of understanding or *good sense* in matters or situations that may be considered common or general to all. This, then, is the purpose of the general-or-mental-type question: it seems to delimn, in objective terms, the basic, clearly definable, mental or intellectual status of the examinee, no matter what his education or his training or his experience or his present position or reputation.

In some cases, and for certain whole fields of job positions, tests of general and mental ability have even supplanted the specialized subject-area or position-information examination.

Moreover, even in the latter type of examination, e.g., the specific position-type, it will be found that questions testing general qualities study the examination at point after point.

This section should be of inestimable value to the candidate as he prepares not only for the job-examination, but also for any other examination that he may take at this time or in the future.

Now the candidate should *take* the tests of general and mental ability that follow, because of this special importance. These, particularly, portray the extended and rounded examination of general and/or mental ability.

The *Tests* that follow also serve to focus the candidate's attention on the variety and types of questions to be encountered, and to familiarize him with answer-patterns-and-nuances.

EXAMINATION SECTION
TEST 1

DIRECTIONS: Each question or incomplete statement is followed by several suggested answers or completions. Select the one that BEST answers the question or completes the statement. *PRINT THE CORRECT ANSWER IN THE SPACE AT THE RIGHT.*

1. The OPPOSITE of defeat is   1.____

    A. glory   B. honor   C. victory
    D. success   E. hope

2. If 3 pencils cost 10 cents, how many pencils can be bought for 50 cents?   2.____

3. A dog does NOT always have   3.____

    A. eyes   B. bones   C. a nose
    D. a collar   E. lungs

4. The OPPOSITE of strange is   4.____

    A. peculiar   B. familiar   C. unusual
    D. quaint   E. extraordinary

5. A lion MOST resembles a   5.____

    A. dog   B. goat   C. cat   D. cow   E. horse

6. Sound is related to quiet in the same way that sunlight is to   6.____

    A. darkness   B. evaporation   C. bright
    D. a cellar   E. noise

7. A party consisted of a man and his wife, his three sons and their wives, and two children in each son's family. How many were there in the party?   7.____

8. A man ALWAYS has   8.____

    A. children   B. nerves   C. teeth
    D. home   E. wife

9. The OPPOSITE of stingy is   9.____

    A. wealthy   B. extravagant   C. poor
    D. economical   E. generous

10. Lead is cheaper than silver because it is   10.____

    A. duller   B. more plentiful   C. softer
    D. uglier   E. less useful

Questions 11-13.

DIRECTIONS: Answer Questions 11 through 13 by choosing the CORRECT proverb meaning given below.

A. Eat heartily at a good feast.
B. Only exceptional misfortunes harm all concerned.
C. Don't invite trouble by stirring it up.
D. Strong winds blow harder than weak ones.
E. Too much of anything is no better than a sufficiency.
F. Tired dogs need lots of sleep.

11. Which statement above explains the proverb, *Let sleeping dogs lie?*   11.____

12. Which statement above explains the proverb, *Enough is as good as a feast?*   12.____

13. Which statement above explains the proverb, *It's an ill wind that blows nobody good?*   13.____

14. A radio is related to a telephone as _____ is to a railroad train.   14.____

   A. a highway   B. an airplane   C. gasoline
   D. speed   E. noise

15. If a boy can run at the rate of 8 feet in 1/3 of a second, how far can he run in 10 seconds?   15.____

16. A debate ALWAYS involves   16.____

   A. an audience   B. judges   C. a prize
   D. a controversy   E. an auditorium

17. Of the five words below, four are alike in a certain way. Which one is NOT like these four?   17.____

   A. Walk   B. Run   C. Kneel   D. Skip   E. Jump

18. The OPPOSITE of frequently is   18.____

   A. seldom   B. occasionally   C. never
   D. sometimes   E. often

19. A thermometer is related to temperature as a speedometer is to   19.____

   A. fast   B. automobile   C. velocity
   D. time   E. heat

20. Which word makes the TRUEST sentence? Women are _____ shorter than their hus-   20.____
    bands.

   A. always   B. usually   C. much
   D. rarely   E. never

21. 1 6 2 7 3 8 4 9 5 10 7 11   21.____
    One number is wrong in the above series.
    What should that number be?

22. All children in this class are good students.   22.____
    John is not a good student.
    John is a member of this class.
    If the first two statements are true, the third is

   A. true   B. false   C. not certain

23. A boat race ALWAYS has   23.____

    A. oars   B. spectators   C. victory
    D. contestants   E. sails

24. 4 2 3 1 5 6 8 7 3 4 6 6 4 3 2 5 1 8 6 7 9   24.____
   Which number in this row appears a second time nearest the beginning?

25. The sun is related to the earth as the earth is to   25.____

    A. clouds   B. rotation   C. the universe
    D. the moon   E. circumference

KEY (CORRECT ANSWERS)

1.	C	11.	C
2.	15	12.	E
3.	D	13.	B
4.	B	14.	B
5.	C	15.	240
6.	A	16.	D
7.	14	17.	C
8.	B	18.	A
9.	E	19.	C
10.	B	20.	B

21.	6
22.	B
23.	D
24.	3
25.	D

TEST 2

DIRECTIONS: Each question or incomplete statement is followed by several suggested answers or completions. Select the one that BEST answers the question or completes the statement. *PRINT THE CORRECT ANSWER IN THE SPACE AT THE RIGHT.*

1. Which word makes the TRUEST sentence?
   A youth is _____ wiser than his father.

   A. never
   D. usually
   B. rarely
   E. always
   C. much

   1.____

2. The OPPOSITE of graceful is

   A. weak
   D. awkward
   B. ugly
   E. uncanny
   C. slow

   2.____

3. A grandmother is always _____ than her granddaughter.

   A. smarter
   D. smaller
   B. more quiet
   E. slower
   C. older

   3.____

Questions 4-6.

DIRECTIONS: Answer Questions 4 through 6 by choosing the CORRECT proverb meaning given below.

   A. Even the darkest situations have their bright aspects.
   B. The final result is more important than the intermediate steps.
   C. Handsome persons always do pleasing things.
   D. All comes out well in the end.
   E. Persons whose actions please us seem good-looking.
   F. Clouds shimmer as if they were made of silver.

4. Which statement above explains the proverb, *All's well that ends well?*   4.____

5. Which statement above explains the proverb, *Every cloud has a silver lining?*   5.____

6. Which statement above explains the proverb, *Handsome is that handsome does?*   6.____

7. If the settlement of a difference between two parties is made by a third party, it is called a(n)

   A. compromise
   D. injunction
   B. truce
   E. arbitration
   C. promise

   7.____

8. Oil is to toil as _____ is to hate.

   A. love   B. work   C. boil   D. ate   E. hat

   8.____

9. Of the five words below, four are alike in a certain way.
   Which one is NOT like these four?

   A. Push   B. Hold   C. Lift   D. Drag   E. Pull

   9.____

10. If 10 boxes full of apples weigh 300 pounds and each box when empty weighs 3 pounds, how many pounds do all the apples weigh?

10.____

11. The OPPOSITE of sorrow is

11.____

    A. fun   B. success   C. hope
    D. prosperity   E. joy

12. A B C D E F G H I J K L M N O P Q R S T U V W X Y Z
If all the odd-numbered letters in the alphabet were crossed out, what would be the twelfth letter NOT crossed out?

12.____

13. What letter in the word *unfortunately* is the same number in the word (counting from the beginning) as it is in the alphabet?

13.____

14. Such traits as honesty, sincerity, and loyalty constitute one's

14.____

    A. personality   B. reputation   C. wisdom
    D. character   E. success

15. If 3 1/3 yards of cloth cost 25 cents, what will 10 yards cost?

15.____

16. same means small little the as
If the above words were arranged to make a good sentence, with what letter would the second word of the sentence begin? (Make it like a printed capital.)

16.____

17. George is younger than Frank.
James is younger than George.
Frank is older than James.
If the first two statements are true, the third is

17.____

    A. true   B. false   C. not certain

18. Suppose that the first and second letters in the word *abolitionist* were interchanged, also the third and fourth letters, the fifth and sixth, etc.
Print the letter that would be the tenth letter counting to the right.

18.____

19. 0 1 3 6 10 15 21 29 36
One number is wrong in the above series.
What should that number be?

19.____

20. If 3 1/2 yards of cloth cost 70 cents, what will 4 1/2 yards cost?

20.____

21. A person who never pretends to be anything other than what he is, is said to be

21.____

    A. loyal   B. hypocritical   C. sincere
    D. meek   E. courageous

22. Which of these words is related to many as exceptional is to ordinary?

22.____

    A. None   B. Each   C. More   D. Much   E. Few

23. The OPPOSITE of cowardly is

23.____

    A. brave   B. strong   C. treacherous
    D. loyal   E. friendly

24. Which one of the five words below is MOST unlike the other four?   24.____

    A. Fast   B. Agile   C. Quick   D. Run   E. Speedy

25. Some of Brown's friends are Catholics.   25.____
Some of Brown's friends are lawyers.
Some of Brown's friends are Catholic lawyers.
If the first two statements are true, the third is

    A. true   B. false   C. not certain

KEY (CORRECT ANSWERS)

1. B	11. E		
2. D	12. X		
3. C	13. L		
4. B	14. D		
5. A	15. 75		
6. E	16. M		
7. E	17. A		
8. D	18. N		
9. B	19. 28		
10. 270	20. 90		

21. C
22. E
23. A
24. D
25. C

TEST 3

DIRECTIONS: Each question or incomplete statement is followed by several suggested answers or completions. Select the one that BEST answers the question or completes the statement. *PRINT THE CORRECT ANSWER IN THE SPACE AT THE RIGHT.*

1. How many of the following words can be made from the letters in the word *strangle,* using any letter any number of times: greatest, tangle, garage, stresses, related, grease, nearest, reeling?

   1.____

2. To insist that trees can talk to one another is

   2.____

   A. absurd   B. misleading   C. improbable
   D. unfair   E. wicked

3. Of the things following, four are alike in a certain way.
   Which one is NOT like these four?

   3.____

   A. Snow   B. Soot   C. Cotton   D. Ivory   E. Milk

4. A square is related to a circle in the same way in which a pyramid is related to

   4.____

   A. a solid   B. Egypt   C. height
   D. a cone   E. a circumference

5. If the following words were seen on a wall by looking in a mirror on the opposite wall, which word would appear exactly the same as if seen directly?

   5.____

   A. Meet   B. Rotor   C. Mama   D. Deed   E. Toot

6. If a strip of cloth 32 inches long will shrink to 28 inches when washed, how many inches long will a 24-inch strip of the same cloth be after shrinking?

   6.____

7. Which of the following is a trait of character?

   7.____

   A. Ability   B. Reputation   C. Hate
   D. Stinginess   E. Nervousness

8. Find the two letters in the word *coming* which have just as many letters between them in the word as in the alphabet. Print the one of these letters that comes FIRST in the alphabet.

   8.____

9. Modern is to ancient as _____ is to yesterday.

   9.____

   A. tomorrow   B. time   C. up-to-date
   D. history   E. today

10. 1 2 4 8 16 32 64 96
    One number is wrong in the above series.
    What should that number be?

    10.____

11. If George can ride a bicycle 40 feet while Frank runs 30 feet, how far can George ride while Frank runs 45 feet?

    11.____

12. L U L R V E L U R E U L U U L V E L L U V L U R U L O E V L U E   12._____
Count each L in this series that is followed by a U next to it if the U is not followed by an R next to it.
Tell how many L's you count.

13. A man who is in favor of marked change is said to be   13._____

    A. democratic   B. conservative   C. radical
    D. anarchistic   E. republican

14. Print the letter which is the fourth letter to the left of the letter midway between N and R in   14._____
the alphabet.

Questions 15-17.

DIRECTIONS: Questions 15 through 17 are to be answered on the basis of the following figure.

15. What number is in the space which is in the rectangle but not in the triangle or in the cir-   15._____
cle?

16. What number is in the same geometrical figure or figures (and no other) as the number   16._____
3?

17. How many spaces are there that are in any one but only one geometrical figure?   17._____

18. A line is related to a surface as a point is to a   18._____

    A. circle   B. line   C. solid
    D. dot   E. intersection

19. One cannot become a good lawyer without diligent study.   19._____
George studies law diligently.
George will become a good lawyer.
If the first two statements are true, the third is

    A. true   B. false   C. not certain

20. honesty traits Generosity character of desirable and are   20._____
If the above words are arranged to make the BEST sentence, with what letter will the
last word of the sentence end? (Print the letter as a capital.)

21. A man who carefully considers all available information before making a decision is said to be   21.____

    A. influential   B. prejudiced   C. decisive
    D. hypocritical   E. impartial

22. A hotel serves a mixture of 2 parts cream and 3 parts milk.   22.____
How many pints of milk will it take to make 25 pints of the mixture?

23. _____ is related to stars as physiology is to blood.   23.____

    A. Telescope   B. Darkness   C. Astronomy
    D. Light waves   E. Chemistry

24. A statement based upon a supposition is said to be   24.____

    A. erroneous   B. ambiguous   C. distorted
    D. hypothetical   E. doubtful

25. If a wire 40 inches long is to be cut so that one piece is 2/3 as long as the other piece, how many inches long must the shorter piece be?   25.____

KEY (CORRECT ANSWERS)

1.	6	11.	60
2.	A	12.	4
3.	B	13.	C
4.	D	14.	L
5.	E	15.	5
6.	21	16.	12
7.	D	17.	7
8.	G	18.	B
9.	E	19.	C
10.	128	20.	R

21.	E
22.	15
23.	C
24.	D
25.	16

EXAMINATION SECTION
TEST 1

DIRECTIONS: Each question or incomplete statement is followed by several suggested answers or completions. Select the one that BEST answers the question or completes the statement. *PRINT THE LETTER OF THE CORRECT ANSWER IN THE SPACE AT THE RIGHT.*

Questions 1-10.

DIRECTIONS: Select the alternative that means the *same as* or the *opposite* of the word in italics.

1. *acquire*   1._____

    A. judge   B. identify   C. surrender
    D. educate   E. happen

2. *begrudge*   2._____

    A. envy   B. hate   C. annoy
    D. obstruct   E. punish

3. *obsolete*   3._____

    A. fatal   B. modern   C. distracting
    D. untouched   E. broken

4. *inflexible*   4._____

    A. weak   B. righteous   C. harmless
    D. unyielding   E. secret

5. *nominal*   5._____

    A. just   B. slight   C. cheerful
    D. familiar   E. ceaseless

6. *debt*   6._____

    A. insane   B. artificial   C. skillful
    D. determined   E. humble

7. *censure*   7._____

    A. focus   B. exclude   C. baffle
    D. portray   E. praise

8. *nebulous*   8._____

    A. imaginary   B. spiritual   C. distinct
    D. starry-eyed   E. unanswerable

9. *impart*   9._____

    A. hasten   B. adjust   C. gamble
    D. address   E. communicate

10. *terminate*   10.____

    A. gain   B. graduate   C. harvest
    D. start   E. paralyze

Questions 11-20.

DIRECTIONS: Select the word which, if inserted in the blank space, agrees *most closely* with the thought of the sentence.

11. Every good story is carefully contrived; the elements of the story are _____ to fit with   11.____
one another in order to make an effect on the reader.

    A. read   B. learned   C. emphasized
    D. reduced   E. planned

12. Their work was commemorative in character and consisted largely of _____ erected   12.____
upon the occasion of victories.

    A. towers   B. tombs   C. monuments
    D. castles   E. fortresses

13. Before criticizing the work of an artist, one needs to _____ the artist's purpose.   13.____

    A. understand   B. reveal   C. defend
    D. correct   E. change

14. Because in the administration it hath respect not to the group but to the _____ , our   14.____
form of government is called a democracy.

    A. courts   B. people   C. majority
    D. individual   E. law

15. Deductive reasoning is that form of reasoning in which the conclusion must necessarily   15.____
follow if we accept the premise as true. In deduction, it is _____ for the premise to be
true and the conclusion false.

    A. impossible   B. inevitable   C. reasonable
    D. surprising   E. unlikely

16. Mathematics is the product of thought operating by means of _____ for the purpose of   16.____
expressing general laws.

    A. reasoning   B. symbols   C. words
    D. examples   E. science

17. No other man loses so much, so _____ , so absolutely, as the beaten candidate for high   17.____
public office.

    A. bewilderingly   B. predictably   C. disgracefully
    D. publicly   E. cheerfully

18. Many television watchers enjoy stories which contain violence. Consequently, those tele-   18.____
vision producers who are dominated by rating systems aim to _____ the popular taste.

    A. raise   B. control   C. gratify
    D. ignore   E. lower

19. The latent period for the contractile response to direct stimulation of the muscle has quite   19.____
another and shorter value, encompassing only a utilization period. Hence, it is that the
term *latent period* must be _____ carefully each time that it is used.

    A. checked   B. timed   C. introduced
    D. defined   E. selected

20. A man who cannot win honor in his own _____ will have a very small chance of winning   20.____
it from posterity.

    A. right   B. field   C. country   D. way   E. age

Questions 21-35.

DIRECTIONS: Select the word that BEST completes the analogy.

21. Albino is to color as traitor is to   21.____

    A. patriotism   B. treachery   C. socialism
    D. integration   E. liberalism

22. Senile is to infantile as supper is to   22.____

    A. snack   B. breakfast   C. dinner
    D. daytime   E. evening

23. Snow shovel is to sidewalk as eraser is to   23.____

    A. writing   B. pencil   C. paper
    D. desk   E. mistake

24. Lawyer is to court as soldier is to   24.____

    A. battle   B. victory   C. training
    D. rifle   E. discipline

25. Faucet is to water as mosquito is to   25.____

    A. swamp   B. butterfly   C. cistern
    D. pond   E. malaria

26. Astronomy is to geology as steeplejack is to   26.____

    A. mailman   B. surgeon   C. pilot
    D. miner   E. skindiver

27. Chimney is to smoke as guide is to   27.____

    A. snare   B. compass   C. hunter
    D. firewood   E. wild game

28. Prodigy is to ability as ocean is to   28.____

    A. water   B. waves   C. ships
    D. icebergs   E. current

29. War is to devastation as microbe is to   29.____

    A. peace   B. flea   C. dog
    D. germ   E. pestilence

30. Blueberry is to pea as sky is to   30.____

    A. storm   B. world   C. star   D. grass   E. purity

31. Pour is to spill as lie is to   31.____

    A. deception   B. misstatement   C. falsehood
    D. perjury   E. fraud

32. Disparage is to despise as praise is to   32.____

    A. dislike   B. adore   C. acclaim
    D. advocate   E. compliment

33. Wall is to mortar as nation is to   33.____

    A. family   B. people   C. patriotism
    D. geography   E. boundaries

34. Servant is to butler as pain is to   34.____

    A. cramp   B. hurt   C. illness
    D. itch   E. anesthesia

35. Fan is to air as newspaper is to   35.____

    A. literature   B. reporter   C. information
    D. subscription   E. reader

Questions 36-45.

DIRECTIONS: Select the *alternative* that BEST answers the question.

36. A set of papers is arranged and numbered from 1 to 49. If the paper numbered 3 is   36.____
drawn first and every ninth paper thereafter, what will be the number of the last paper
drawn?

    A. 45   B. 46   C. 47   D. 48   E. 49

37. Which quantity can be measured *exactly* from a tank of water by using only a 10-pint can   37.____
and an 8-pint can? _____ pint(s).

    A. 1   B. 6   C. 3   D. 7   E. 5

38. If city R has more fires than city S, and city T has more fires than cities P and S com-   38.____
bined, then the number of fires in city

    A. P must be less than in city T
    B. T must be less than in city R
    C. T must be greater than in city R
    D. R must be greater than in city P
    E. S must be greater than in city T

39. The average of three numbers is 25.   39.____
If one of the numbers is increased by 4, the average will remain unchanged if each of
the other two numbers is reduced by

    A. 1   B. 2   C. 2/3   D. 4   E. 1 1/3

40. Below are the first six rows of a triangular array constructed according to a fixed law. What number does the letter X represent?   40._____

```
                    1
                 1     1
              1     2     1
           1     3     3     1
        1     4     6     4     1
     1     5    10     X     5     1
```

   A. 8   B. 10   C. 15   D. 20   E. 5

41. If all A are C and no C are B, it necessarily follows that   41._____

   A. all B are C   B. all B are A   C. no A are B
   D. no C are A   E. some B are A

42. What number is missing in the series 7, _____ , 63, 189?   42._____

   A. 9   B. 11   C. 19   D. 21   E. 24

43. A clock that gains one minute each hour is synchronized at noon with a clock that loses   43._____
    two minutes an hour.
    How many minutes apart will the minute hands of the two clocks be at midnight?

   A. 0   B. 12   C. 14   D. 24   E. 30

44. The pages of a typewritten report are numbered by hand from 1 to 100.   44._____
    How many times will it be necessary to write the numeral 5?

   A. 10   B. 11   C. 12   D. 19   E. 20

45. The number 6 is called a *perfect* number because it is the sum of all its integral divisors   45._____
    except itself. Another *perfect* number is

   A. 12   B. 16   C. 24   D. 28   E. 36

KEY (CORRECT ANSWERS)

1.	C	11.	E	21.	A	31.	B	41.	C
2.	A	12.	C	22.	B	32.	B	42.	D
3.	B	13.	A	23.	C	33.	C	43.	D
4.	D	14.	D	24.	A	34.	A	44.	E
5.	B	15.	A	25.	E	35.	C	45.	D
6.	C	16.	B	26.	D	36.	D		
7.	E	17.	D	27.	C	37.	B		
8.	C	18.	C	28.	A	38.	A		
9.	E	19.	D	29.	E	39.	B		
10.	D	20.	E	30.	D	40.	B		

WORD MEANING

EXAMINATION SECTION
TEST 1

Questions 1-20.

DIRECTIONS: Each question consists of a statement. You are to indicate whether the statement is TRUE (T) or FALSE (F). *PRINT THE LETTER OF THE CORRECT
ANSWER IN THE SPACE AT THE RIGHT.*

1. *To eliminate hand pumping* means NEARLY the same as *to do away with hand pumping.*   1._____

2. *Discarding a ladder with a cracked rung* means NEARLY the same as *repairing a ladder*   2._____
    with a cracked rung.

3. A *projecting* stub is USUALLY a stub which sticks out.   3._____

4. A *nitrogen deficiency* in the soil is an oversupply of nitrogen in the soil.   4._____

5. Saying that a soil has a heavy *texture* is NEARLY the same as saying that the soil has a   5._____
    deep color.

6. A *neutral* soil is one in which no useful plants will grow.   6._____

7. A plant which is *dormant* is USUALLY in an inactive period of growth.   7._____

8. Saying that sun is *detrimental* to ferns is NEARLY the same as saying that sun is harmful   8._____
    to ferns.

9. *Vendors are permitted only in certain park areas.* In this sentence, the word *vendors*   9._____
    means NEARLY the same as *sellers.*

10. *The Assistant Gardener was confident that he would be able to learn the new work*   10._____
    quickly. In this sentence, the word *confident* means NEARLY the same as *sure.*

11. *The employee's behavior on the job was improper.* In this sentence, the word *improper*   11._____
    means NEARLY the same as *good.*

12. *The foreman's oral instructions were always clear and to the point.* In this sentence, the   12._____
    word *oral* means NEARLY the same as *spoken.*

13. *A covering with paper will prevent excessive loss of moisture from the surface soil.* In this   13._____
    sentence, the word *excessive* means NEARLY the same as *unnecessary.*

14. *In making a permanent hotbed, the ground should be excavated to a depth of fifteen*   14._____
    inches. In this sentence, the word *excavated* means NEARLY the same as *dug out.*

15. *After the seed has been sown, an application of water will help it to germinate.* In this   15._____
    sentence, the word *germinate* means NEARLY the same as *start growing.*

16. *A sandy soil may be greatly improved through the incorporation of organic materials.* In   16._____
    this sentence, the word *incorporation* means NEARLY the same as *removal.*

17. *Manures are considered a concentrated form of fertilizer.*
    In this sentence, the word *concentrated* means NEARLY the same as *natural.*   17.____

18. *Ventilation of some kind must be given the plants.* In this sentence, the word *ventilation*   18.____
    means NEARLY the same as *heat.*

19. *When rain water enters soil, it penetrates air spaces.* In this sentence, the word *pene-*   19.____
    trates means NEARLY the same as *fills.*

20. *The metal was corroded.* In this sentence, the word *corroded* means NEARLY the same   20.____
    as *polished.*

Questions 21-40.

DIRECTIONS: In answering Questions 21 through 40, select the lettered word which means
             MOST NEARLY the same as the capitalized word. *PRINT THE LETTER OF*
             THE CORRECT ANSWER IN THE SPACE AT THE RIGHT.

21. ACCURATE   21.____

    A. correct   B. useful   C. afraid   D. careless

22. ALTER   22.____

    A. copy   B. change   C. repeat   D. agree

23. DOCUMENT   23.____

    A. outline   B. agreement   C. blueprint   D. record

24. INDICATE   24.____

    A. listen   B. show   C. guess   D. try

25. INVENTORY   25.____

    A. custom   B. discovery   C. warning   D. list

26. ISSUE   26.____

    A. annoy   B. use up   C. give out   D. gain

27. NOTIFY   27.____

    A. inform   B. promise   C. approve   D. strengthen

28. ROUTINE   28.____

    A. path   B. mistake   C. habit   D. journey

29. TERMINATE   29.____

    A. rest   B. start   C. deny   D. end

30. TRANSMIT   30.____

    A. put in   B. send   C. stop   D. go across

44

31. QUARANTINE   31._____

    A. feed   B. keep separate
    C. clean   D. give an injection to

32. HERD   32._____

    A. group   B. pair   C. person   D. ear

33. SPECIES   33._____

    A. few   B. favorite   C. kind   D. small

34. INJURE   34._____

    A. hurt   B. need   C. protect   D. help

35. ANNOY   35._____

    A. like   B. answer   C. rest   D. bother

36. EXTINCT   36._____

    A. likely   B. no longer exists
    C. tired   D. gradually dying out

37. CONFINE   37._____

    A. fly about freely   B. free
    C. keep within limits   D. care

38. ENVIRONMENT   38._____

    A. distant   B. surroundings
    C. disease   D. lake

39. AVIARY   39._____

    A. pig pen   B. large bird cage
    C. elephant cage   D. snake pit

40. CRATE   40._____

    A. make   B. report   C. box   D. truck

———

KEY (CORRECT ANSWERS)

1.	T	11.	F	21.	A	31.	B
2.	F	12.	T	22.	B	32.	A
3.	T	13.	F	23.	D	33.	C
4.	F	14.	T	24.	B	34.	A
5.	F	15.	T	25.	D	35.	D
6.	F	16.	F	26.	C	36.	B
7.	T	17.	F	27.	A	37.	C
8.	T	18.	F	28.	C	38.	B
9.	T	19.	F	29.	D	39.	B
10.	T	20.	F	30.	B	40.	C

TEST 2

Questions 1-6.

DIRECTIONS: Questions 1 through 6 are to be answered on the basis of the following paragraph.

It is important that traffic signals be regularly and _effectively_ maintained. Signals with _impaired_ efficiency cannot be expected to command _desired_ respect. Poorly maintained traffic signs create disrespect in the minds of those who are to obey them and thereby reduce the effectiveness and authority of the signs. Maintenance should receive _paramount_ consideration in the design and purchase of traffic signal equipment. The _initial_ step in a good maintenance program for traffic signals is the establishment of a maintenance record. This record should show the cost of operation and maintenance of different types of equipment. It should give complete information regarding signal operations and indicate where _defective_ planning exists in maintenance programs.

1. The word _effectively,_ as used in the above paragraph, means MOST NEARLY   1.____

   A. occasionally   B. properly
   C. expensively   D. cheaply

2. The word _impaired,_ as used in the above paragraph, means MOST NEARLY   2.____

   A. reduced   B. increased   C. constant   D. high

3. The word _desired,_ as used in the above paragraph, means MOST NEARLY   3.____

   A. public   B. complete   C. wanted   D. enough

4. The word _paramount,_ as used in the above paragraph, means MOST NEARLY   4.____

   A. little   B. chief   C. excessive   D. some

5. The word _initial,_ as used in the above paragraph, means MOST NEARLY   5.____

   A. first   B. final
   C. determining   D. most important

6. The word _defective,_ as used in the above paragraph, means MOST NEARLY   6.____

   A. suitable   B. real   C. good   D. faulty

Questions 7-31.

DIRECTIONS: Each of Questions 7 through 31 consists of a capitalized word followed by four suggested meanings of the word. For each question, choose the word or phrase which means MOST NEARLY the same as the capitalized word.

7. ABOLISH   7.____

   A. count up   B. do away with
   C. give more   D. pay double for

8. ABUSE   8.____

   A. accept   B. mistreat   C. respect   D. touch

9. ACCURATE   9.____

  A. correct   B. lost   C. neat   D. secret

10. ASSISTANCE   10.____

  A. attendance   B. belief
  C. help   D. reward

11. CAUTIOUS   11.____

  A. brave   B. careful   C. greedy   D. hopeful

12. COURTEOUS   12.____

  A. better   B. easy   C. polite   D. religious

13. CRITICIZE   13.____

  A. admit   B. blame   C. check on   D. make dirty

14. DIFFICULT   14.____

  A. capable   B. dangerous   C. dull   D. hard

15. ENCOURAGE   15.____

  A. aim at   B. beg for   C. cheer on   D. free from

16. EXTENT   16.____

  A. age   B. size   C. truth   D. wildness

17. EXTRAVAGANT   17.____

  A. empty   B. helpful   C. over   D. wasteful

18. FALSE   18.____

  A. absent   B. colored
  C. not enough   D. wrong

19. INDICATE   19.____

  A. point out   B. show up
  C. shrink from   D. take to

20. NEGLECT   20.____

  A. disregard   B. flatten
  C. likeness   D. thoughtfulness

21. PENALIZE   21.____

  A. make   B. notice   C. pay   D. punish

22. POSTPONED   22.____

  A. put off   B. repeated   C. taught   D. went to

23. PUNCTUAL   23.____

    A. bursting   B. catching
    C. make a hole in   D. on time

24. RARE   24.____

    A. large   B. ride up   C. unusual   D. young

25. REVEAL   25.____

    A. leave   B. renew   C. soften   D. tell

26. EXCESSIVE   26.____

    A. excusable   B. immoderate
    C. ethereal   D. intentional

27. VOLUNTARY   27.____

    A. common   B. paid   C. sharing   D. willing

28. WHOLESOME   28.____

    A. cheap   B. healthful   C. hot   D. together

29. SERIOUS   29.____

    A. important   B. order   C. sharp   D. tight

30. TRIVIAL   30.____

    A. alive   B. empty   C. petty   D. troublesome

31. VENTILATE   31.____

    A. air out   B. darken
    C. last   D. take a chance

Questions 32-40.

DIRECTIONS: Each question consists of a statement. You are to indicate whether the statement is TRUE (T) or FALSE (F).

32. *The price of this merchandise fluctuates from day to day.* In this sentence, the word *fluctuates* means the OPPOSITE of *remains steady.*   32.____

33. *The patient was in acute pain.* In this sentence, the word *acute* means the OPPOSITE of *slight.*   33.____

34. *The essential data appear in the report.* In this sentence, the word *data* means the OPPOSITE of *facts.*   34.____

35. *The open lounge is spacious.* In this sentence, the word *spacious* means the OPPOSITE of *well-lighted.*   35.____

36. *The landscaping work was a prolonged task.* In this sentence, the word *prolonged* means NEARLY the same as *difficult.*   36.____

37. *A transparent removable cover was placed over the flower bed.* In this sentence, the   37.____
word *transparent* means NEARLY the same as *wooden.*

38. *The prompt action of the employee saved many lives.* In this sentence, the word *prompt*   38.____
means NEARLY the same as *quick.*

39. *The attendant's request for a vacation was approved.* In this sentence, the word   39.____
approved means NEARLY the same as *refused.*

40. *The paycheck was received in the mail.* In this sentence, the *word received* means   40.____
NEARLY the same as *lost.*

———

KEY (CORRECT ANSWERS)

1.	B	11.	B	21.	D	31.	A
2.	A	12.	C	22.	A	32.	T
3.	C	13.	B	23.	D	33.	T
4.	B	14.	D	24.	C	34.	F
5.	A	15.	C	25.	D	35.	F
6.	D	16.	B	26.	B	36.	F
7.	B	17.	D	27.	D	37.	F
8.	B	18.	D	28.	B	38.	T
9.	A	19.	A	29.	A	39.	F
10.	C	20.	A	30.	C	40.	F

———

TEST 3

Questions 1-50.

DIRECTIONS: Each question consists of a statement. You are to indicate whether the statement is TRUE (T) or FALSE (F). *PRINT THE LETTER OF THE CORRECT
ANSWER IN THE SPACE AT THE RIGHT.*

1. *A few men were assisting the attendant.* In this sentence, the word *assisting* means
NEARLY the same as *helping.*

1.____

2. *He opposed the idea of using a vacuum cleaner for this job.*
In this sentence, the word *opposed* means NEARLY the same as *suggested.*

2.____

3. *Four employees were selected.* In this sentence, the word *selected* means NEARLY the
same as *chosen.*

3.____

4. *This man is constantly supervised.* In this sentence, the word *constantly* means NEARLY
the same as *rarely.*

4.____

5. *One part of soap to two parts of water is sufficient.* In this sentence, the word *sufficient*
means NEARLY the same as *enough.*

5.____

6. *The fire protection system was inadequate.* In this sentence, the word *inadequate* means
NEARLY the same as *very good.*

6.____

7. *The nozzle of the hose was clogged.* In this sentence, the word *clogged* means NEARLY
the same as *brass.*

7.____

8. *He resembles the man who worked here before.* In this sentence, the word *resembles*
means NEARLY the same as *replaces.*

8.____

9. *They eliminated a number of items.* In this sentence, the word *eliminated* means
NEARLY the same as *bought.*

9.____

10. *He is a dependable worker.* In this sentence, the word *dependable* means NEARLY the
same as *poor.*

10.____

11. *Some wood finishes color the wood and conceal the natural grain.* In this sentence, the
word *conceal* means NEARLY the same as *hide.*

11.____

12. *Paint that is chalking sometimes retains its protective value.* In this sentence, the word
retains means NEARLY the same as *keeps.*

12.____

13. *Wood and trash had accumulated.* In this sentence, the word *accumulated* means
NEARLY the same as *piled up.*

13.____

14. An *inflammable* liquid is one that is easily set on fire.

14.____

15. *The amounts were then compared.* In this sentence, the word *compared* means NEARLY
the same as *added.*

15.____

16. *The boy had fallen into a shallow pool.* In this sentence, the word *shallow* means NEARLY the same as *deep.*   16.____

17. *He acquired a new instrument.* In this sentence, the word *acquired* means NEARLY the same as *got.*   17.____

18. *Several men were designated for this activity.* In this sentence, the word *designated* means NEARLY the same as *laid off.*   18.____

19. *The drawer had been converted into a file.* In this sentence, the word *converted* means NEARLY the same as *changed.*   19.____

20. *The patient has recuperated.* In this sentence, the word *recuperated* means NEARLY the same as *died.*   20.____

21. *A rigid material should be used.* In this sentence, the word *rigid* means NEARLY the same as *stiff.*   21.____

22. *Only half the supplies were utilized.* In this sentence, the word *utilized* means NEARLY the same as *used.*   22.____

23. *In all these years, he had never obstructed any change.* In this sentence, the word *obstructed* means NEARLY the same as *suggested.*   23.____

24. *Conditions were aggravated when he left.* In this sentence, the word *aggravated* means NEARLY the same as *improved.*   24.____

25. *The autopsy room is now available.* In this sentence, the word *available* means NEARLY the same as *clean.*   25.____

26. An investigation which *precedes* a report is one which comes before the report.   26.____

27. *Another word was inserted.* In this sentence, the word *inserted* means NEARLY the same as *put in.*   27.____

28. *He reversed the recommended steps in the procedure.* In this sentence, the word *reversed* means NEARLY the same as *explained.*   28.____

29. *His complaint was about a trivial matter.* In this sentence, the word *trivial* means NEARLY the same as *petty.*   29.____

30. *Using the proper tool will aid a worker in doing a better job.* In this sentence, the word *aid* means NEARLY the same as *help.*   30.____

31. *The application form has a space for the name of the former employer.* In this sentence, the word *former* means NEARLY the same as *new.*   31.____

32. *The exterior of the building needed to be painted.* In this sentence, the word *exterior* means NEARLY the same as *inside.*   32.____

33. *The smoke from the fire was dense.* In this sentence, the word *dense* means NEARLY the same as *thick.*   33.____

34. *Vacations should be planned in advance.* In this sentence, vacations should be planned ahead of time.   34.____

35. *The employee denied that he would accept another job.*
    In this sentence, the word *denied* means NEARLY the same as *admitted.*   35.____

36. *An annual report is made by the central stockroom.* In this sentence, the word *annual* means NEARLY the same as *monthly.*   36.____

37. *Salaries were increased in the new budget.* In this sentence, the word *increased* means NEARLY the same as *cut.*   37.____

38. *All excess oil is to be removed from tools.* In this sentence, the word *excess* means NEARLY the same as *extra.*   38.____

39. *The new employee did similar work on his last job.* In this sentence, the word *similar* means NEARLY the same as *interesting.*   39.____

40. *Helpful employees make favorable impressions on the public.* In this sentence, the word *favorable* means NEARLY the same as *poor.*   40.____

41. *Some plants are grown for the decorative value of their leaves.* In this sentence, the word *decorative* means NEARLY the same as *ornamental.*   41.____

42. *They made a circular flower garden.* In this sentence, the word *circular* means NEARLY the same as *square.*   42.____

43. *The gardener was a conscientious worker.* In this sentence, the word *conscientious* means NEARLY the same as *lazy.*   43.____

44. *The instructions received were contradictory.* In this sentence, the word *contradictory* means NEARLY the same as *alike.*   44.____

45. *His application for the job was rejected.* In this sentence, the word *rejected* means NEARLY the same as *accepted.*   45.____

46. *This plant reaches maturity quickly.* In this sentence, the word *maturity* means NEARLY the same as *full development.*   46.____

47. *The garden was provided with a system of underground irrigation.* In this sentence, the word *irrigation* means NEARLY the same as *watering.*   47.____

48. *In some plants, the flowers often appear before the foliage.* In this sentence, the word *foliage* refers to the leaves of the plant.   48.____

49. *The new horticultural society was organized through the merger of two previous groups.* In this sentence, the word *merger* means NEARLY the same as *breakup.*   49.____

50. *The stem of the plant measured three inches in diameter.* In this sentence, the word *diameter* means NEARLY the same as *height.*   50.____

KEY (CORRECT ANSWERS)

1.	T	11.	T	21.	T	31.	F	41.	T
2.	F	12.	T	22.	T	32.	F	42.	F
3.	T	13.	T	23.	F	33.	T	43.	F
4.	F	14.	T	24.	F	34.	T	44.	F
5.	T	15.	F	25.	F	35.	F	45.	F
6.	F	16.	F	26.	T	36.	F	46.	T
7.	F	17.	T	27.	T	37.	F	47.	T
8.	F	18.	F	28.	F	38.	T	48.	T
9.	F	19.	T	29.	T	39.	F	49.	F
10.	F	20.	F	30.	T	40.	F	50.	F

EXAMINATION SECTION
TEST 1

DIRECTIONS: Select the word or phrase which has the same meaning, or most nearly the same meaning, as the CAPITALIZED word. *PRINT THE LETTER OF THE CORRECT ANSWER IN THE SPACE AT THE RIGHT.*

1. A CAR is to

    A. start fires with   B. eat on   C. take pictures with
    D. ride in   E. draw with

1.____

2. INK is used to

    A. walk on   B. .write with   C. cut with
    D. serve with   E. stand on

2.____

3. POOR means having very little

    A. money   B. hair   C. sun   D. time   E. snow

3.____

4. COMBAT

    A. point   B. report   C. fight   D. start   E. admit

4.____

5. A MISTAKE is something done

    A. first   B. wrong   C. next   D. often   E. alone

5.____

6. HOWL

    A. roar   B. design   C. propose   D. depart   E. succeed

6.____

7. PHONY

    A. tough   B. neutral   C. vivid   D. fake   E. hasty

7.____

8. ADVICE

    A. record   B. visit   C. bridge   D. opinion   E. minute

8.____

9. BURLAP

    A. tunnel   B. medicine   C. soil   D. engine   E. fabric

9.____

10. A SEAMSTRESS is a woman who

    A. writes   B. sews   C. sings   D. paints   E. bakes

10.____

11. APPROACH means to come

    A. through   B. with   C. into   D. between   E. near

11.____

12. ABANDON

    A. look over   B. hold on   C. lift up   D. fall down   E. give up

12.____

13. BARELY

    A. generally   B. scarcely   C. completely
    D. especially   E. gradually

13.____

14. SNEER   14.____

    A. listen with interest   B. practice with care   C. look with scorn
    D. lift with ease   E. dance with joy

15. ELIGIBLE   15.____

    A. lonesome   B. careless   C. qualified   D. inferior   E. profound

16. EXCLUDE   16.____

    A. educate   B. excite   C. eliminate   D. encourage   E. ensure

17. JUVENILE   17.____

    A. haunted   B. youthful   C. intimate   D. favorable   E. unable

18. JOLT   18.____

    A. justify   B. join   C. judge   D. jar   E. journey

19. GRATIFY   19.____

    A. heat   B. shout   C. hope   D. charge   E. please

20. RAFTER   20.____

    A. angel   B. canal   C. beam   D. lamb   E. trunk

21. LANK   21.____

    A. slender   B. grateful   C. musical   D. lively   E. rare

22. CONSOLE   22.____

    A. compare   B. conclude   C. comfort   D. command   E. collect

23. MANIPULATE   23.____

    A. reserve   B. devote   C. handle   D. inquire   E. introduce

24. CONCRETE   24.____

    A. clean   B. mean   C. low   D. nice   E. real

25. DESTITUTE   25.____

    A. respectful   B. divine   C. urgent   D. slippery   E. needy

26. BASTION   26.____

    A. fortification   B. qualification   C. appropriation
    D. legislation   E. illustration

27. FOREGO   27.____

    A. represent   B. sacrifice   C. justify
    D. determine   E. display

28. MACKINTOSH   28.____

    A. raincoat   B. tractor   C. honeybee
    D. cartoon   E. saucepan

29. TRAJECTORY   29.____

    A. curved path   B. ill health   C. bold type
    D. glorious spirit   E. strong back

30. A TRIPHTHONG is a combination of three   30.____

    A. fossils   B. cables   C. diagrams
    D. vowels   E. atoms

31. WHIST   31.____

    A. captain   B. game   C. soul   D. finger   E. rock

32. FETID   32.____

    A. exhausted   B. stinking   C. pathetic
    D. meager   E. insane

33. BEZANT   33.____

    A. hotel   B. coin   C. mill   D. harbor   E. desk

34. SCINTILLATE   34.____

    A. develop   B. whistle   C. ruin   D. breathe   E. flash

35. GLIB   35.____

    A. unaware   B. fluent   C. reluctant
    D. philosophical   E. inquisitive

36. DINT   36.____

    A. supply   B. wish   C. force   D. price   E. demand

37. SARCOPHAGUS   37.____

    A. coffin   B. insect   C. interview
    D. wharf   E. mushroom

38. DIABOLO   38.____

    A. bed   B. dance   C. game   D. mark   E. record

39. LEMPIRA   39.____

    A. chair   B. money   C. salt   D. earth   E. music

40. PYROPE   40.____

    A. reptile   B. heather   C. slogan   D. mantle   E. garnet

KEY (CORRECT ANSWERS)

1.	D	11.	E	21.	A	31.	B
2.	B	12.	E	22.	C	32.	B
3.	A	13.	B	23.	C	33.	B
4.	C	14.	C	24.	E	34.	E
5.	B	15.	C	25.	E	35.	B
6.	A	16.	C	26.	A	36.	C
7.	D	17.	B	27.	B	37.	A
8.	D	18.	D	28.	A	38.	C
9.	E	19.	E	29.	A	39.	B
10.	B	20.	C	30.	D	40.	E

SPELLING
EXAMINATION SECTION
TEST 1

DIRECTIONS: In each of the following tests in this part, select the letter of the one MIS-SPELLED word in each of the following groups of words. *PRINT THE LETTER OF THE CORRECT ANSWER IN THE SPACE AT THE RIGHT.*

1. A. grateful   B. fundimental   1.____
   C. census   D. analysis

2. A. installment   B. retrieve   2.____
   C. concede   D. dissapear

3. A. accidentaly   B. dismissal   3.____
   C. conscientious   D. indelible

4. A. perceive   B. carreer   C. anticipate   D. acquire   4.____

5. A. facillity   B. reimburse   C. assortment   D. guidance   5.____

6. A. plentiful   B. across   6.____
   C. advantagous   D. similar

7. A. omission   B. pamphlet   C. guarrantee   D. repel   7.____

8. A. maintenance   B. always   8.____
   C. liable   D. anouncement

9. A. exaggerate   B. sieze   C. condemn   D. commit   9.____

10. A. pospone   B. altogether   C. grievance   D. excessive   10.____

11. A. banana   B. trafic   C. spectacle   D. boundary   11.____

12. A. commentator   B. abbreviation   12.____
    C. battaries   D. monastery

13. A. practically   B. advise   13.____
    C. pursuade   D. laboratory

14. A. fatigueing   B. invincible   14.____
    C. strenuous   D. ceiling

15. A. propeller   B. reverence   C. piecemeal   D. underneth   15.____

16. A. annonymous   B. envelope   C. transit   D. variable   16.____

17. A. petroleum   B. bigoted   C. meager   D. resistence   17.____

18. A. permissible   B. indictment   18.____
    C. fundemental   D. nowadays

19. A. thief   B. bargin   C. nuisance   D. vacant   19.____

20. A. technique   B. vengeance   C. aquatic   D. heighth   20.____

_____

KEY (CORRECT ANSWERS)

1. B. fundamental
2. D. disappear
3. A. accidentally
4. B. career
5. A. facility

6. C. advantageous
7. C. guarantee
8. D. announcement
9. B. seize
10. A. postpone

11. B. traffic
12. C. batteries
13. C. persuade
14. A. fatiguing
15. D. underneath

16. A. anonymous
17. D. resistance
18. C. fundamental
19. B. bargain
20. D. height

TEST 2

DIRECTIONS: In each of the following tests in this part, select the letter of the one MIS-
SPELLED word in each of the following groups of words. *PRINT THE LETTER
OF THE CORRECT ANSWER IN THE SPACE AT THE RIGHT.*

1.   A.   apparent   B.   superintendent   1.____
     C.   releive   D.   calendar

2.   A.   foreign   B.   negotiate   C.   typical   D.   disipline   2.____

3.   A.   posponed   B.   argument   3.____
     C.   susceptible   D.   deficit

4.   A.   preferred   B.   column   C.   peculiar   D.   equiped   4.____

5.   A.   exaggerate   B.   disatisfied   5.____
     C.   repetition   D.   already

6.   A.   livelihood   B.   physician   C.   obsticle   D.   strategy   6.____

7.   A.   courageous   B.   ommission   C.   ridiculous   D.   awkward   7.____

8.   A.   sincerely   B.   abundance   C.   negligable   D.   elementary   8.____

9.   A.   obsolete   B.   mischievous   9.____
     C.   enumerate   D.   atheletic

10. A.   fiscel   B.   beneficiary   10.____
     C.   concede   D.   translate

11. A.   segregate   B.   excessivly   C.   territory   D.   obstacle   11.____

12. A.   unnecessary   B.   monopolys   12.____
     C.   harmonious   D.   privilege

13. A.   sinthetic   B.   intellectual   13.____
     C.   gracious   D.   archaic

14. A.   beneficial   B.   fulfill   C.   sarcastic   D.   disolve   14.____

15. A.   umbrella   B.   sentimental   15.____
     C.   inefficent   D.   psychiatrist

16. A.   noticable   B.   knapsack   C.   librarian   D.   meant   16.____

17. A.   conference   B.   upheaval   C.   vulger   D.   odor   17.____

18. A.   surmount   B.   pentagon   C.   calorie   D.   inumerable   18.____

19. A.   classifiable   B.   moisturize   19.____
     C.   monitor   D.   assesment

20. A.   thermastat   B.   corrupting   C.   approach   D.   thinness   20.____

KEY (CORRECT ANSWERS)

1. C. relieve
2. D. discipline
3. A. postponed
4. D. equipped
5. B. dissatisfied

6. C. obstacle
7. B. omission
8. C. negligible
9. D. athletic
10. A. fiscal

11. B. excessively
12. B. monopolies
13. A. synthetic
14. D. dissolve
15. C. inefficient

16. A. noticeable
17. C. vulgar
18. D. innumerable
19. D. assessment
20. A. thermostat

———

TEST 3

DIRECTIONS: In each of the following tests in this part, select the letter of the one MIS-SPELLED word in each of the following groups of words. *PRINT THE LETTER OF THE CORRECT ANSWER IN THE SPACE AT THE RIGHT.*

1. A. typical   B. descend   C. summarize   D. continuel   1.____
2. A. courageous   B. recomend   C. omission   D. eliminate   2.____
3. A. compliment   B. illuminate   3.____
    C. auxilary   D. installation
4. A. preliminary   B. aquainted   4.____
    C. syllable   D. analysis
5. A. accustomed   B. negligible   C. interupted   D. bulletin   5.____
6. A. summoned   B. managment   C. mechanism   D. sequence   6.____
7. A. commitee   B. surprise   C. noticeable   D. emphasize   7.____
8. A. occurrance   B. likely   C. accumulate   D. grievance   8.____
9. A. obstacle   B. particuliar   9.____
    C. baggage   D. fascinating
10. A. innumerable   B. seize   10.____
    C. applicant   D. dictionery
11. A. monkeys   B. rigid   C. unnatural   D. roomate   11.____
12. A. surveying   B. figurative   C. famous   D. curiosety   12.____
13. A. rodeo   B. inconcievable   13.____
    C. calendar   D. magnificence
14. A. handicaped   B. glacier   C. defiance   D. emperor   14.____
15. A. schedule   B. scrawl   C. seclusion   D. sissors   15.____
16. A. tissues   B. tomatos   C. tyrants   D. tragedies   16.____
17. A. casette   B. graceful   C. penicillin   D. probably   17.____
18. A. gnawed   B. microphone   C. clinicle   D. batch   18.____
19. A. amateur   B. altitude   C. laborer   D. expence   19.____
20. A. mandate   B. flexable   C. despise   D. verify   20.____

KEY (CORRECT ANSWERS)

1. D. continual
2. B. recommend
3. C. auxiliary
4. B. acquainted
5. C. interrupted

6. B. management
7. A. committee
8. A. occurrence
9. B. particular
10. D. dictionary

11. D. roommate
12. D. curiosity
13. B. inconceivable
14. A. handicapped
15. D. scissors

16. B. tomatoes
17. A. cassette
18. C. clinical
19. D. expense
20. B. flexible

TEST 4

DIRECTIONS: In each of the following tests in this part, select the letter of the one MIS-SPELLED word in each of the following groups of words. *PRINT THE LETTER OF THE CORRECT ANSWER IN THE SPACE AT THE RIGHT.*

1.   A. primery   B. mechanic   C. referred   D. admissible   1._____

2.   A. cessation   B. beleif   C. aggressive   D. allowance   2._____

3.   A. leisure   B. authentic   3._____
     C. familiar   D. contemptable

4.   A. volume   B. forty   C. dilemma   D. seldum   4._____

5.   A. discrepancy   B. aquisition   5._____
     C. exorbitant   D. lenient

6.   A. simultanous   B. penetrate   6._____
     C. revision   D. conspicuous

7.   A. ilegible   B. gracious   C. profitable   D. obedience   7._____

8.   A. manufacturer   B. authorize   8._____
     C. compelling   D. pecular

9.   A. anxious   B. rehearsal   C. handicaped   D. tendency   9._____

10. A. meticulous   B. accompaning   10._____
     C. initiative   D. shelves

11. A. hammaring   B. insecticide   11._____
     C. capacity   D. illogical

12. A. budget   B. luminous   C. aviation   D. lunchon   12._____

13. A. moniter   B. bachelor   13._____
     C. pleasurable   D. omitted

14. A. monstrous   B. transistor   C. narrative   D. anziety   14._____

15. A. engagement   B. judical   C. pasteurize   D. tried   15._____

16. A. fundimental   B. innovation   16._____
     C. perpendicular   D. extravagant

17. A. bookkeeper   B. brutality   C. gymnaseum   D. cemetery   17._____

18. A. sturdily   B. pretentious   18._____
     C. gourmet   D. enterance

19. A. resturant   B. tyranny   19._____
     C. kindergarten   D. ancestry

20. A. benefit   B. possess   C. speciman   D. noticing   20._____

KEY (CORRECT ANSWERS)

1. A. primary
2. B. belief
3. D. contemptible
4. D. seldom
5. B. acquisition

6. A. simultaneous
7. A. illegible
8. D. peculiar
9. C. handicapped
10. B. accompanying

11. A. hammering
12. D. luncheon
13. A. monitor
14. D. anxiety
15. B. judicial

16. A. fundamental
17. C. gymnasium
18. D. entrance
19. A. restaurant
20. C. specimen

TEST 5

DIRECTIONS: In each of the following tests in this part, select the letter of the one MIS-SPELLED word in each of the following groups of words. *PRINT THE LETTER OF THE CORRECT ANSWER IN THE SPACE AT THE RIGHT.*

1. A. arguing   B. correspondance   1.____
   C. forfeit   D. dissension

2. A. occasion   B. description   2.____
   C. prejudice   D. elegible

3. A. accomodate   B. initiative   C. changeable   D. enroll   3.____

4. A. temporary   B. insistent   C. benificial   D. separate   4.____

5. A. achieve   B. dissappoint   5.____
   C. unanimous   D. judgment

6. A. procede   B. publicly   C. sincerity   D. successful   6.____

7. A. deceive   B. goverment   C. preferable   D. repetitive   7.____

8. A. emphasis   B. skillful   C. advisible   D. optimistic   8.____

9. A. tendency   B. rescind   C. crucial   D. noticable   9.____

10. A. privelege   B. abbreviate   C. simplify   D. divisible   10.____

11. A. irresistible   B. varius   11.____
    C. mutual   D. refrigerator

12. A. amateur   B. distinguish   12.____
    C. rehearsal   D. poision

13. A. biased   B. ommission   C. precious   D. coordinate   13.____

14. A. calculated   B. enthusiasm   C. sincerely   D. parashute   14.____

15. A. sentry   B. materials   C. incredable   D. budget   15.____

16. A. chocolate   B. instrument   C. volcanoe   D. shoulder   16.____

17. A. ancestry   B. obscure   C. intention   D. ninty   17.____

18. A. artical   B. bracelet   C. beggar   D. hopeful   18.____

19. A. tournament   B. sponsor   19.____
    C. perpendiclar   D. dissolve

20. A. yeild   B. physician   C. greasiest   D. admitting   20.____

KEY (CORRECT ANSWERS)

1. B. correspondence
2. D. eligible
3. A. accommodate
4. C. beneficial
5. B. disappoint

6. A. proceed
7. B. government
8. C. advisable
9. D. noticeable
10. A. privilege

11. B. various
12. D. poison
13. B. omission
14. D. parachute
15. C. incredible

16. C. volcano
17. D. ninety
18. A. article
19. C. perpendicular
20. A. yield

———

TEST 6

DIRECTIONS: In each of the following tests in this part, select the letter of the one MIS-SPELLED word in each of the following groups of words. *PRINT THE LETTER OF THE CORRECT ANSWER IN THE SPACE AT THE RIGHT.*

1. A. achievment   B. maintenance   1._____
   C. questionnaire   D. all are correct

2. A. prevelant   B. pronunciation   2._____
   C. separate   D. all are correct

3. A. permissible   B. relevant   3._____
   C. seize   D. all are correct

4. A. corroborate   B. desparate   4._____
   C. eighth   D. all are correct

5. A. exceed   B. feasibility   5._____
   C. psycological   D. all are correct

6. A. parallel   B. aluminum   C. calendar   D. eigty   6._____

7. A. microbe   B. ancient   C. autograph   D. existance   7._____

8. A. plentiful   B. skillful   C. amoung   D. capsule   8._____

9. A. erupt   B. quanity   C. opinion   D. competent   9._____

10. A. excitement   B. discipline   C. luncheon   D. regreting   10._____

11. A. magazine   B. expository   C. imitation   D. permenent   11._____

12. A. ferosious   B. machinery   12._____
    C. precise   D. magnificent

13. A. conceive   B. narritive   C. separation   D. management   13._____

14. A. muscular   B. witholding   C. pickle   D. glacier   14._____

15. A. vehicel   B. mismanage   15._____
    C. correspondence   D. dissatisfy

16. A. sentince   B. bulletin   C. notice   D. definition   16._____

17. A. appointment   B. exactly   17._____
    C. typest   D. light

18. A. penalty   B. suparvise   C. consider   D. division   18._____

19. A. schedule   B. accurate   C. corect   D. simple   19._____

20. A. suggestion   B. installed   C. proper   D. agincy   20._____

KEY (CORRECT ANSWERS)

1. A. achievement
2. A. prevalent
3. D all are correct
4. B. desperate
5. C. psychological

6. D. eighty
7. D. existence
8. C. among
9. B. quantity
10. D. regretting

11. D. permanent
12. A. ferocious
13. B. narrative
14. B. withholding
15. A. vehicle

16. A. sentence
17. C. typist
18. B. supervise
19. C. correct
20. D. agency

———

TEST 7

DIRECTIONS: In each of the following tests in this part, select the letter of the one MIS-SPELLED word in each of the following groups of words. *PRINT THE LETTER OF THE CORRECT ANSWER IN THE SPACE AT THE RIGHT.*

1. A. symtom   B. serum   C. antiseptic   D. aromatic   1.____

2. A. register   B. registrar   C. purser   D. burser   2.____

3. A. athletic   B. tragedy   C. batallion   D. sophomore   3.____

4. A. latent   B. godess   C. aisle   D. whose   4.____

5. A. rhyme   B. rhythm   C. thime   D. thine   5.____

6. A. eighth   B. exaggerate   C. electorial   D. villain   6.____

7. A. statute   B. superintendent   7.____
   C. iresistible   D. colleague

8. A. sieze   B. therefor   C. auxiliary   D. changeable   8.____

9. A. siege   B. knowledge   C. lieutenent   D. weird   9.____

10. A. acquitted   B. polititian   C. professor   D. conqueror   10.____

11. A. changeable   B. chargeable   C. salable   D. useable   11.____

12. A. promissory   B. prisoner   C. excellent   D. tyrrany   12.____

13. A. conspicuous   B. essance   13.____
    C. comparative   D. brilliant

14. A. notefying   B. accentuate   C. adhesive   D. primarily   14.____

15. A. exercise   B. sublime   C. stuborn   D. shameful   15.____

16. A. presume   B. transcript   C. strech   D. wizard   16.____

17. A. specify   B. regional   17.____
    C. arbitrary   D. segragation

18. A. requirement   B. happiness   18.____
    C. achievement   D. gentlely

19. A. endurance   B. fusion   C. balloon   D. enormus   19.____

20. A. luckily   B. schedule   C. simplicity   D. sanwich   20.____

――――――

KEY (CORRECT ANSWERS)

1. A. symptom
2. D. bursar
3. C. battalion
4. B. goddess
5. C. thyme

6. C. electoral
7. C. irresistible
8. A. seize
9. C. lieutenant
10. B. politician

11. D. usable
12. D. tyranny
13. B. essence
14. A. notifying
15. C. stubborn

16. C. stretch
17. D. segregation
18. D. gently
19. D. enormous
20. D. sandwich

TEST 8

DIRECTIONS: In each of the following tests in this part, select the letter of the one MIS-SPELLED word in each of the following groups of words. *PRINT THE LETTER OF THE CORRECT ANSWER IN THE SPACE AT THE RIGHT.*

1. A. maintain   B. maintainance   1.____
    C. sustain   D. sustenance

2. A. portend   B. portentious   2.____
    C. pretend   D. pretentious

3. A. prophesize   B. prophesies   3.____
    C. farinaceous   D. spaceous

4. A. choose   B. chose   C. choosen   D. chasten   4.____

5. A. censure   B. censorious   5.____
    C. pleasure   D. pleasurible

6. A. cover   B. coverage   C. adder   D. adege   6.____

7. A. balloon   B. diregible   C. direct   D. descent   7.____

8. A. whemsy   B. crazy   C. flimsy   D. lazy   8.____

9. A. derision   B. pretention   C. sustention   D. contention   9.____

10. A. question   B. questionaire   10.____
    C. legion   D. legionary

11. A. chattle   B. cattle   C. dismantle   D. kindle   11.____

12. A. canal   B. cannel   C. chanel   D. colonel   12.____

13. A. hemorrage   B. storage   C. manage   D. foliage   13.____

14. A. surgeon   B. sturgeon   C. luncheon   D. stancheon   14.____

15. A. diploma   B. commission   C. dependent   D. luminious   15.____

16. A. likelihood   B. blizzard   C. machanical   D. suppress   16.____

17. A. commercial   B. releif   C. disposal   D. endeavor   17.____

18. A. operate   B. bronco   C. excaping   D. grammar   18.____

19. A. orchard   B. collar   C. embarass   D. distant   19.____

20. A. sincerly   B. possessive   C. weighed   D. waist   20.____

KEY (CORRECT ANSWERS)

1.   B. maintenance
2.   B. portentous
3.   D. spacious
4.   C. chosen
5.   D. pleasurable

6.   D. adage
7.   B. dirigible
8.   A. whimsy
9.   B. pretension
10.   B. questionnaire

11.   A. chattel
12.   C. channel
13.   A. hemorrhage
14.   D. stanchion
15.   D. luminous

16.   C. mechanical
17.   B. relief
18.   C. escaping
19.   C. embarrass
20.   A. sincerely

TEST 9

DIRECTIONS: In each of the following tests in this part, select the letter of the one MIS-
SPELLED word in each of the following groups of words. *PRINT THE LETTER
OF THE CORRECT ANSWER IN THE SPACE AT THE RIGHT.*

1.	A. statute			B. stationary				1._____
	C. staturesque			D. stature				
2.	A. practicible			B. practical				2._____
	C. particle			D. reticule				
3.	A. plague	B. plaque	C. ague	D. aigrete				3._____
4.	A. theology	B. idealogy	C. psychology	D. philology				4._____
5.	A. dilema	B. stamina	C. feminine	D. strychnine				5._____
6.	A. deceit	B. benefit	C. grieve	D. hienous				6._____
7.	A. commensurable			B. measurable				7._____
	C. duteable			D. salable				
8.	A. homogeneous			B. heterogeneous				8._____
	C. advantageous			D. religeous				
9.	A. criticize	B. dramatise	C. exorcise	D. exercise				9._____
10.	A. ridiculous	B. comparable	C. merciful	D. cotten				10._____
11.	A. antebiotic	B. stitches	C. pitiful	D. sneaky				11._____
12.	A. amendment			B. candadate				12._____
	C. accountable			D. recommendation				
13.	A. avocado	B. recruit	C. tripping	D. probally				13._____
14.	A. calendar	B. desirable	C. familar	D. vacuum				14._____
15.	A. deteriorate			B. elligible				15._____
	C. liable			D. missile				
16.	A. amateur			B. competent				16._____
	C. mischeivous			D. occasion				
17.	A. friendliness			B. saleries				17._____
	C. cruelty			D. ammunition				
18.	A. wholesome	B. cieling	C. stupidity	D. eligible				18._____
19.	A. comptroller			B. traveled				19._____
	C. accede			D. procede				
20.	A. Britain			B. Brittainica				20._____
	C. conductor			D. vendor				

KEY (CORRECT ANSWERS)

1. C. statuesque
2. A. practicable
3. D. aigrette
4. B. ideology
5. A. dilemma

6. D. heinous
7. C. dutiable
8. D. religious
9. B. dramatize
10. D. cotton

11. A. antibiotic
12. B. candidate
13. D. probably
14. C. familiar
15. B. eligible

16. C. mischievous
17. B. salaries
18. B. ceiling
19. D. proceed
20. B. Brittanica

TEST 10

DIRECTIONS: In each of the following tests in this part, select the letter of the one MIS-SPELLED word in each of the following groups of words. *PRINT THE LETTER OF THE CORRECT ANSWER IN THE SPACE AT THE RIGHT.*

1. A. lengthen B. region C. gases D. inspecter 1._____

2. A. imediately C. complimentary B. forbidden D. aeronautics 2._____

3. A. continuous B. paralel C. opposite D. definite 3._____

4. A. Antarctic B. Wednesday C. Febuary D. Hungary 4._____

5. A. transmission C. pistol B. exposure D. customery 5._____

6. A. juvinile C. deceive B. martyr D. collaborate 6._____

7. A. unnecessary C. cancellation B. repetitive D. airey 7._____

8. A. transit B. availible C. objection D. galaxy 8._____

9. A. ineffective C. arrangement B. believeable D. aggravate 9._____

10. A. possession B. progress C. reception D. predjudice 10._____

11. A. congradulate C. major B. percolate D. leisure 11._____

12. A. convenience C. emerge B. privilige D. immerse 12._____

13. A. erasable C. audable B. inflammable D. laudable 13._____

14. A. final B. fines C. finis D. Finish 14._____

15. A. emitted C. discipline B. representative D. insistance 15._____

16. A. diphthong B. rarified C. library D. recommend 16._____

17. A. compel C. successful B. belligerent D. sargeant 17._____

18. A. dispatch B. dispise C. dispose D. dispute 18._____

19. A. administrator C. diner B. adviser D. celluler 19._____

20. A. ignite B. ignision C. igneous D. ignited 20._____

KEY (CORRECT ANSWERS)

1. D. inspector
2. A. immediately
3. B. parallel
4. C. February
5. D. customary

6. A. juvenile
7. D. airy
8. B. available
9. B. believable
10. D. prejudice

11. A. congratulate
12. B. privilege
13. C. audible
14. D. Finnish
15. D. insistence

16. B. rarefied
17. D. sergeant
18. B. despise
19. D. cellular
20. B. ignition

TEST 11

DIRECTIONS: In each of the following tests in this part, select the letter of the one MIS-SPELLED word in each of the following groups of words. *PRINT THE LETTER OF THE CORRECT ANSWER IN THE SPACE AT THE RIGHT.*

1. A. repellent   B. secession   C. sebaceous   D. saxaphone   1. ____

2. A. navel   B. counteresolution   2. ____
    C. marginalia   D. perceptible

3. A. Hammerskjold   B. Nehru   3. ____
    C. U Thamt   D. Khrushchev

4. A. perculate   B. periwinkle   4. ____
    C. perigee   D. retrogression

5. A. buccaneer   B. tobacco   C. buffalo   D. oscilate   5. ____

6. A. siege   B. wierd   C. seize   D. cemetery   6. ____

7. A. equaled   B. bigoted   7. ____
    C. benefited   D. kaleideoscope

8. A. blamable   B. bullrush   8. ____
    C. questionnaire   D. irascible

9. A. tobagganed   B. acquiline   9. ____
    C. capillary   D. cretonne

10. A. daguerrotype   B. elegiacal   10. ____
    C. iridescent   D. inchoate

11. A. bayonet   B. braggadocio   11. ____
    C. corollary   D. connoiseur

12. A. equinoctial   B. fusillade   12. ____
    C. fricassee   D. potpouri

13. A. octameter   B. impressario   13. ____
    C. hyetology   D. hieroglyphics

14. A. innanity   B. idyllic   C. fylfot   D. inimical   14. ____

15. A. liquefy   B. rarefy   C. putrify   D. sapphire   15. ____

16. A. canonical   B. stupified   16. ____
    C. millennium   D. memorabilia

17. A. paraphenalia   B. odyssey   17. ____
    C. onomatopoeia   D. osseous

18. A. peregrinate   B. pecadillo   18. ____
    C. reptilian   D. uxorious

19. A. pharisaical   B. vicissitude   19. ____
    C. puissance   D. wainright

20. A. holocaust   B. tesselate   C. scintilla   D. staccato   20. ____

KEY (CORRECT ANSWERS)

1. D. saxophone
2. B. counterresolution
3. C. U Thant
4. A. percolate
5. D. oscillate

6. B. weird
7. D. kaleidoscope
8. B. bulrush
9. B. aquiline
10. A. daguerreotype

11. D. connoisseur
12. D. potpourri
13. B. impresario
14. A. inanity
15. C. putrefy

16. B. stupefied
17. A. paraphernalia
18. B. peccadillo
19. D. wainwright
20. B. tessellate

TEST 12

DIRECTIONS: In each of the following tests in this part, select the letter of the one MIS-SPELLED word in each of the following groups of words. *PRINT THE LETTER OF THE CORRECT ANSWER IN THE SPACE AT THE RIGHT.*

1. A. questionnaire   B. gondoleer   C. chandelier   D. acquiescence   1._____

2. A. surveillance   B. surfeit   C. vaccinate   D. belligerent   2._____

3. A. occassionally   B. recurrence   C. silhouette   D. incessant   3._____

4. A. transferral   B. benefical   C. descendant   D. dependent   4._____

5. A. separately   B. flouresence   C. deterrent   D. parallel   5._____

6. A. acquittal   B. enforceable   C. counterfeit   D. indispensible   6._____

7. A. susceptible   B. accelarate   C. exhilarate   D. accommodation   7._____

8. A. impedimenta   B. collateral   C. liason   D. epistolary   8._____

9. A. inveigle   B. panegyric   C. reservoir   D. manuver   9._____

10. A. synopsis   B. paraphernalia   C. affidavit   D. subpoena   10._____

11. A. grosgrain   B. vermilion   C. abbatoir   D. connoiseur   11._____

12. A. gabardine   B. camoflage   C. hemorrhage   D. contraband   12._____

13. A. opprobrious   B. defalcate   13._____
    C. fiduciery   D. recommendations

14. A. nebulous   B. necessitate   C. impricate   D. discrepancy   14._____

15. A. discrete   B. condesension   C. condign   D. condiment   15._____

16. A. cavalier   B. effigy   C. legitimatly   D. misalliance   16._____

17. A. rheumatism   B. vaporous   C. cannister   D. hallucinations   17._____

18. A. paleonthology   B. octogenarian   C. gradient   D. impingement   18._____

19. A. fusilade   B. fusilage   C. ensilage   D. desiccate   19._____

20. A. rationale   B. raspberry   C. reprobate   D. varigated   20._____

KEY (CORRECT ANSWERS)

1. B. gondolier
2. A. surveillance
3. A. occasionally
4. B. beneficial
5. B. fluorescence

6. D. indispensable
7. B. accelerate
8. C. liaison
9. D. maneuver
10. B. paraphernalia

11. D. connoisseur
12. B. camouflage
13. C. fiduciary
14. C. imprecate
15. B. condescension

16. C. legitimately
17. C. canister
18. A. paleontology
19. A. fusillade
20. D. variegated

VERBAL ANALOGIES

EXAMINATION SECTION
TEST 1

DIRECTIONS: In Questions 1 to 10, the first two *italicized* words have a relationship to each other. Determine that relationship, and then match the third *italicized* word with the one of the lettered choices with which it has the same relationship as the words of the first pair have to each other. *PRINT THE LETTER OF THE CORRECT ANSWER IN THE SPACE AT THE RIGHT.*

In order to help you understand the procedure, a sample question is given:

SAMPLE: *dog* is to *bark* as *cat* is to
    A. animal   B. small   C. meow
    D. pet   E. snarl

The relationship between *dog* and *bark* is that the sound which a dog normally emits is a bark. In the same way, the sound which a cat emits is a meow. Thus, C is the CORRECT answer.

1. *Fine* is to *speeding* as *jail* is to   1.____

    A. bars   B. prisoner   C. warden
    D. confinement   E. steal

2. *Orchid* is to *rose* as *gold* is to   2.____

    A. watch   B. copper   C. mine   D. coin   E. mint

3. *Pistol* is to *machine gun* as *button* is to   3.____

    A. coat   B. bullet   C. zipper
    D. tailor   E. needle and thread

4. *Spontaneous* is to *unrehearsed* as *planned* is to   4.____

    A. completed   B. organized   C. restricted
    D. understood   E. informal

5. *Friendly* is to *hostile* as *loyalty* is to   5.____

    A. fealty   B. evil   C. devotion
    D. warlike   E. treachery

6. *Fear* is to *flight* as *bravery* is to   6.____

    A. courage   B. danger   C. resistance
    D. injury   E. unyielding

7. *Economical* is to *stingy* as *sufficient* is to   7.____

    A. abundant   B. adequate   C. expensive
    D. needy   E. greedy

8. *Astronomer* is to *observation* as *senator* is to   8.____

    A. caucus   B. election   C. convention
    D. legislation   E. patronage

9. *Hunger* is to *food* as *exhaustion* is to   9.____

    A. labor   B. play   C. illness
    D. debility   E. rest

10. *Entertainment* is to *boredom* as *efficiency* is to   10.____

    A. ignorance   B. government   C. waste
    D. expert   E. time and motion stud-
                                  ies

KEY (CORRECT ANSWERS)

1.	E	6.	C
2.	B	7.	A
3.	C	8.	D
4.	B	9.	E
5.	E	10.	C

TEST 2

DIRECTIONS: In Questions 1 to 10, the first two *italicized* words have a relationship to each other. Determine that relationship, and then match the third *italicized* word with the one of the lettered choices with which it has the same relationship as the words of the first pair have to each other. *PRINT THE LETTER OF THE CORRECT ANSWER IN THE SPACE AT THE RIGHT.*

1. *Diamond* is to *glass* as *platinum* is to   1._____

    A. jewelry   B. metal   C. aluminum
    D. mine   E. white

2. *Water* is to *aqueduct* as *electricity* is to   2._____

    A. meter   B. battery   C. fuse   D. wire   E. solenoid

3. *Oratory* is to *filibuster* as *reign* is to   3._____

    A. tyrant   B. terror   C. government
    D. bluster   E. confusion

4. *Gravity* is to *gaiety* as *taunt* is to   4._____

    A. ridicule   B. console   C. avoid
    D. amuse   E. condone

5. *Electron* is to *atom* as *earth* is to   5._____

    A. sun   B. solar system   C. moon
    D. planet   E. center

6. *Flattery* is to *adulation* as *cruelty* is to   6._____

    A. pain   B. barbarity   C. censorious
    D. compassion   E. duality

7. *Rowboat* is to *oar* as *automobile* is to   7._____

    A. land   B. engine   C. driver
    D. passenger   E. piston

8. *Friction* is to *oil* as *war* is to   8._____

    A. conference   B. peace   C. munitions
    D. satellite   E. retaliation

9. *Disease* is to *infection* as *reaction* is to   9._____

    A. control   B. injury   C. relapse
    D. stipulation   E. sensation

10. *Persecution* is to *martyr* as *swindle* is to   10._____

    A. embezzler   B. refuge   C. confidence man
    D. bank   E. dupe

KEY (CORRECT ANSWERS)

1. C
2. D
3. E
4. B
5. B

6. B
7. B
8. A
9. E
10. E

———

TEST 3

DIRECTIONS: In Questions 1 to 10, the first two *italicized* words have a relationship to each other. Determine that relationship, and then match the third *italicized* word with the one of the lettered choices with which it has the same relationship as the words of the first pair have to each other. *PRINT THE LETTER OF THE CORRECT ANSWER IN THE SPACE AT THE RIGHT.*

1. *Woman* is to *man* as *Mary* is to   1._____

    A. woman   B. child   C. female   D. John   E. male

2. *Land* is to *ocean* as *soldier* is to   2._____

    A. river   B. sailor   C. shore   D. uniform   E. sailing

3. *Sugar* is to *candy* as *flour* is to   3._____

    A. eat   B. cook   C. candy   D. bread   E. sweet

4. *Sorrow* is to *joy* as *laugh* is to   4._____

    A. amuse   B. tears   C. fun   D. weep   E. cry

5. *Heat* is to *fire* as *pain* is to   5._____

    A. injury   B. wind   C. weather   D. cool   E. summer

6. *Grass* is to *cattle* as *milk* is to   6._____

    A. growing   B. lawn   C. baby   D. green   E. sun

7. *Winter* is to *spring* as *autumn* is to   7._____

    A. summer   B. winter   C. warm   D. cold   E. flower

8. *Rising* is to *falling* as *smile* is to   8._____

    A. climbing   B. baking   C. scolding
    D. frown   E. laughing

9. *Day* is to *night* as *succeed* is to   9._____

    A. fail   B. sunshine   C. evening
    D. afternoon   E. morning

10. *Apple* is to *fruit* as *corn* is to   10._____

    A. orange   B. eat   C. grain   D. cereal   E. food

———————

KEY (CORRECT ANSWERS)

1.	D	6.	C
2.	B	7.	B
3.	D	8.	D
4.	E	9.	A
5.	A	10.	C

———

TEST 4

DIRECTIONS: In Questions 1 to 10, the first two *italicized* words have a relationship to each other. Determine that relationship, and then match the third *italicized* word with the one of the lettered choices with which it has the same relationship as the words of the first pair have to each other. *PRINT THE LETTER OF THE CORRECT ANSWER IN THE SPACE AT THE RIGHT.*

1. *Robin* is to *feathers* as *cat* is to   1._____

    A. sing   B. fur   C. eat   D. bird   E. fly

2. *Late* is to *end* as *early* is to   2._____

    A. prompt   B. enter   C. begin   D. start   E. end

3. *Beginning* is to *end* as *horse* is to   3._____

    A. cart   B. automobile   C. wagon
    D. travel   E. ride

4. *Kitten* is to *cat* as *baby* is to   4._____

    A. rabbit   B. mother   C. dog   D. cow   E. lamb

5. *Little* is to *weak* as *big* is to   5._____

    A. boy   B. man   C. tall   D. baby   E. strong

6. *Arm* is to *hand* as *leg* is to   6._____

    A. knee   B. toe   C. elbow   D. foot   E. finger

7. *Alive* is to *dead* as *well* is to   7._____

    A. grow   B. sick   C. decay   D. sleep   E. play

8. *In* is to *out* as *bad* is to   8._____

    A. up   B. open   C. good   D. shut   E. on

9. *Dust* is to *dry* as *mud* is to   9._____

    A. wet   B. blow   C. splash   D. fly   E. settle

10. *Width* is to *wide* as *height* is to   10._____

    A. high   B. low   C. tall   D. brief   E. short

KEY (CORRECT ANSWERS)

1. B
2. C
3. A
4. B
5. E

6. D
7. B
8. C
9. A
10. C

———

TEST 5

DIRECTIONS: In Questions 1 to 10, the first two *italicized* words have a relationship to each other. Determine that relationship, and then match the third *italicized* word with the one of the lettered choices with which it has the same relationship as the words of the first pair have to each other. *PRINT THE LETTER OF THE CORRECT ANSWER IN THE SPACE AT THE RIGHT.*

1. *Above* is to *below* as *before* is to   1._____

    A. beyond   B. behind   C. beside   D. between   E. after

2. *Start* is to *stop* as *begin* is to   2._____

    A. go   B. run   C. wait   D. finish   E. work

3. *Everything* is to *nothing* as *always* is to   3._____

    A. forever   B. usually   C. never
    D. sometimes   E. something

4. *Search* is to *find* as *question* is to   4._____

    A. answer   B. reply   C. study
    D. problem   E. explain

5. *Top* is to *spin* as *spear* is to   5._____

    A. bottom   B. roll   C. throw   D. sharp   E. pin

6. *Scale* is to *weight* as *thermometer* is to   6._____

    A. weather   B. temperature   C. pounds
    D. spring   E. chronometer

7. *Congress* is to *senator* as *convention* is to   7._____

    A. election   B. chairman   C. delegate
    D. nominee   E. representative

8. *Dividend* is to *investor* as *wage* is to   8._____

    A. employee   B. salary   C. consumer
    D. price   E. employer

9. *Terminate* is to *commence* as *adjourn* is to   9._____

    A. enact   B. convene   C. conclude
    D. veto   E. prorogue

10. *Administrator* is to *policy* as *clerk* is to   10._____

    A. subornation   B. organization   C. coordination
    D. direction   E. application

KEY (CORRECT ANSWERS)

1.	E	6.	B
2.	D	7.	C
3.	C	8.	A
4.	A	9.	B
5.	C	10.	E

———

READING COMPREHENSION
UNDERSTANDING AND INTERPRETING WRITTEN MATERIAL
EXAMINATION SECTION
TEST 1

DIRECTIONS: Each question has five suggested answers, lettered A to E. Decide which one
is the BEST answer. *PRINT THE LETTER OF THE CORRECT ANSWER IN
THE SPACE AT THE RIGHT.*

1. Some specialists are willing to give their services to the Government entirely free of
charge; some feel that a nominal salary, such as will cover traveling expenses, is sufficient for a position that is recognized as being somewhat honorary in nature; many other
specialists value their time so highly that they will not devote any of it to public service
that does not repay them at a rate commensurate with the fees that they can obtain from
a good private clientele.
*The paragraph BEST supports the statement that the use of specialists by the Govern-
ment*

    A. is rare because of the high cost of securing such persons
    B. may be influenced by the willingness of specialists to serve
    C. enables them to secure higher salaries in private fields
    D. has become increasingly common during the past few years
    E. always conflicts with private demands for their services

1.____

2. The fact must not be overlooked that only about one-half of the international trade of the
world crosses the oceans. The other half is merely exchanges of merchandise between
countries lying alongside each other or at least within the same continent.
The paragraph BEST supports the statement that

    A. the most important part of any country's trade is transoceanic
    B. domestic trade is insignificant when compared with foreign trade
    C. the exchange of goods between neighborhing countries is not considerd interna-
tional trade
    D. foreign commerce is not necessarily carried on by water
    E. about one-half of the trade of the world is international

2.____

3. Individual differences in mental traits assume importance in fitting workers to jobs
because such personal characteristics are persistent and are relatively little influenced
by training and experience.
The paragraph BEST supports the statement that training and experience

    A. are limited in their effectiveness in fitting workers to jobs
    B. do not increase a worker's fitness for a job
    C. have no effect upon a person's mental traits
    D. have relatively little effect upon the individual's chances for success
    E. should be based on the mental traits of an individual

3.____

4. The competition of buyers tends to keep prices up, the competition of sellers to send them down. Normally the pressure of competition among sellers is stronger than that among buyers since the seller has his article to sell and must get rid of it, whereas the buyer is not committed to anything.
The paragraph BEST supports the statement that low prices are caused by

    4._____

    A. buyer competition
    B. competition of buyers with sellers
    C. fluctuations in demand
    D. greater competition among sellers than among buyers
    E. more sellers than buyers

5. In seventeen states, every lawyer is automatically a member of the American Bar Association. In some other states and localities, truly representative organizations of the Bar have not yet come into being, but are greatly needed.
The paragraph IMPLIES that

    5._____

    A. representative Bar Associations are necessary in states where they do not now exist
    B. every lawyer is required by law to become a member of the Bar
    C. the Bar Association is a democratic organization
    D. some states have more lawyers than others
    E. every member of the American Bar Association is automatically a lawyer in seventeen states.

_____

KEY (CORRECT ANSWERS)

    1. B
    2. D
    3. A
    4. D
    5. A

_____

TEST 2

DIRECTIONS: Each question has five suggested answers, lettered A to E. Decide which one
is the BEST answer. *PRINT THE LETTER OF THE CORRECT ANSWER IN
THE SPACE AT THE RIGHT.*

1. We hear a great deal about the new education, and see a great deal of it in action. But   1._____
the school house, though prodigiously magnified in scale, is still very much the same old
school house.
The paragraph IMPLIES that

    A.   the old education was, after all, better than the new
    B.   although the modern school buildings are larger than the old ones, they have not
changed very much in other respects
    C.   the old school houses do not fit in with modern educational theories
    D.   a fine school building does not make up for poor teachers
    E.   schools will be schools

2. No two human beings are of the same pattern — not even twins and the method of bring-   2._____
ing out the best in each one necessarily varies according to the nature of the child.
The paragraph IMPLIES that

    A.   individual differences should be considered in dealing with children
    B.   twins should be treated impartially
    C.   it is an easy matter to determine the special abilities of children
    D.   a child's nature varies from year to year
    E.   we must discover the general technique of dealing with children

3. Man inhabits today a world very different from that which encompassed even his parents   3._____
and grandparents. It is a world geared to modern machinery—automobiles, airplanes,
power plants; it is linked together and served by electricity.
The paragraph IMPLIES that

    A.   the world has not changed much during the last few generations
    B.   modern inventions and discoveries have brought about many changes in man's
way of living
    C.   the world is run more efficiently today than it was in our grandparents' time
    D.   man is much happier today than he was a hundred years ago
    E.   we must learn to see man as he truly is, underneath the veneers of man's contriv-
ances

4. Success in any study depends largely upon the interest taken in that particular subject by   4._____
the student. This being the case, each teacher earnestly hopes that her students will
realize at the very outset that shorthand can be made an intensely fascinating study.
The paragraph IMPLIES that

    A.   everyone is interested in shorthand
    B.   success in a study is entirely impossible unless the student finds the study very
interesting
    C.   if a student is eager to study shorthand, he is likely to succeed in it
    D.   shorthand is necessary for success
    E.   anyone who is not interested in shorthand will not succeed in business

5. The primary purpose of all business English is to move the reader to agreeable and 5.____
mutually profitable action. This action may be indirect or direct, but in either case a highly
competitive appeal for business should be clothed with incisive diction tending to replace
vagueness and doubt with clarity, confidence, and appropriate action.
The paragraph IMPLIES that the

   A. ideal business letter uses words to conform to the reader's language level
   B. business correspondent should strive for conciseness in letter writing
   C. keen competition of today has lessened the value of the letter as an appeal for business
   D. writer of a business letter should employ incisive diction to move the reader to compliant and gainful action
   E. the writer of a business letter should be himself clear, confident, and Forceful

---

KEY (CORRECT ANSWERS)

1. B
2. A
3. B
4. C
5. D

TEST 3

DIRECTIONS: Each question has five suggested answers, lettered A to E. Decide which one is the BEST answer. *PRINT THE LETTER OF THE CORRECT ANSWER IN THE SPACE AT THE RIGHT.*

1. To serve the community best, a comprehensive city plan must coordinate all physical improvements, even at the possible expense of subordinating individual desires, to the end that a city may grow in a more orderly way and provide adequate facilities for its people.
   The paragraph IMPLIES that

   A. city planning provides adequate facilities for recreation
   B. a comprehensive city plan provides the means for a city to grow in a more orderly fashion
   C. individual desires must always be subordinated to civic changes
   D. the only way to serve a community is to adopt a comprehensive city plan
   E. city planning is the most important function of city government

   1.____

2. Facility in writing letters, the knack of putting into these quickly written letters the same personal impression that would mark an interview, and the ability to boil down to a one-page letter the gist of what might be called a five- or ten-minute conversation—all these are essential to effective work under conditions of modern business organization.
   The paragraph IMPLIES that

   A. letters are of more importance in modern business activities than ever before
   B. letters should be used in place of interviews
   C. the ability to write good letters is essential to effective work in modern business organization
   D. business letters should never be more than one page in length
   E. the person who can write a letter with great skill will get ahead more readily than others

   2.____

3. The general rule is that it is the city council which determines the amount to be raised by taxation and which therefore determines, within the law, the tax rates. As has been pointed out, however, no city council or city authority has the power to determine what kinds of taxes should be levied.
   The paragraph IMPLIES that

   A. the city council has more authority than any other municipal body
   B. while the city council has a great deal of authority in the levying of taxes, its power is not absolute
   C. the kinds of taxes levied in different cities vary greatly
   D. the city council appoints the tax collectors
   E. the mayor determines the kinds of taxes to be levied

   3.____

4. The growth of modern business has made necessary mass production, mass distribution, and mass selling. As a result, the problems of personnel and industrial relations have increased so rapidly that grave injustices in the handling of personal relationships have frequently occurred. Personnel administration is complex because, as in all human problems, many intangible elements are involved. Therefore a thorough, systematic, and continuous study of the psychology of human behavior is essential to the intelligent handling of personnel.
   The paragraph IMPLIES that

   4.____

A. complex modern industry makes impossible the personal relationships which formerly existed between employer and employee
B. mass decisions are successfully applied to personnel problems
C. the human element in personnel administration makes continuous study necessary to its intelligent application
D. personnel problems are less important than the problems of mass production and mass distribution
E. since personnel administration is so complex and costly, it should be sub-ordinated to the needs of good industrial relations

5. The Social Security Act is striving toward the attainment of economic security for the individual and for his family. It was stated, in outlining this program, that security for the individual and for the family concerns itself with three factors: (1) decent homes to live in; (2) development of the natural resources of the country so as to afford the fullest opportunity to engage in productive work; and (3) safeguards against the major misfortunes of life. The Social Security Act is concerned with the third of these factors – "safeguards against misfortunes which cannot be wholly eliminated in this man-made world of ours."
    The paragraph IMPLIES that the   5._____

A. Social Security Act is concerned primarily with supplying to families decent homes in which to live
B. development of natural resources is the only means of offering employment to the
C. masses of the unemployed
    Social Security Act has attained absolute economic security for the individual and his family
D. Social Security Act deals with the first (1) factor as stated in the paragraph above
E. Social Security Act deals with the third (3) factor as stated in the paragraph above

---

KEY (CORRECT ANSWERS)

1. B
2. C
3. B
4. C
5. E

TEST 4

Free unrhymed verse has been practiced for some thousands of years and reaches back to the incantation which linked verse with the ritual dance. It provided a communal emotion; the aim of the cadenced phrases was to create a state of mind. The general coloring of free rhythms in the poetry of today is that of speech rhythm, composed in the sequence of the musical phrase, not in the sequence of the metronome, the regular beat. In the twenties, conventional rhyme fell into almost complete disuse. This liberation from rhyme became as well a liberation of rhyme. Freed of its exacting task of supporting lame verse, it would be applied with greater effect where wanted for some special effect. Such break in the tradition of rhymed verse had the healthy effect of giving it a fresh start, released from the hampering convention of too familiar cadences. This refreshing and subtilizing of the use of rhyme can be seen everywhere in the poetry today.

1. The title below that BEST expresses the ideas of this paragraph is: 1.____

    A. Primitive Poetry
    B. The Origin of Poetry
    C. Rhyme and Rhythm in Modern Verse
    D. Classification of Poetry
    E. Purposes in All Poetry

2. Free verse had its origin in primitive   2.____

    A. fairytales   B. literature   C. warfare
    D. chants   E. courtship

3. The object of early free verse was to   3.____

    A. influence the mood of the people   B. convey ideas
    C. produce mental pictures   D. create pleasing sounds
    E. provide enjoyment

PASSAGE 2

Control of the Mississippi had always been goals of nations having ambitions in the New World. La Salle claimed it for France in 1682. Iberville appropriated it to France when he colonized Louisiana in 1700. Bienville founded New Orleans, its principal port, as a French city in 1718. The fleur-de-lis were the blazon of the delta country until 1762. Then Spain claimed all of Louisiana. The Spanish were easy neighbors. American products from western Pennsylvania and the North west Territory were barged down the Ohio and Mississippi to New Orleans, here they were reloaded on ocean-going vessels that cleared for the great seaports of the world.

1. The title below that BEST expresses the ideas of this paragraph is: 1.____

    A. Importance of seaports
    B. France and Spain in the New World
    C. Early control of the Mississippi
    D. Claims of European nations
    E. American trade on the Mississippi

2. Until 1762 the lower Mississippi area was held by   2.____

    A. England   B. Spain   C. the United States
    D. France   E. Indians

3. In doing business with Americans the Spaniards were   3.____

    A. easy to outsmart
    B. friendly to trade
    C. inclined to charge high prices for use of their ports
    D. shrewd
    E. suspicious

PASSAGE 3

Our humanity is by no means so materialistic as foolish talk is continually asserting it to be. Judging by what I have learned about men and women, I am convinced that there is far more in them of idealistic willpower than ever comes to the surface of the world. Just as the water of streams is small in amount compared to that which flows underground, so the idealism which becomes visible is small in amount compared with that which men and women bear locked in their hearts, unreleased or scarcely released. To unbind what is bound, to bring the underground waters to the surface — mankind is waiting and longing for men who can do that.

1. The title below that BEST expresses the ideas of this paragraph is   1.____

    A. Releasing Underground Riches
    B. The Good and Bad in Man
    C. Materialism in Humanity
    D. The Surface and the Depths of Idealism
    E. Unreleased Energy

2. Human beings are more idealistic than   2.____

    A. the water in underground streams
    B. their waiting and longing proves
    C. outward evidence shows
    D. the world
    E. other living creatures

PASSAGE 4

The total impression made by any work of fiction cannot be rightly understood without a sympathetic perception of the artistic aims of the writer. Consciously or unconsciouly, he has accepted certain facts, and rejected or suppressed other facts, in order to give unity to the particular aspect of human life which he is depicting. No novelist possesses the impartiality, the indifference, the infinite tolerance of nature. Nature displays to use, with complete unconcern, the beautiful and the ugly, the precious and the trivial, the pure and the impure. But a writer must select the aspects of nature and human nature which are demanded by the work in hand. He is forced to select, to combine, to create.

1. The title below that BEST expresses the ideas of this paragraph is: 1.____

    A. Impressionists in Literature
    B. Nature as an Artist
    C. The Novelist as an Imitator
    D. Creative Technic of the Novelist
    E. Aspects of Nature

2. A novelist rejects some facts because they 2.____

    A. are impure and ugly
    B. would show he is not impartial
    C. are unrelated to human nature
    D. would make a bad impression
    E. mar the unity of his story

3. It is important for a reader to know 3.____

    A. the purpose of the author
    B. what facts the author omits
    C. both the ugly and the beautiful
    D. something about nature
    E. what the author thinks of human nature

PASSAGE 5

If you watch a lamp which is turned very rapidly on and off, and you keep your eyes open, "persistence of vision" will bridge the gaps of darkness between the flashes of light, and the lamp will seem to be continuously lit. This "topical afterglow" explains the magic produced by the stroboscope, a new instrument which seems to freeze the swiftest motions while they are still going on, and to stop time itself dead in its tracks. The "magic" is all in the eye of the beholder.

1. The "magic" of the stroboscope is due to 1.____

    A. continuous lighting   B. intense cold
    C. slow motion   D. behavior of the human eye
    E. a lapse of time

2. "Persistence of vision" is explained by 2.____

    A. darkness   B. winking   C. rapid flashes
    D. gaps   E. after impression

KEY (CORRECT ANSWERS)

PASSAGE 1

1. C
2. D
3. A

PASSAGE 2

1. C
2. D
3. B

PASSAGE 3

1. D
2. C

PASSAGE 4

1. D
2. E
3. A

PASSAGE 5

1. D
2. E

TEST 5

PASSAGE 1

During the past fourteen years, thousands of top-lofty United States elms have been marked for death by the activities of the tiny European elm bark beetle. The beetles, however, do not do fatal damage. Death is caused by another importation, Dutch elm disease, a fungus infection which the beetles carry from tree to tree. Up to 1941, quarantine and tree-sanitation measures kept the beetles and the disease pretty well confined within 510 miles around metropolitan New York. War curtailed these measures and made Dutch elm disease a wider menace. Every house hold and village that prizes an elm-shaded lawn or commons must now watch for it. Since there is as yet no cure for it, the infected trees must be pruned or felled, and the wood must be burned in order to protect other healthy trees.

1. The title below that BEST expresses the ideas of this paragraph is: 1.____

   A. A Menace to Our Elms
   C. Our Vanishing Elms
   E. How Elms are Protected
   B. Pests and Diseases of the Elm
   D. The Need to Protect Dutch Elms

2. The danger of spreading the Dutch elm disease was increased by   2.____

   A. destroying infected trees
   C. the lack of a cure
   E. quarantine measures
   B. the war
   D. a fungus infection

3. The European elm bark beetle is a serious threat to our elms because it   3.____

   A. chews the bark
   B. kills the trees
   C. is particularly active on the eastern seaboard
   D. carries infection
   E. cannot be controlled

PASSAGE 2

It is elemental that the greater the development of man, the greater the problems he has to concern him. When he lived in a cave with stone implements, his mind no less than his actions was grooved into simple channels. Every new invention, every new way of doing things posed fresh problems for him. And, as he moved along the road, he questioned each step, as indeed he should, for he trod upon the beliefs of his ancestors. It is equally elemental to say that each step upon this later road posed more questions than the earlier ones. It is only the edcated man who realizes the results of his actions; it is only the thoughtful one who questions his own decisions.

1. The title below that BEST expresses the ideas of this paragraph is: 1.____

   A. Channels of Civilization
   B. The Mark of a Thoughtful Man
   C. The Cave Man in Contrast with Man Today
   D. The Price of Early Progress
   E. Man's Never-Ending Challenge

PASSAGE 3

Spring is one of those things that man has no hand in, any more than he has a part in sunrise or the phases of the moon. Spring came before man was here to enjoy it, and it will go right on coming even if man isn't here some time in the future. It is a matter of solar mechanics and celestial order. And for all our knowledge of astronomy and terrestrial mechanics, we haven't yet been able to do more than bounce a radar beam off the moon. We couldn't alter the arrival of the spring equinox by as much as one second, if we tried.

Spring is a matter of growth, of chlorophyll, of bud and blossom.   We can alter growth and change the time of blossoming in individual plants; but the forests still grow in nature's way, and the grass of the plains hasn't altered its nature in a thousand years. Spring is a magnificent phase of the cycle of nature; but man really hasn't any guiding or controlling hand in it. He is here to enjoy it and benefit by it. And April is a good time to realize it; by May perhaps we will want to take full credit.

1. The title below that BEST expresses the ideas of this passage is:　　　　　1.___

    A. The Marvels of the Spring Equinox
    B. Nature's Dependence on Mankind
    C. The Weakness of Man Opposed to Nature
    D. The Glories of the World
    E. Eternal Growth

2. The author of the passage states that　　　　　2.___

    A. man has a part in the phases of the moon
    B. April is a time for taking full-credit
    C. April is a good time to enjoy nature
    D. man has a guiding hand in spring
    E. spring will cease to be if civilization ends

PASSAGE 4

The walled medieval town was as characteristic of its period as the cut of a robber baron's beard. It sprang out of the exigencies of war, and it was not without its architectural charm, whatever its hygienic deficiencies may have been. Behind its high, thick walls not only the normal inhabitants but the whole countryside fought and cowered in an hour of need. The capitals of Europe now forsake the city when the sirens scream and death from the sky seems imminent. Will the fear of bombs accelerate the slow decentralization which began with the automobile and the wide distribution of electrical energy and thus reverse the medieval flow to the city?

1. The title below that BEST expresses the ideas in this paragraph is.　　　　　1.___

    A. A Changing Function of the Town　　B. The Walled Medieval Town
    C. The Automobile's Influence on City　　D. Forsaking the City
        Life
    E. Bombs Today and Yesterday

2. Conditions in the Middle Ages made the walled town　　　　　2.___

    A. a natural development　　　　B. the most dangerous of all places
    C. a victim of fires　　　　　　D. lacking in architectural charm
    E. healthful

3.   Modern conditions may   3._____

    A. make cities larger   B. make cities more hygienic
    C. protect against floods   D. cause people to move from population
    E. encourage good architecture   centers

PASSAGE 5

The literary history of this nation began when the first settler from abroad of sensitive mind paused in his adventure long enough to feel that he was under a different sky, breathing new air, and that a New World was all before him with only his strength and Providence for guides. With him began a new emphasis upon an old theme in literature, the theme of cutting loose and faring forth, renewed, under the powerful influence of a fresh continent for civilized man. It has provided, ever since those first days, a strong current in our native literature, whose other flow has come from a nostalgia for the rich culture of Europe, so much of which was perforce left behind.

1.   The title below that BEST expresses the ideas of this paragraph is: 1._____

    A. America's Distinctive Literature   B. Pioneer Authors
    C. The Dead Hand of the Past   D. Europe's Literary Grandchild
    E. America Comes of Age

2.   American writers, according to the author, because of their colonial experiences   2._____

    A. were antagonistic to European writers
    B. cut loose from Old World influences
    C. wrote only on New World events and characters
    D. created new literary themes
    E. gave fresh interpretation to an old literary idea

KEY (CORRECT ANSWERS)

PASSAGE 1	PASSAGE 2
1. A	1. E
2. B	
3. D	

PASSAGE 3	PASSAGE 4
1. C	1. A
2. C	2. A
	3. D

PASSAGE 5

1. A
2. E

TEST 6

1. Any business not provided with capable substitutes to fill all important positions is a weak business. Therefore a foreman should train each man not only to perform his own particular duties but also to do those of two or three positions.
   The paragraph BEST supports the statement that

   A. dependence on substitutes is a sign of weak organization
   B. training will improve the strongest organization
   C. the foreman should be the most expert at any particular job under him
   D. every employee can be trained to perform efficiently work other than his own
   E. vacancies in vital positions should be provided for in advance

1.____

2. The coloration of textile fabrics composed of cotton and wool generally requires two processes, as the process used in dyeing wool is seldom capable of fixing the color upon cotton. The usual method is to immerse the fabric in the requisite baths to dye the wool and then to treat the partially dyed material in the manner found suitable for cotton.
   The paragraph BEST supports the statement that the dyeing of textile fabrics composed of cotton and wool

   A. is less complicated than the dyeing of wool alone
   B. is more successful when the material contains more cotton than wool
   C. is not satisfactory when solid colors are desired
   D. is restricted to two colors for any one fabric
   E. is usually based upon the methods required for dyeing the different materials

2.____

3. The serious investigator must direct his whole effort toward. success in his work. If he wishes to succeed in each investigation, his work will be by no means easy, smooth, or peaceful; on the contrary, he will have to devote himself completely and continuously to a task that requires all his ability.
   The paragraph BEST supports the statement that an investigator's success depends most upon

   A. ambition to advance rapidly in the service
   B. persistence in the face of difficulty
   C. training and experience
   D. willingness to obey orders without delay
   E. the number of investigations which he conducts

3.____

4. Honest people in one nation find it difficult to understand the viewpoint of honest people in another. State departments and their ministers exist for the purpose of explaining the viewpoints of one nation in terms understood by another. Some of their most important work lies in this direction.
   The paragraph BEST supports the statement that

   A. people of different nations may not consider matters in the same light
   B. it is unusual for many people to share similar ideas
   C. suspicion prevents understanding between nations
   D. the chief work of state departments is to guide relations between nations united by a common cause
   E. the people of one nation must sympathize with the view points of others

4.____

5. Economy once in a while is just not enough. I expect to find it at every level of responsi-   5.____
bility, from cabinet member to the newest and youngest recruit. Controlling waste is
something like bailing a boat; you have to keep at it. I have no intention of easing up on
my insistence on getting a dollar of value for each dollar we spend.
The paragraph BEST supports the statement that

    A.   we need not be concerned about items which cost less than a dollar
    B.   it is advisable to buy the cheaper of two items
    C.   the responsibility of economy is greater at high levels than at low levels
    D.   economy becomes easy with practice
    E.   economy is a continuing responsibility

KEY (CORRECT ANSWERS)

    1. E
    2. E
    3. B
    4. A
    5. E

TEST 7

1. On all permit imprint mail the charge for postage has been printed by the mailer before he presents it for mailing and pays the postage. Such mail of any class is mailable only at the post office that issued a permit covering it. Since the postage receipts for such mail represent only the amount of permit imprint mail detected and verified, employees in receiving, handling, and outgoing sections must be alert constantly to route such mail to the weighing section before it is handled or dispatched.

   The paragraph BEST supports the statement that, at post offices where permit mail is received for dispatch,

   A. dispatching units make a final check on the amount of postage payable on permit imprint mail
   B. employees are to check the postage chargeable on mail received under permit
   C. neither more nor less postage is to be collected than the amount printed on permit imprint mail
   D. the weighing section is primarily responsible for failure to collect postage on such mail
   E. unusual measures are taken to prevent unstamped mail from being accepted

   1.____

2. Education should not stop when the individual has been prepared to make a livelihood and to live in modern society. Living would be mere existence were there no appreciation and enjoyment of the riches of art, literature, and science.

   The paragraph BEST supports the statement that true education

   A. is focused on the routine problems of life
   B. prepares one for full enjoyment of life
   C. deals chiefly with art, literature and science
   D. is not possible for one who does not enjoy scientific literature
   E. disregards practical ends

   2.____

3. Insured and c.o.d. air and surface mail is accepted with the understanding that the sender guarantees any necessary forwarding or return postage. When such mail is forwarded or returned, it shall be rated up for collection of postage; except that insured or c.o.d. air mail weighing 8 ounces or less and subject to the 40 cents an ounce rate shall be forwarded by air if delivery will be advanced, and returned by surface means, without additional postage.

   The paragraph BEST supports the statement that the return postage for undeliverable insured mail is

   A. included in the original prepayment on air mail parcels
   B. computed but not collected before dispatching surface patrol post mail to sender
   C. not computed or charged for any air mail that is returned by surface transportation
   D. included in the amount collected when the sender mails parcel post
   E. collected before dispatching for return if any amount due has been guaranteed

   3.____

4. All undeliverable first-class mail, except first-class parcels and parcel post paid with first-class postage, which cannot be returned to the sender, is sent to a dead-letter branch. Undeliverable matter of the third-and fourth-classes of obvious value for which the sender does not furnish return postage and undeliverable first-class parcels and parcel-post matter bearing postage of the first-class, which cannot be returned, is sent to a dead parcel-post branch.

   4.____

The paragraph BEST supports the statement that matter that is sent to a dead parcel-post branch includes all undeliverable

    A.   mail, except first-class letter mail, that appears to be valuable
    B.   mail, except that of the first-class, on which the sender failed to prepay the original mailing costs
    C.   parcels on which the mailer prepaid the first-class rate of postage
    D.   third-and fourth-class matter on which the required return postage has not been paid
    E.   parcels on which first-class postage has been prepaid, when the sender's address is not known

5.   Civilization started to move rapidly when man freed himself of the shackles that restricted his search for truth.
    The paragraph BEST supports the statement that the progress of civilization   5._____

    A.   came as a result of man's dislike for obstacles
    B.   did not begin until restrictions on learning were removed
    C.   has been aided by man's efforts to find the truth
    D.   is based on continually increasing efforts
    E.   continues at a constantly increasing rate

KEY (CORRECT ANSWERS)

1. B
2. B
3. B
4. E
5. C

TEST 8

1. E-mails should be clear, concise, and brief. Omit all unnecessary words. The parts of speech most often used in e-mails are nouns, verbs, adjectives, and adverbs. If possible, do without pronouns, prepositions, articles, and copulative verbs. Use simple sentences, rather than complex and compound.

   The paragraph BEST supports the statement that in writing e-mails one should always use

   A. common and simple words
   B. only nouns, verbs, adjectives, and adverbs
   C. incomplete sentences
   D. only words essential to the meaning
   E. the present tense of verbs

   1.____

2. The function of business is to increase the wealth of the country and the value and happiness of life. It does this by supplying the material needs of men and women. When the nation's business is successfully carried on, it renders public service of the highest value.

   The paragraph BEST supports the statement that

   A. all businesses which render public service are successful
   B. human happiness is enhanced only by the increase of material wants
   C. the value of life is increased only by the increase of wealth
   D. the material needs of men and women are supplied by welt-conducted business
   E. business is the only field of activity which increases happiness

   2.____

3. In almost every community, fortunately, there are certain men and women known to be public-spirited. Others, however, may be selfish and act only as their private interests seem to require.

   The paragraph BEST supports the statement that those citizens who disregard others are

   A. fortunate
   C. found only in small communities
   E. not public-spirited
   B. needed
   D. not known

   3.____

KEY (CORRECT ANSWERS)

1. D
2. D
3. E

Basic Mathematics

EXAMINATION SECTION
TEST 1

DIRECTIONS: Each question or incomplete statement is followed by several suggested answers or completions. Select the one that BEST answers the question or completes the statement. *PRINT THE LETTER OF THE CORRECT ANSWER IN THE SPACE AT THE RIGHT.*

1. 534
   18
   +1291   1.____

    A. 1733   B. 1743   C. 1833   D. 1843   E. 1853

2. $(17 \times 23) - 16 + 20 =$ 2.____

    A. 459   B. 427   C. 411   D. 395   E. 355

3. $3/7 + 5/11 =$ 3.____

    A. 33/35   B. 4/9   C. 8/18   D. 68/77   E. 15/77

4. $4832 \div 6 =$ 4.____

    A. 905 1/3   B. 805 1/3   C. 95 1/3   D. 95   E. 85 1/3

5. $62.3 - 4.9 =$ 5.____

    A. 5.74   B. 7.4   C. 57.4   D. 58.4   E. 67.4

6. $3/5 \times 4/9 =$ 6.____

    A. 4/15   B. 7/45   C. 27/20   D. 12/14   E. 15/4

7. $14/16 - 5/16 =$ 7.____

    A. 8/16   B. 9/16   C. 11/16   D. 8   E. 9

8. $5.03 + 2.7 + 40 =$ 8.____

    A. .570   B. 4.773   C. 5.70   D. 11.73   E. 47.73

9. $5.37 \times 21.4 =$ 9.____

    A. 11491.8   B. 1149.18   C. 114.918   D. 11.4918   E. 1.14918

10. $5 1/4 + 2 7/8 =$ 10.____

    A. 8 1/4   B. 8 1/8   C. 7 2/3   D. 7 1/4   E. 7 1/8

11. $-14 + 5 =$ 11.____

    A. -19   B. -9   C. 9   D. 19   E. 70

12. 2/7 of 28 =

    A. 98   B. 16   C. 14   D. 8   E. 4

12.____

13. 2/5 =

    A. .10   B. .20   C. .25   D. .40   E. .52

13.____

14. 20% of _____ is 38.

    A. 7.6   B. 19   C. 76   D. 190   E. 760

14.____

15. $\dfrac{8.4}{400} =$

    A. .0021   B. .021   C. .21   D. 2.1   E. 21

15.____

16. $\dfrac{4}{5} = \dfrac{?}{60}$

    A. 240   B. 48   C. 20   D. 15   E. 12

16.____

17. What is the area of the rectangle shown at the right?

    A. 47 mm^2
    B. 94 mm^2
    C. 240 mm^2
    D. 480 mm^2
    E. 960 mm^2

15 mm

32 mm

17.____

18. What number does □ represent in this equation?

    25 − □ − □ − □ − □ = 13

    A. 13   B. 12   C. 7   D. 4   E. 3

18.____

19. Approximate lengths are given in the right triangles shown at the right. What does length x equal?

    A. 48
    B. 39
    C. 37
    D. 35
    E. 32

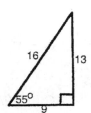

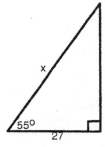

19.____

20. What is the perimeter of the triangle shown at the right?
    A. 10 x 15 x 17
    B. 10 + 15 + 17
    C. 1/2 x 10 x 15
    D. 1/2 x 10 x 17
    E. 1/2(10 + 15 + 17)

20._____

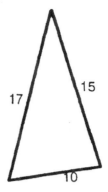

21. Which of the following expressions will give the same answer as 45 x 9?

    A. 5×3^3
    B. (4x9) + (5x9)
    C. (40+9) x 5
    D. (45x3) + (45x3)
    E. (45x10) - (45x1)

21._____

22. Find the average of 19, 21, 21, 22, and 27.

    A. 23   B. 22   C. 21   D. 20   E. 19

22._____

23. In the triangle at the right, how many degrees is <T?
    A. 75°
    B. 85°
    C. 95°
    D. 115°
    E. 180°

23._____

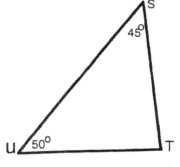

24.

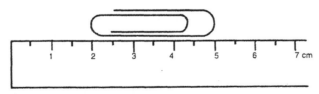

About how long is the paper clip?

    A. 5 cm   B. 4 cm   C. 3 cm   D. 2 cm   E. 1 cm

24._____

25. Five stores sell the same size cans of tomato soup. Their prices are listed below. Which sells the soup for the LOWEST price per can?
    _____ cans for _____

    A. 6; 99¢   B. 6; 90¢   C. 5; 93¢   D. 3; 56¢   E. 3; 50¢

25._____

26. Rock star Peter Giles receives $1.97 royalty on each of his albums that is sold. 14,127 albums are sold.
    Estimate how much Peter Giles will receive.

    A. $7,000   B. $14,000   C. $20,000   D. $26,000   E. $28,000

26._____

27. An amplifier is advertised for 20% off the list price of $430.   27._____
    What is the sale price?

    A. $516   B. $454   C. $354   D. $344   E. $215

28. If 9 dozen eggs cost $3.60, what do 25 dozen eggs cost?   28._____

    A. $90.00   B. $10.00   C. $9.00   D. $2.54   E. $.40

29. The distance between New York and San Antonio is 1860 miles. If a jet averages 465   29._____
    miles per hour, how many hours will it take to travel the distance?

    A. 9   B. 5   C. 4   D. 3   E. 2

30. In a high school homeroom of 32 students, 24 are girls. What percent are girls?   30._____

    A. 3/4%   B. 24%   C. 25%   D. 75%   E. 80%

31. Which problem could give the answer   31._____
    shown on the calculator?
    A. 2 + .3
    B. 2 x 3/10
    C. 2 x 1/3
    D. 33333 + .2
    E. 7 ÷ 3

    ```
    | 2.33333 |

    [7] [8] [9] [+]
    [4] [5] [6] [-]
    [1] [2] [3] [x]
    [0] [.] [=] [÷]
    ```

32. According to the table at the right, how   32._____
    much will it cost in a typical week for the
    3 members of the Wright family to eat at
    home? Mr. Wright is 56 years old; Mrs.
    Wright, 52; and their son Harry, 17.
    A. $125
    B. $52
    C. $49
    D. $42
    E. $40

    Cost of Eating at Home
    (one week)

Age	Male	Female
6-11 yrs.	$14	$14
12-19 yrs.	$19	$16
20-54 yrs.	$20	$16
55 and up	$14	$14

33. According to the table shown in the previous question, how much does it cost in a typical   33._____
    four-week month to feed a 12-year-old girl?

    A. $4   B. $16   C. $48   D. $64   E. $78

34. Reverend Wilhite jogs for 11/2 hours each day, 6 days a week. If he burns 800 calories   34._____
    per hour of jogging, how many calories does he burn in a week?

    A. 4800   B. 5600   C. 7200   D. 8400   E. 9000

35. Ground meat costs 90¢ per pound. How much does the meat on the scale cost?
    A. $1.80
    B. $1.60
    C. $1.54
    D. $1.44
    E. $.90

35._____

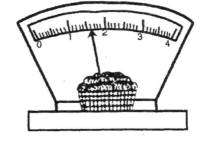

36. According to the graph at the right, about when did the weekly wages for a minimum wage worker go over $100?
    A. 1965
    B. 1970
    C. 1975
    D. 1979
    E. 1980

36._____

Weekly wages For a Minimum-Wage Employee

37. According to the bar graph at the right, what is the approximate height of the Crystal Beach Comet?
    A. 40 ft.
    B. 90 ft.
    C. 92 ft.
    D. 94 ft.
    E. 98 ft.

37._____

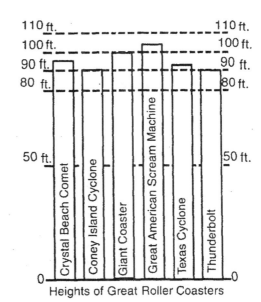

Heights of Great Roller Coasters

38. According to the bar graph shown in the previous question, what is the difference in height between the tallest and shortest roller coasters?
    _____ feet.

    A. 5   B. 10   C. 15   D. 20   E. 50

38._____

39. How much change will you receive from a $10 bill when you buy 4 grapefruits at 90¢ each and 3 apples at 40¢ each?

    A. $6.20   B. $5.20   C. $4.80   D. $4.20   E. $4.00

39._____

40. A medical supplier packages medicine in boxes. The cost of packaging is computed with the flow chart at the right. What is the cost of packaging medicine in a box that is 30 cm long, 20 cm wide, and 20 cm high?

   A. $.20
   B. $.24
   C. $2.00
   D. $2.40
   E. $3.00

40.____

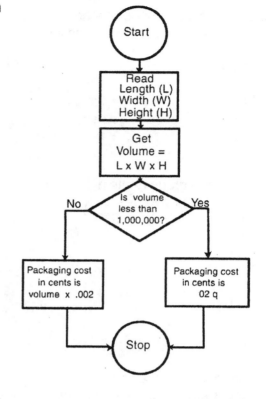

KEY (CORRECT ANSWERS)

1.	D	11.	B	21.	E	31.	E
2.	D	12.	D	22.	B	32.	C
3.	D	13.	D	23.	B	33.	D
4.	B	14.	D	24.	C	34.	C
5.	C	15.	B	25.	B	35.	D
6.	A	16.	B	26.	E	36.	C
7.	B	17.	D	27.	D	37.	D
8.	E	18.	E	28.	B	38.	C
9.	C	19.	A	29.	C	39.	B
10.	B	20.	B	30.	D	40.	A

SOLUTIONS TO PROBLEMS

1. $534 + 18 + 1291 = 1843$

2. $(17 \times 23) - 16 + 20 = 391 - 16 + 20 = 395$

3. $\dfrac{3}{7} + \dfrac{5}{11} = \dfrac{33}{77} + \dfrac{35}{77} = \dfrac{68}{77}$

4. $4832 \div 6 = 805\dfrac{1}{3}$

5. $62.3 - 4.9 = 57.4$

6. $\dfrac{3}{5} \times \dfrac{4}{9} = \dfrac{12}{45} = \dfrac{4}{15}$

7. $\dfrac{14}{16} - \dfrac{5}{16} = \dfrac{9}{16}$

8. $5.03 + 2.7 + 40 = 47.73$

9. $5.37 \times 21.4 = 114.918$

10. $5\dfrac{1}{4} + 2\dfrac{7}{8} = 7\dfrac{9}{8} = 8\dfrac{1}{8}$

11. $-14 + 5 = -9$

12. $\dfrac{2}{7}$ of $28 = (\dfrac{2}{7})(\dfrac{28}{1}) = 8$

13. $\dfrac{2}{5} = .40$ as a decimal

14. Let x = missing number. Then, $.20x = 38$. Solving, $x = 190$

15. $\dfrac{8.4}{400} = .021$

16. Let x = missing number. Then, $\dfrac{4}{5} = \dfrac{x}{60}$. $5x = 240$, so $x = 48$

17. Area $= (15)(32) = 480\text{mm}^2$

18. Let $x = \square$. Then, $25 - 4x = 13$. So, $-4x = -12$. Solving, $x = 3$

19. $\frac{9}{27} = \frac{16}{X}$. Then, 9x = 432. Solving, x = 48.

20. Perimeter = 17 + 10 + 15 = 42

21. 45 x 9 = 405 = (45x10) - (45x1)

22. 19 + 21 + 21 + 22 + 27 = 110. Then, 110 ÷ 5 = 22

23. $\angle T = 180° - 50° - 45° = 85°$

24. The paper clip's length is about 5 - 2 = 3 cm.

25. For A: price per can = $\frac{.99}{6} = .165$;

    For B: price per can = $\frac{.90}{6} = .15$

    For C: price per can = $\frac{.93}{5} = .186$

    For D: price per can = $\frac{.56}{3} = .18\overline{6}$

    For E: price per can = $\frac{.50}{3} = .1\overline{6}$

    Lowest price is for B.

26. $1.97 = $2.00. Then, ($2.00) (14,127) = $28,254 = $28,000.

27. Sale price = ($430) (.80) = $344

28. Let x = cost. Then, 9x=$90, so x =$10.00

29. $\frac{1860}{465} = 4$ hours

30. $\frac{24}{32} = 75\%$

31. $\frac{7}{3} = 2.\overline{3} = 2.33333$ on this calculator shown.

32. Total cost = $14 + $16 + $19 = $49

33. Cost = ($16)(4) = $64

34. $(800)(1\frac{1}{2})(6) = 7200$ calories

35. $(.90)(1.6) = \$1.44$

36. Around 1975, the minimum weekly wages exceeded $100.

37. The Crystal Beach Comet's height is about 94 ft.

38. Tallest = 105 ft. and the shortest = 90 ft.
    Difference = 15 ft.

39. $\$10 - (4)(.90) - (3)(.40) = \$5.20$ change

40. $(30)(20)(20) = 12,000$ cm^3. Since $12,000 < 1,000,000$, the price is 20 cents.

EXAMINATION SECTION
TEST 1

DIRECTIONS: Each question or incomplete statement is followed by several suggested answers or completions. Select the one that BEST answers the question or completes the statement. *PRINT THE LETTER OF THE CORRECT ANSWER IN THE SPACE AT THE RIGHT.*

1. Which of the following fractions is the SMALLEST?   1._____

    A. 2/3   B. 4/5   C. 5/7   D. 5/11

2. 40% is equivalent to which of the following?   2._____

    A. 4/5   B. 4/6   C. 2/5   D. 4/100

3. How many 100's are in 10,000?   3._____

    A. 10   B. 100   C. 10,000   D. 100,000

4. $\dfrac{6}{7}+\dfrac{11}{12}$ is approximately   4._____

    A. 1   B. 2   C. 17   D. 19

5. The time required to heat water to a certain temperature is directly proportional to the volume of water being heated.
If it takes 12 minutes to heat 1 1/2 gallons of water, how many minutes will it take to heat 2 gallons of water?   5._____

    A. 12   B. 16   C. 18   D. 24

6. The cost of an item increased by 25%.
If the original cost was C dollars, identify the expression which gives the new cost of that item.   6._____

    A. C + 0.25   B. 1/4 C   C. 25C   D. 1.25C

7. Given the formula PV = nRT, all of the following are true EXCEPT   7._____

    A. T = PV/nR   B. P = nRT/V   C. V = P/nRT   D. n = PV/RT

8. If a Fahrenheit (F) temperature reading is 104, find its Celsius (C) equivalent, given that C = i(F-32)   8._____

    A. 36   B. 40   C. 72   D. 76

9. If 40% of a graduating class plans to go directly to work after graduation, which of the following must be TRUE?   9._____

    A.   Less than half of the class plans to go directly to work.
    B.   Forty members of the class plan to enter the job market.
    C.   Most of the class plans to go directly to work.
    D.   Six in ten members of the class are expected not to graduate.

10. Given a multiple-choice test item which has 5 choices, what is the probability of guessing the correct answer if you know nothing about the item content?

    A. 5%   B. 10%   C. 20%   D. 25%

10._____

11. Which graph BEST represents the data shown in the table at the right?

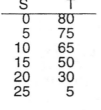

S	T
0	80
5	75
10	65
15	50
20	30
25	5

11._____

A.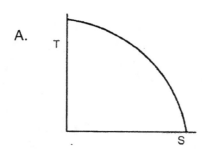

B.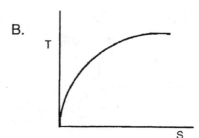

C.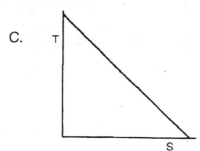

D.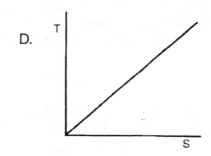

12. If 3(X + 5Y) = 24, find Y when X = 3.

    A. 1   B. 3   C. 33/5   D. 7

12._____

13. The payroll of a grocery store for its 23 clerks is $395,421. Which expression below shows the average salary of a clerk?

    A. 395,421 x 23   B. 23 ÷ 395,421

    C. (395,421x14) ÷ 23   D. 395,421 ÷ 23

13._____

14. If 12.8 pounds of coffee cost $50.80, what is the APPROXIMATE price per pound?

    A. $2.00   B. $3.00   C. $4.00   D. $5.00

14._____

15. A road map has a scale where 1 inch corresponds to 150 miles. A distance of 3 3/4 inches on the map corresponds to what actual distance?

    _____ miles

    A. 153.75   B. 375   C. 525   D. 562.5

15._____

16. How many square feet of plywood are needed to construct the back and 4 adjacent sides of the box shown at the right?
_____ square feet.

16._____

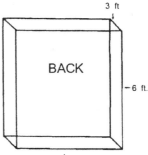

3 ft

BACK

— 6 ft.

5 ft.

A. 63
B. 90
C. 96
D. 126

17. One thirty pound bag of lawn fertilizer costs $20.00 and will cover 600 square feet of lawn. Terry's lawn is a 96 foot by 75 foot rectangle. How much will it cost Terry to buy enough bags of fertilizer for her lawn?
Which of the following do you NOT need in order to solve this problem?
The

17._____

A. product of 96 and 75
B. fact that one bag weighs 30 pounds
C. fact that one bag covers 600 square feet
D. fact that one bag costs $20.00

18. On the graph shown at the right, between which hours was the drop in temperature GREATEST?

18._____

A. 11:00 - Noon
B. Noon - 1:00
C. 1:00 - 2:00
D. 2:00 - 3:00

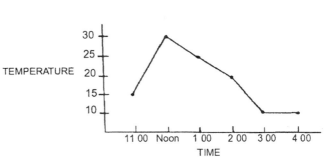

19. If on a typical railroad track, the distance from the center of one railroad tie to the next is 30 inches, approximately how many ties would be needed for one mile of track?

19._____

A. 180   B. 2,110   C. 6,340   D. 63,360

20. Which of the following is MOST likely to be the volume of a wine bottle?

20._____

A. 750 milliliters   B. 7 kilograms
C. 7 milligrams   D. 7 liters

21. What is the reading on the gauge shown at the right?

21._____

A. -7
B. -3
C. 1
D. 3

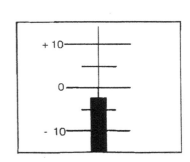

123

22. Which statement below disproves the assertion, *All students in Mrs. Marino's 10th grade geometry class are planning to go to college?*   22.____

    A. Albert is in Mrs, Marino's class, but he is not planning to take mathematics next year.
    B. Jorge is not in Mrs. Marino's class, but he is still planning to go to college.
    C. Pierre is in Mrs. Marino's class but says he will not be attending school anymore after this year.
    D. Crystal is in Mrs. Marino's class and plans to attend Yale University when she graduates.

23. A store advertisement reads, *Buy now while our prices are low. There will never be a better time to buy.* The customer reading this advertisement should assume that   23.____

    A. the prices at the store will probably never be lower
    B. right now, this store has the best prices in town
    C. prices are higher at other stores
    D. prices are always lowest at this store

24. *Given any positive integer A, there is always a positive number B such that A x B is less than 1.*   24.____
    Which statement below supports this generalization?

    A. $8 \times 1/16 = 1/2$ B. $8 \times 1/2 = 4$
    C. $5/2 \times 1/10 = 1/4$ D. $1/2 \times 1/2 = 1/2$

25. Of the following expressions, which is equivalent to $4C + D = 12E$?   25.____

    A. $C = 4(12E - D)$ B. $4 + D = 12E - C$

    C. $4C + 12E = -D$ D. $C = \dfrac{12E - D}{4}$

KEY (CORRECT ANSWERS)

1.	D	11.	A
2.	C	12.	A
3.	B	13.	D
4.	B	14.	C
5.	B	15.	D
6.	D	16.	C
7.	C	17.	B
8.	B	18.	D
9.	A	19.	B
10.	C	20.	A

21. B
22. C
23. A
24. A
25. D

SOLUTIONS TO PROBLEMS

1. Converting to decimals, we get $.\overline{6}$, .8, .714 (approx), $.\overline{45}$. The smallest is $.\overline{45}$ corresponding to 5/11.

2. 40% = 40/100 = 2/5

3. 10,000 ÷ 100 = 100

4. $\dfrac{6}{7} + \dfrac{11}{12} = (72 + 77) \div 84 = \dfrac{149}{84} \approx 1.77 \approx 2$

5. Let x = required minutes. Then, 12/1 1/2 = x/2 This reduces to 1 1/2x = 24. Solving, x = 16

6. New cost is C + .25C = 1.25C

7. For PV = nRT, V = nRT/P

8. C = 5/9 (104-32) = 5/9 (72) = 40

9. Since 40% is less than 50% (or half), we conclude that less than half of the class plans to go to work directly after graduation.

10. The probability of guessing right is 1/5 or 20%.

11. Curve A is most accurate since as S increases, we see that T decreases. Note, however, that the relationship is NOT linear. Although S increases in equal amounts, the decrease in T is NOT in equal amounts.

12. 3(3+5Y) = 24. This simplifies to 9 + 15Y = 24 Solving, Y = 1

13. The average salary is $395,421 ÷ 23

14. The price per pound is $50.80 ÷ 12.8 = $3.96875 or approximately $4.

15. Actual distance is (3 3/4)(l50) = 562.5 miles

16. The area of the back = (6)(5) = 30 sq.ft. The combined area of the two vertical sides is (2)(6)(3) = 36 sq.ft. The combined area of the horizontal sides is (2)(5)(3) = 30 sq.ft. Total area = 30 + 36 + 30 = 96 square feet.

17. Choice B is not relevant to solving the problem since the cost will be [(96)(75) / 600][$20] = $240. So, the weight per bag is not needed.

18. For the graph, the largest temperature drop was from 2:00 P.M. to 3:00 P.M. The temperature dropped 20 - 10 = 10 degrees.

19. 1 mile = 5280 feet = 63,360 inches. Then, 63,360 ÷ 30 = 2112 or about 2110 ties are needed.

20. Since 1 liter = 1.06 quarts, 750 milliliters = (750/1000)(1.06) = .795 quarts. This is a reasonable volume for a wine bottle.

21. The reading is -3.

22. Statement C contradicts the given information, since Pierre is in Mrs. Marino's class. Then he should plan to go to college.

23. Since there will never be a better time to buy at this particular store, the customer can assume the current prices will probably never be lower.

24. Statement A illustrates this concept. Note that in general, if n is a positive integer, then

$$(n)\left(\frac{1}{n+1}\right) < 1$$

Example: (100)(1/100)< 1

———

TEST 2

DIRECTIONS: Each question or incomplete statement is followed by several suggested answers or completions. Select the one that BEST answers the question or completes the statement. *PRINT THE LETTER OF THE CORRECT ANSWER IN THE SPACE AT THE RIGHT.*

1. Which of the following lists numbers in INCREASING order?

    A. 0.4, 0.04, 0.004   B. 2.71, 3.15, 2.996
    C. 0.7, 0.77, 0.777   D. 0.06, 0.5, 0.073

1.____

2. $\dfrac{4}{10} + \dfrac{7}{100} + \dfrac{5}{1000} =$

    A. 4.75   B. 0.475   C. 0.0475   D. 0.00475

2.____

3. 700 times what number equals 7?

    A. 10   B. 0.1   C. 0.01   D. 0.001

3.____

4. 943 - 251 is approximately

    A. 600   B. 650   C. 700   D. 1200

4.____

5. The time needed to set up a complicated piece of machinery is inversely proportional to the number of years' experience of the worker.
If a worker with 10 years' experience needs 6 hours to do the job, how long will it take a worker with 15 years' experience?

    A. 4   B. 5   C. 9   D. 25

5.____

6. Let W represent the number of waiters and D, the number of diners in a particular restaurant.
Identify the expression which represents the statement: There are 10 times as many diners as waiters.

    A. 10W = D   B. 10D = W
    C. 10D + 10W   D. 10 = D + W

6.____

7. Which of the following is equivalent to the formula $F = XC + Y$?

    A. F-C=X+Y   B. $Y = F + XC$
    C. $C = \dfrac{F-Y}{X}$ D. $C = \dfrac{F-X}{Y}$

7.____

8. Given the formula $A = BC / D$, if A = 12, B = 6, and D = 3, what is the value of C?

    A. 2/3   B. 6   C. 18   D. 24

8.____

9. 5 is to 7 as X is to 35. X =

    A. 7   B. 12   C. 25   D. 49

9.____

10. Kramer Middle School has 5 seventh grade mathematics teachers: two of the math teachers are women and three are men.
If you are assigned a teacher at random, what is the probability of getting a female teacher?

   A. 0.2   B. 0.4   C. 0.6   D. 0.8

10.____

11. Which statement BEST describes the graph shown at the right? Temperature

   A. and time decrease at the same rate
   B. and time increase at the same rate
   C. increases over time
   D. decreases over time

11.____

12. If $3X + 4 = 2Y$, find Y when $X = 2$.

   A. 0   B. 3   C. 4 1/2   D. 5

12.____

13. A car goes 243 miles on 8.7 gallons of gas. Which numeric expression should be used to determine the car's miles per gallon?

   A. 243 x 87   B. 8.7 ÷ 243
   C. 243 ÷ 8.7   D. 243 - 8.7

13.____

14. What is the average cost per book if you buy six books at $4.00 each and four books at $5.00 each?

   A. $4.40   B. $4.50   C. $4.60   D. $5.40

14.____

15. A publisher's sale offers a 15% discount to anyone buying more than 100 workbooks. What will be the discount on 200 workbooks selling at $2.25 each?

   A. $15.00   B. $30.00   C. $33.75   D. $67.50

15.____

16. A road crew erects 125 meters of fencing in one workday. How many workdays are required to erect a kilometer of fencing?

   A. 0.8   B. 8   C. 80   D. 800

16.____

17. Last month Kim made several telephone calls to New York City totaling 45 minutes in all. What does Kim need in order to calculate the average duration of her New York City calls?
The

   A. total number of calls she made to New York City
   B. cost per minute of a call to New York City
   C. total cost of her telephone bill last month
   D. days of the week on which the calls were made

17.____

18.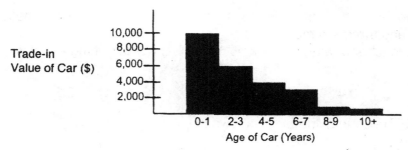

The chart above relates a car's age to its trade-in value. Based on the chart, which of the following is TRUE?

A. A 4- to 5-year old car has a trade-in value of about $2,000.
B. The trade-in value of an 8- to 9-year old car is about 1/3 that of a 2- to 3-year old car.
C. A 6- to 7-year old car has no trade-in value.
D. A 4- to 5-year old car's trade-in value is about $2,000 less than that of a 2- to 3-year old car.

18.____

19. Which of the following expressions could be used to determine how many seconds are in a 24-hour day?

A. 60 x 60 x 24   B. 60 x 12 x 24
C. 60 x 2 x 24   D. 60 x 24

19.____

20. For measuring milk, we could use each of the following EXCEPT

A. liters   B. kilograms
C. millimeters   D. cubic centimeters

20.____

21. What is the reading on the gauge shown at the right?

A. 51
B. 60
C. 62.5
D. 70

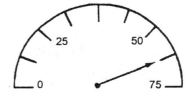

21.____

22. Bill is taller than Yvonne. Yvonne is shorter than Sue. Sue is 5'4" tall. Which of the following conclusions must be TRUE?

A. Bill is taller than Sue.
B. Yvonne is taller than 5'4".
C. Sue is taller than Bill.
D. Yvonne is the shortest.

22.____

23. The Bass family traveled 268 miles during the first day of their vacation and another 300 miles on the next day. Maria Bass said they were 568 miles from home. Which of the following facts did Maria assume?

A. They traveled faster on the first day and slower on the second.
B. If she plotted the vacation route on a map, it would be a straight line.
C. Their car used more gasoline on the second day.
D. They traveled faster on the second day than they did on the first day.

23.____

24. *The word LEFT in a mathematics problem indicates that it is a subtraction problem.*   24._____
Which of the following mathematics problems proves this statement FALSE?

    A. I want to put 150 bottles into cartons which hold 8 bottles each. After I completely fill as many cartons as I can, how many bottles will be left?
    B. Sarah had 5 books but gave one to John. How many books did Sarah have left?
    C. Carlos had $4.25 but spent $3.75. How much did he have left?
    D. We had 38 models in stock but after yesterday's sale, only 12 are left. How many did we sell?

25. Let Q represent the number of miles Dave can jog in 15 minutes.   25._____
Identify the expression which represents the number of miles Dave can jog between 3:00 PM and 4:45 PM?

    A. 1 3/4 Q   B. 7Q

    C. $15 \times 1\frac{3}{4} \times Q$ D. Q/7

KEY (CORRECT ANSWERS)

1.	C		11.	D
2.	B		12.	D
3.	C		13.	C
4.	C		14.	A
5.	A		15.	D
6.	A		16.	B
7.	C		17.	A
8.	B		18.	D
9.	C		19.	A
10.	B		20.	C

21.	C
22.	D
23.	B
24.	A
25.	B

SOLUTIONS TO PROBLEMS

1. Choice C is in ascending order since .7 < .77 < .777

2. Rewrite in decimal form: .4 + .07 + .005 = .475

3. Let x = missing number. Then, 700x = 7. Solving, x = 7/700 = .01

4. 943 - 251 = 692 ≈ 700

5. Let x = hours needed. Then, 10/15 = x/6. Solving, x = 4

6. The number of diners (D) is 10 times as many waiters (10W). So, D = 10W or 10W = D

7. Given F = XC + Y, subtract Y from each side to get F - Y = XC. Finally, dividing by X, we get (F-Y)/X = C

8. 12 = 6C/3. Then, 12 = 2C, so C = 6

9. 5/7 = X/35 Then, 7x = 175, so x = 25

10. Probability of a female teacher = 2/5 = .4

11. Statement D is best, since as time increases, the temperature decreases

12. (3)(2) + 4 = 2Y. Then, 10 = 2Y, so Y = 5

13. Miles per gallon = 243 / 8.7

14. Total purchase is (6)($4) + (4)($5) = $44. The average cost per book is $44 ÷ 10 = $4.40

15. (220)($2.25) = $450. The discount is (.15)($450) = $67.50

16. The number of workdays is 1000 ÷ 125 = 8

17. Choice A is correct because the average duration of the phone calls = total time ÷ total number of calls

18. Statement D is correct since a 4-5 year-old car's value is $4,000, whereas a 2-3 year-old car's value is $6000.

19. 60 seconds = 1 minute and 60 minutes = 1 hour. Thus, 24 hours = (24)(60)(60) or (60)(60)(24) seconds

20. We can't use millimeters in measuring milk since millimeters is a linear measurement

21. The reading shows the average of 50 and 75 = 62.5

22. Since Yvonne is shorter than both Bill and Sue, Yvonne is the shortest.

23. Statement B is assumed correct since 568 = 268 + 300 could only be true if the mileage traveled represents a straight line

24. To find the number of bottles left, we look only for the remainder when 150 is divided by 8 (which happens to be 6)

———

ARITHMETICAL REASONING
EXAMINATION SECTION
TEST 1

DIRECTIONS: Briefly and concisely, solve each of the following problems, using the processes of arithmetic ONLY.

1. It is believed that every even number is the sum of two prime numbers. Two prime numbers whose sum is 32 are

    A. 7, 25   B. 11, 21   C. 13, 19   D. 17, 15

1.____

2. To divide a number by 3000, we should move the decimal point 3 places to the _____ by 3.

    A. right and divide   B. left and divide
    C. right and multiply   D. left and multiply

2.____

3. The difference between the area of a rectangle 6 ft. by 4 ft. and the area of a square having the same perimeter is

    A. 1 sq. ft.   B. 2 sq. ft.
    C. 4 sq. ft.   D. none of the above

3.____

4. The ratio of 1/4 to 3/8 is the same as the ratio of

    A. 1 to 3   B. 2 to 3   C. 3 to 2   D. 3 to 4

4.___

5. If 7 1/2 is divided by 1 1/5, the quotient is

    A. 6 1/4   B. 9   C. 7 1/10   D. 6 3/5

5.____

6. A farmer has a cylindrical metal tank for watering his stock. It is 10 ft. in diameter and 3 ft. deep.
If one cubic foot contains about 7.5 gallons, the APPROXIMATE capacity of the tank, in gallons, is

    A. 12   B. 225   C. 4   D. 1707

6.____

7. The fraction which fits in the following series, 1/2, 1/10, _____ , 1/250 is

    A. 1/20   B. 1/100   C. 1/10   D. 1/50

7.____

8. In two years $200 with interest compounded semi-annually at 4% will amount to

    A. $216.48   B. $233.92   C. $208   D. $216

8.____

9. With a tax rate of .0200, a tax bill of $1050 corresponds to an assessed valuation of

    A. $21,000   B. $52,500   C. $21   D. $1029

9.____

10. A sales agent, after deducting his commission of 6%, remits $2491 to his principal. The sale amounted to

    A. $2809   B. $2640   C. $2650   D. $2341.54

10.____

11. The percent equivalent of .0295 is   11.____

    A. 2.95%   B. 29.5%   C. .295%   D. 295%

12. An angle of 105° is a(n) _____ angle.   12.____

    A. straight   B. acute   C. obtuse   D. reflex

13. A quart is approximately sixty cubic inches. A cubic foot of water weighs approximately   13.____
sixty pounds.
Therefore, a quart of water weighs APPROXIMATELY _____ lbs.

    A. 2   B. 3   C. 4   D. 5

14. If the same number is added to both the numerator and the denominator of a proper frac-   14.____
tion, the

    A. value of the fraction is decreased
    B. value of the fraction is increased
    C. value of the fraction is unchanged
    D. effect of the operation depends on the original fraction

15. The LEAST common multiple of 3, 8, 9, 12 is   15.____

    A. 36   B. 72   C. 108   D. 144

16. On a bill of $100, the difference between a discount of 30% and 20% and a discount of   16.____
40% and 10% is

    A. nothing   B. $2   C. $20   D. 20%

17. 1/3 percent of a number is 24.   17.____
The number is

    A. 8   B. 72   C. 800   D. 7200

18. The cost of importing five dozen china dinner sets, billed at $32 per set and paying a duty   18.____
of 40%, is

    A. $224   B. $2688   C. $768   D. $1344

19. The net price of a television set is $756.   19.____
If bought with a trade discount of 20%, and 10% for cash, the list price is

    A. $925.00   B. $957.80   C. $982.80   D. $1050.00

20. If Bob can complete a job in 6 hours and Steven can finish it in 8 hours, together they can   20.____
complete the job in_____ hrs. _____ min .

    A. 2; 45   B. 3; 10   C. 3; 25   D. 4; 5

21. If the diameter is 80', the APPROXIMATE area of a skating rink is _____ square feet.   21.____

    A. 251.33   B. 1281.74   C. 2538.77   D. 5026.56

22. If an employer is subject to the Unemployment Insurance Fund and his quarterly   22.____
    payroll totals to $18,000, the quarterly tax payable to the Fund would be _____
    (assuming the tax to be 2.7%).

    A. $233   B. $486   C. $977   D. $1,944

23. During a certain year, the weekly pay of John Smith was $900, his withholding tax 15%,   23.____
    and his Social Security tax was 4.4%.
    Then, Mr. Smith's take-home pay amounted to

    A. $685.85   B. $711.00   C. $725.40   D. $755.65

24. A 5% mortgage of $90,000 is for sale.   24.____
    What will the buyer have to pay for it to net 9%?

    A. $50,000   B. $85,500   C. $65,000   D. $81,900

25. If the passenger rate is $54, the operating cost per passenger to the railroad on the basis   25.____
    of 12 1/2% profit on fares is

    A. $6.75   B. $38.95   C. $47.25   D. $49.68

26. What is the amount of premium refunded to the insured if the insurance company can-   26.____
    cels a 3-year policy at the end of 15 months?
    The rate is $30 per year.

    A. $37.50   B. $41.50   C. $43.00   D. $43.75

27. Suits originally selling for $200 were marked down to yield 20% on cost.   27.____
    If the original profit was 33 1/3% on cost, the new sales price will be

    A. $134   B. $160   C. $171   D. $180

28. If he works 10 hours on Tuesday and 12 hours on Friday, and regular hours on the other   28.____
    days, for an 8-hour day, 5 days per week, daily pay $120, Samuels will earn _____ (time
    and a half for overtime).

    A. $600   B. $735   C. $750   D. $785

29. To provide 10,000 typewriting sheets (8 1/2 x 11), the mill will have to cut how many   29.____
    reams of folio stock which measures 17 x 22?

    A. 5   B. 6 1/2   C. 8   D. 10

30. Property worth $1.6 million was insured for $1 million under a policy containing the 80%   30.____
    co-insurance clause. The damage amounted to $960,000.
    The insured will collect

    A. $480,000   B. $650,000   C. $750,000   D. $780,000

31. At the rate of $1.68 for the Sterling, what will the traveler require in American currency to   31.____
    meet expenses and purchases of goods calling for £20 6s. 6d?

    A. $21.34   B. $34.15   C. $38.21   D. $57.12

32. The proceeds of a 6% interest-bearing note for $800 due in 45 days and discounted 15   32.____
    days after it was dated, at the rate of 5%, will be

    A. $796.25   B. $802.64   C. $804.93   D. $805.92

33. $4.80 is .08% of   33.____

    A. $600   B. $6000   C. $6500   D. $60,000

34. If 25% of a classroom register consists of boys, the ratio of girls to boys is   34.____

    A. 4:1   B. 3:1   C. 1:4   D. 1:3

35. If a wage earner who is over 65 years of age, married (wife's age 55) and 2 other depen-   35.____
dents whose earnings are below $2,300, pays his Federal income tax, what will his
TOTAL exemptions add up to?

    A. 2   B. 3   C. 4   D. 5

36. An equality of ratios is another term for   36.____

    A. proportion   B. equilibrium
    C. summation   D. inversion

37. A kilometer is APPROXIMATELY what part of a mile?   37.____

    A. 0.059   B. 0.062   C. 0.064   D. 0.067

38. Two liters is a_____ quantity than two quarts.   38.____

    A. smaller dry quart/larger liquid quart
    B. larger dry quart/smaller liquid quart
    C. smaller dry quart/smaller liquid quart
    D. larger dry quart/larger liquid quart

39. The square root of 46.24 is   39.____

    A. 6.793   B. 6.800   C. 7.984   D. 9.248

40. Ordinary interest is _____ than exact interest for the same time and at the same rate.   40.____

    A. less   B. more   C. equal   D. variable

41. After all taxes have been added on, what will the coat cost the purchaser if the advertised   41.____
price of a natural mink coat is $8,000? (Assume Federal Sales Tax is 10% and the Local
Sales Tax is 8 1/4%.)

    A. $8660   B. $9460   C. $9526   D. $9548

42. A ring bearing the mark 12K on the inside contains _____ parts gold and 12 parts alloy.   42.____

    A. 2   B. 12   C. 6   D. 14

43. The sounding line recorded a depth of 20 fathoms or _____ feet.   43.____

    A. 110   B. 120   C. 130   D. 140

44. If a pound of green peanuts costs $1.25 and peanuts lose 1/6 of its weight in the roasting   44.____
process, what is the cost of the roasted peanuts?

    A. $1.00   B. $1.20   C. $1.25   D. $1.50

45. A cubic foot (liquid measure) is APPROXIMATELY how many gallons?   45.____

    A. 7.48   B. 7.55   C. 7.65   D. 7.80

46. If the closing price of USX Corp. reads 76 1/2 followed by -1/4, it indicates that the previous day's closing price was 46._____

    A. 76 3/4   B. 76 1/2   C. 76 5/8   D. 76 3/8

47. An inscription on the cornerstone of a building reads MDCXCIV. This means that the cornerstone was placed there in the year 47._____

    A. 1484   B. 1594   C. 1694   D. 1794

48. 12 plus 6 x 6 less 24 ÷ 6 plus 10 equals 48._____

    A. 44   B. 64   C. 54   D. 14

49. A motorist travels 120 miles to his destination at the average speed of 60 miles per hour and returns to the starting point at the average speed of 40 miles per hour. His AVERAGE speed for the entire trip is _____ miles per hour. 49._____

    A. 53   B. 50   C. 48   D. 45

50. A snapshot measures 2 1/2 inches by 1 7/8 inches. It is to be enlarged so that the longer dimension will be 4 inches. The length of the enlarged shorter dimension will be _____ inches. 50._____

    A. 2 1/2   B. 3 3/8
    C. 3   D. none of the above

KEY (CORRECT ANSWERS)

1. C	11. A	21. D	31. B	41. B
2. B	12. C	22. D	32. B	42. B
3. A	13. A	23. C	33. B	43. B
4. B	14. B	24. A	34. B	44. D
5. A	15. B	25. C	35. C	45. A
6. B	16. B	26. D	36. A	46. A
7. D	17. D	27. D	37. B	47. C
8. A	18. B	28. B	38. A	48. C
9. B	19. D	29. A	39. B	49. C
10. C	20. C	30. C	40. B	50. C

SOLUTIONS TO PROBLEMS

1. CORRECT ANSWER: C
    A prime number is an integer which cannot be divided except by itself and one integer; a whole number as opposed to a fraction or a decimal.

2. CORRECT ANSWER: B

    $$3\overline{)6.000}\;\;\overset{2}{}$$ Example: Divide 6000 by 3000

3. CORRECT ANSWER: A

    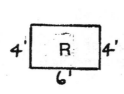   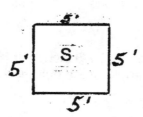

    P = 20 ft.   P = 20 ft.
    A = 24 sq. ft.   A = 25 sq. ft.

    $$\begin{array}{r} 25 \\ -24 \\ \hline 1 \end{array}$$

4. CORRECT ANSWER: B

    $$\frac{1/4}{3/8} = 1/4 \div 3/8 = 1/4 \times 8/3 = 2/3$$

5. CORRECT ANSWER: A

    $$\frac{7\frac{1}{2}}{1\,1/5} = \frac{15}{2} \div \frac{6}{5} = \frac{15}{2} \times \frac{5}{6} = \frac{25}{4} = 6\frac{1}{4}$$

    OR

    $$1.2\overline{)7.5}\;\;\overset{6\;\frac{\cancel{3}\;\;1}{\cancel{12}\;\;4}}{}$$

6. CORRECT ANSWER: B

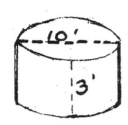

$A = \pi R^2$

$= 3(5)^2$

$= 75$ sq. ft.

$$\begin{array}{r} 225 \\ \times 7.5 \\ \hline 1125 \\ 1575 \\ \hline 1687.5 \end{array} \text{ gal.}$$

$\pi = \dfrac{22}{7} = 3$ (approx.)

Volume of tank $= 75 \times 3 =$ 225 cu. ft.
(approximate capacity of tank in gallons)

7. CORRECT ANSWER: D
A geometric series: each number is multiplied by the same number to get the succeeding number. (Multiply each number by 1/5.)

1/2, 1/10, 1/50, 1/250

8. CORRECT ANSWER: A
Compound Interest
4% a year compounded semi-annually is the same as 2% for a half year.

(a) $200
     × .02
     $4.00 Interest for 1st half year

     $200
     + 4
     $204 Principal for 1st half year

(b) $204
     × .02
     $4.08 Interest for 2nd half year

     $204.00
     + 4.08
     $208.08 Principal for 1st half
              of 2nd year

(c) $208.08
     ×   .02
     $4.1616 Interest for 1st half
              of 2nd year

     $208.08
     + 4.16
     $212.24 Principal for 2nd
              half of 2nd year

(d) $212.24
     ×   .02
     $4.2448 Interest for 2nd half
              of 2nd year

     $212.24
     + 4.24
     $216.48 Principal at end of
              2nd half of 2nd year

9. CORRECT ANSWER: B

$$\begin{array}{rcl} .0200x &=& \$1050 \\ 200x &=& \$10,500,000 \\ 2x &=& \$105,000 \\ x &=& \$52,500 \text{ (assessed valuation)} \end{array}$$

10. CORRECT ANSWER: C

$2491 + .06x = x   Proof
x = 2491 + .06x $2650 $2491
1.00x - .06x = 2491   x .06   + 159
.94x = 2491 $159.00 $2650
94x = 249,100

$$94 \overline{)249,100} = \$2,650$$

11. CORRECT ANSWER: A
.0295 = 2.95%

12. CORRECT ANSWER: C

An obtuse angle is an angle greater than $90°$.

13. CORRECT ANSWER: A

A quart   = 60 cu. in.
80 lbs.   = 1 cu. ft. (or 1728 cu.in.)(12x12x12)
             (Keep like units of measure together)
60 lbs.   = 1728 cu.in.

$$1 \text{ lb.} = \frac{1728}{60} = \text{approximately .29 cu. in.}$$

If 29 cu.in. weigh 1 lb., then 60 cu.in. weighs 2 lbs. (approx). Therefore, a quart weighs 2 lbs. (approx.).

14. CORRECT ANSWER: B
(1) Start with the fraction 2/3

(2) $\dfrac{2+2}{3+2} = \dfrac{4}{5}$ (Adding 2 to the numerator and the denominator)

(3) $\dfrac{2}{3} = \dfrac{10}{15}$

(4) $\dfrac{4}{5} = \dfrac{12}{15}$

15. CORRECT ANSWER: B
Common multiple: can be evenly divided by all the numbers. Least common multiple: the lowest of these numbers (72).

16. CORRECT ANSWER: B
Formula
    Step 1. Express percentages as decimals
    Step 2. Subtract each discount from one
    Step 3. Multiply all the results
    Step 4. Subtract the product from one

    Step 1. .3, .2, and .4, .1

Step 2. .7, .8, and .6, .9
Step 3. .7 x .8 = .56 (represents percent remaining after the .6 x .9 = .54 discounts are taken)

Step 4.
$$
\begin{array}{cc}
1.00 & 1.00 \\
-.56 & -.54 \\
\hline
.44 & .46
\end{array}
$$

The difference is 2%

Then, $100 x .02 = $2.00.

17. CORRECT ANSWER: D

$$\frac{1}{300}x = 24$$

x = 24 x 300

x = 7200

18. CORRECT ANSWER: B

$$
\begin{array}{r}
\$32 \\
\times\ 60 \\
\hline
\$1920
\end{array}
$$ (Cost of dinner sets before paying duty)

$$
\begin{array}{r}
\$1920 \\
\times\ .40 \\
\hline
\$768.00
\end{array}
$$ (Duty)

$$
\begin{array}{r}
\$1920 \\
+\ 768 \\
\hline
\$2688
\end{array}
$$

19. CORRECT ANSWER: D

Single discount for 20% and 10% = 28%

$$
\begin{array}{rcl}
20 + 10 & = & 30 \\
20 \times 10\% & = & 2.0 \\
\hline
& & 28.0
\end{array}
$$

List Price - Discount = Net Price
100% - 28% = 72%
$756 = 72% of List Price

$$
\begin{array}{r}
1050 \\
72\overline{)\$75600} \\
72 \\
\hline
360 \\
360
\end{array}
$$

20. CORRECT ANSWER: C

$$\frac{1}{6} + \frac{1}{8} = \frac{7}{24} \text{ (job done in 1 hour by both)}$$

$$\therefore 24 \div 7 = 3\frac{3}{7} \text{ (hours together)}$$

$$= 3 \text{ hours, 25 minutes}$$

21. CORRECT ANSWER: D

$$\text{Area} = \pi r^2$$

$$= 3.1416 \times (40')^2 = 3.1416 \times 1600 = 5026.56 \text{ sq. ft.}$$

22. CORRECT ANSWER: B

18,000 x 2.7% = $486 (quarterly) or $1,944 (annually)

23. CORRECT ANSWER: C

1) $900 x 15% = $135 (Withholding Tax)
2) $900 x 4.4% = $39.60 (Social Security Tax)
$174.60 (Total Tax Deduction)
$900 - $174.60 = $725.40 (Take-home Pay)

24. CORRECT ANSWER: A

5% of $90,000 = $4,500 (income for one year)
To obtain 9%, the cost of the mortgage must be:

$$4,500 = \frac{9}{100} \text{ of the mortgage}$$

$$4,500 \times \frac{100}{9} = \$50,000 \text{ (cost of mortgage)}$$

25. CORRECT ANSWER: C

Passenger rate = $54
Profit   =   6.75 (1/8 of 54)
Operating Cost = $47.25

26. CORRECT ANSWER: D

30 x 2 1/2 = $75 (premium for 3 years)
36 months - 15 months = 21 months unexpired time

$$\frac{21}{36} \times 75 = \$43.75 \text{ (amount to be refunded)}$$

27. CORRECT ANSWER: D

L.P.   = $200 = 133 1/3% of cost
Cost   = 100%
Profit = 33 1/3%

$200 =$ 1 1/3 of the cost
$200 \times 3/4 =$ $150 cost
$150 \times 1/5 =$ $30 new profit
$150 + $30 =$ $180 new marked price

28.   CORRECT ANSWER: B

	Regular Time	Overtime
Monday	8	
Tuesday	8	2
Wednesday	8	
Thursday	8	
Friday	8	4
	40 hours	6 hours

Rate per hour = $120 / 8 hours = $15 per hour
Overtime = 6 hours x 1 1/2 x $15 = $22.50 overtime pay x 6 hrs. = $135
Payment for regular time worked = 40 hours x $15 = $600
Samuels earned $135 + $600 = $735

29.   CORRECT ANSWER: A
500 sheets = 1 ream of paper
1 ream 17x22 = 4 sheets 8 1/2 x 11
500 sheets x 4 = 2000 sheets from 1 ream (17x22)

∴ 10,000 sheets may be obtained from 5 reams (17x22)

30.   CORRECT ANSWER: C

$$\frac{1 \text{ million}}{4/5 \times 1.6 \text{ mil.}} \times 960,000 = \$750,000$$

31.   CORRECT ANSWER: B (12 pence (d) = 1 shilling(s);

6s = .3£   20 s = 1 pound (£);
.5s = .025£   6d = .5s)
.325£

∴ $1.68 x 20.325 = $34.15

32.   CORRECT ANSWER: B
Maturation value of $800 note at 6% interest for 45 days may be computed as follows:
   $800 + (1/8 x .06 x 800) = 800 + 6 = $806 (maturation value)

Interest is $8.06 for   72   days   at   5%
Interest is $4.03 for   36   days   at   5%
Interest is   .67 for   6   days   at   5%
Interest is $3.36 for   30   days   at   5%
Finally, maturation value = $806.00
                  discount =   3.36
                  proceeds = $802.64

33.   CORRECT ANSWER: B
      $4.80 ÷ .0008 = $6000

34.   CORRECT ANSWER: B
      Boys = 1/4 of class
      ∴ Girls = 3/4 of class
      Ratio is 3 to 1 (girls to boys)

35.   CORRECT ANSWER: C
      Exemptions: 1 + 1 + 2 = 4

36.   CORRECT ANSWER: A
      Proportion

37.   CORRECT ANSWER: B
      39.37 inches = 1 meter
      3937 inches = 1 kilometer
      1 kilometer = 3937 ÷ 12 = 328.08 ft.
      ∴ 328.08 ÷ 5280 = .0621

38.   CORRECT ANSWER: A
      1 liter = 0.9081 U.S. dry quart ANSWER: Smaller (U.S. dry quart)
      1 liter = 1.0567 U.S. liquid quarts ANSWER: Larger (U.S. liquid quart)

39.   CORRECT ANSWER: B

$$\begin{array}{r} 6.8 \\ 22\overline{)46.24} \\ \underline{36} \\ 128\overline{)1024} \\ \underline{1024} \end{array}$$

40.   CORRECT ANSWER: B
      More

41.   CORRECT ANSWER: B
      $8000 + $800 (Federal Tax 10%) + $660 (Local Sales Tax 3%) = $9460

42.   CORRECT ANSWER: B
      Gold marked 12K is 12/24 pure and 12/24 alloy.

43.   CORRECT ANSWER: B
      1 fathom = 6 feet

44.   CORRECT ANSWER: D
      Cost = $1.25, which is 5/6 of the cost of the roasted peanuts
      ∴ $1.25 x 6/5 = $1.50, the cost of 1 lb. of roasted peanuts.

45. CORRECT ANSWER: A
    231 cu.in. = 1 gallon
    1 cu.ft. = 12" x 12" x 12" = 1728 cu.in.
    1728 ÷ 231 = 7.48 gallons

46. CORRECT ANSWER: A
    76 1/2 + 1/4 = 76 3/4 (previous day's closing)

47. CORRECT ANSWER: C
    M = 1000
    DC = 600
    XC = 90
    IV = 4
    ‾‾‾‾‾‾
       1694

48. CORRECT ANSWER: C
    12 + 36 - 4 + 10 = 54
    Order of Operations:
    In order to find the value of a number expression:
    1. First, do all the multiplications
    2. Second, do the divisions, taking them in order from left to right
    3. Finally, do the additions and subtractions, taking them in any order

49. CORRECT ANSWER: C
    120 miles = 2 hours (60 mph)
    120 miles = 3 hours (40 mph)
    240 miles = 5 hours = average of 48 mph

50. CORRECT ANSWER: C
    Change 2 1/2 to 20/8

    Change 1 7/8 to 15/8
    Ratio is 20 to 15 or 4 to 3
    If the longer dimension is 4 inches, then the shorter is 3 inches.

ARITHMETICAL REASONING
EXAMINATION SECTION
TEST 1

DIRECTIONS: Each question or incomplete statement is followed by several suggested answers or completions. Select the one that BEST answers the question or completes the statement. *PRINT THE LETTER OF THE CORRECT ANSWER IN THE SPACE AT THE RIGHT.*

1. To check the correctness of the answer to a multiplication example, divide the   1._____

   A. product by the multiplier
   B. multiplier by the product
   C. multiplicand by the multiplier
   D. multiplier by the multiplicand

2. Of the following correct ways to solve .125 x .32, the MOST efficient is to   2._____

   A. write .125 under .32, multiply, point off 5 places
   B. write .32 under .125, multiply, point off 5 places
   C. multiply 125 by 32 and divide by 1000 x 100
   D. divide . 32 by 8

3. If you were to eat each meal in a different restaurant in the city's eating places, assuming   3._____
   that you eat three meals a day, it would take you more than 19 years to cover all of the
   city's eating places.
   On the basis of this information, the BEST of the following choices is that the number
   of restaurants in the city

   A. exceeds 20,500
   B. is closer to 21,000 than 22,000
   C. exceeds 21,000
   D. does not exceed 21,500

4. The cost of electricity for operating an 875 watt toaster, an 1100 watt steam iron, and four   4._____
   75 watt lamps, each for one hour, at 7.5 cents per kilowatt hour (1 kilowatt equals 1000
   watts) is

   A. 15¢   B. 17¢   C. $1.54   D. $1.71

5. Of the following, the pair that is NOT a set of equivalents is   5._____

   A. .021%, .00021   B. 1/4%, .0025
   C. 1.5%, 3/200   D. 225%, .225

6. Assuming that the series will continue in the same pattern, the NEXT number in the   6._____
   series 3, 5, 11, 29, ... is

   A. 41   B. 47   C. 65   D. 83

7. If the total area of a picture measuring 10 inches by 12 inches plus a matting of uniform   7._____
   width surrounding the picture is 224 square inches, the width of the matting is _____
   inches.

   A. 2   B. 2 4/11   C. 3   D. 4

8. The net price of a $25 item after successive discounts of 20% and 30% is   8._____

    A. $11   B. $12.50   C. $14   D. $19

9. The cost of 63 inches of ribbon at 12¢ per yard is   9._____

    A. $.20   B. $.21   C. $.22   D. $.23

10. If 14 cups of cereal are used with 4 1/2 cups of water, the amount of water needed with 3/4 of a cup of cereal is _____ cups.   10._____

    A. 2   B. 2 1/8   C. 2 1/4   D. 2 1/2

11. Under certain conditions, sound travels at about 1100 ft. per second.
If 88 ft. per second is approximately equivalent to 60 miles per hour, the speed of sound, under the above conditions, is, of the following, CLOSEST to _____ miles per hour.   11._____

    A. 730   B. 740   C. 750   D. 760

12. Of the following, the MOST NEARLY accurate set of equivalents is   12._____

    A. 1 foot equals 30.48 centimeters
    B. 1 centimeter equals 2.54 inches
    C. 1 rod equals 3.28 meters
    D. 1 meter equals 1.09 feet

13. If one angle of a triangle is three times a second angle and the third angle is 20° more than the second angle, the second angle is   13._____

    A. 32°   B. 34°   C. 40°   D. 50°

14. Assuming that on a blueprint 1/4 inch equals 12 inches, the ACTUAL length, in feet, of a steel bar represented on the blueprint by a line 3 3/8 inches long is   14._____

    A. 3 3/8   B. 6 3/4.   C. 12 1/2   D. 13 1/2

15. A plane leaves Denver, Colorado on June 1st at 1 P.M. Mountain Standard Time and arrives at New York City on June 2nd at 2 A.M. Eastern Daylight Savings Time.
The ACTUAL time of flight was _____ hours.   15._____

    A. 10   B. 11   C. 12   D. 13

16. Of the following, the CLOSEST to that of 42.10 x .0003/.002   16._____

    A. .063   B. .63   C. 6.3   D. 63

17. If Mrs. Jones bought 3 3/4 yards of dacron at $1.16 per yard and 4 2/3 yards of velvet at $3.87 per yard, the amount of change she receives from $25 is   17._____

    A. $2.12   B. $2.28   C. $2.59   D. $2.63

18. The water level of a swimming pool 75 feet by 42 feet is to be raised 4 inches.
The number of gallons of water needed for this purpose is (1 cubic foot equals 7 1/2 gallons)   18._____

    A. 140   B. 7,875   C. 31,500   D. 94,500

19. The part of the total quantity represented by a 24 degree sector of a circle graph is   19._____

    A. 6 2/3%   B. 12%   C. 13 1/3%   D. 24%

20. If the shipping charges to a certain point are 62 cents for the first 5 oz. and 8 cents for   20._____
    each additional ounce, the weight of a package for which the charges are $1.66 is

    A. 13 oz.   B. 1 1/8 lbs.   C. 14 lbs.   D. 1 1/2 lbs.

21. If 15 cans of food are needed for 7 men for 2 days, the number of cans needed for 4 men   21._____
    for 7 days is

    A. 15   B. 20   C. 25   D. 30

22. The total saving in purchasing thirty 13¢ ice cream pops for a class party at a reduced   22._____
    rate of $1.38 per dozen is

    A. 35¢   B. 40¢   C. 45¢   D. 50¢

23. The quotient for the division of 36 apples among 4 children may be CORRECTLY found   23._____
    by thinking _____

    A. 36 ÷ 1/4   B. $36\overline{)4.0}$

    C. 1/4 of 36   D. 4/36

24. The missing term in the equation 1/3 of ?= 1/2 of 90 is   24._____

    A. 45   B. 30   C. 15   D. 135

25. The fraction CLOSEST to 4/5 is   25._____

    A. 2/3   B. 7/9   C. 8/11   D. 5/8

26. Of the following, the one which may be used CORRECTLY to compute the value of 4 x   26._____
    22 1/2 is

    A. (4 x 45) + (4 x 1/2)
    B. (4 x A) + (4 x 2) + (4 x 2)
    C. (1/2 of 4) + (2 x 4) + (2 x 4)
    D. (4 x 20) + (4 x 2) + (4 x 1/2)

27. 16 1/2 ÷ 1/4 may CORRECTLY be expressed as   27._____

    A. (1/4 x 16) + (1/4 x 1/2)   B. (4 x 16) + (4 x 1/2)
                                         D. 1/4 times 33/2
    C. $4\overline{)16.5}$

28. In computation, 3/4 may be CORRECTLY transformed into 6/8 for the same reason that   28._____

    A. 7(3+4) = 21 +28   B. 3 apples+5 apples = 8
                                 D. 3+4=4+3
    C. $.2\overline{)3.4}$ = $2\overline{)34}$

29. The mathematical law of distribution is illustrated by all of the following EXCEPT   29.____

    A.   B.   C.   D.

$$
\begin{array}{r} 15 \\ \times 12 \\ \hline 150 \\ 30 \\ \hline 180 \end{array}
\qquad
\begin{array}{r} 15 \\ \times 12 \\ \hline 30 \\ 150 \\ \hline 180 \end{array}
\qquad
\begin{array}{r} 15 \\ \times 12 \\ \hline 180 \end{array}
\qquad
\begin{array}{r} 15 \\ \times 12 \\ \hline 30 \\ 15 \\ \hline 180 \end{array}
$$

30. Of the following series of partial sums which might arise in the addition of 36 and 25, the one that is INCORRECT is   30.____

    A. 11, 31, 61   B. 11, 4, 6, 61
    C. 11, 41, 61   D. 36, 56, 61

31. Of the following, the one which equals one million is   31.____

    A. ten hundred thousand
    B. 10^7
    C. 10 x 10 x 10 x 10 x 10 x 10 x 10
    D. 1 plus 6 zeroes

32. Of the following groups, the one containing four terms all associated with one algorismic process is   32.____

    A. addend, quotient, dividend, divisor
    B. dividend, quotient, divisor, minuend
    C. dividend, quotient, addend, minuend
    D. multiplicand, product, minuend, addend

33. Depreciation of a certain machine is estimated, for any year, at 20% of its value at the beginning of the year. If the machine is purchased for $600, its estimated net value at the end of two years is CLOSEST to   33.____

    A. $325   B. $350   C. $375   D. $400

34. Hats are purchased at the rate of $33 per dozen.
If they are sold at a close-out sale for $2.50 each, the percent loss on the cost price is   34.____

    A. 3   B. 3 1/3   C. 9 1/11   D. 10

35. The time 3 hours, 58 minutes after 10:56 A.M. _____ P.M.   35.____

    A. 4:54   B. 2:54   C. 4:14   D. 2:14

36. Mr. Brown had $20.00 when he took his three children on a bus trip. He spent $7.33 for the four tickets and bought each of the children a magazine costing 15¢, a candy bar costing 11¢, and a 5¢ package of chewing gum. His change from the $20.00 was   36.____

    A. $12.74   B. $11.43   C. $11.74   D. $12.84

37. The loan value on a life insurance policy at the end of five years is $30.19/ $1000 of insurance.
The LARGEST amount, to the nearest dollar, that can be borrowed on a $5500 policy at the end of five years is   37.____

    A. $17   B. $151   C. $166   D. $1660

38. Using cups that hold six ounces of milk, the number of cupfuls a person can obtain from 1 1/2 gallons of milk is

    A. 16   B. 24   C. 32   D. 64

38.____

39. A storekeeper purchased an article for $36.
In order to include 10% of cost for overhead and to provide $9 of net profit, the markup should be

    A. 25%   B. 35%   C. 37 1/2%   D. 40%

39.____

40. A rectangular carton has twice the height, one-third the length, and four times the width of a second carton. The ratio of the volume of the first carton to that of the second carton is

    A. 16:3   B. 2:1   C. 8:3   D. 3:8

40.____

41. If $300 is invested at simple interest so as to yield interest income of $18 in 9 months, the amount of money that must be invested at the same rate of interest so as to yield a return of $120 in 6 months is

    A. $3000   B. $3300   C. $2800   D. $2400

41.____

42. If a boy has a number of dimes and quarters in his pocket adding up to $3.10, the LARGEST possible number of dimes he can have is

    A. 16   B. 28   C. 26   D. 21

42.____

43. In a number system using the base 10, the value represented by the first digit 3 reading from the left, in the number 82,364,371 is _____ times the value represented by the second digit 3.

    A. 30   B. 100   C. 1,000   D. 10,000

43.____

44. The number of revolutions made by a bicycle wheel of 28 inch diameter in traveling 1/2 mile is CLOSEST to

    A. 720   B. 180   C. 360   D. 120

44.____

45. Of the following, the property which is TRUE of all parallelograms is that the

    A.   diagonals are equal
    B.   diagonals meet at right angles
    C.   sum of the interior angles is 180°
    D.   diagonals bisect each other

45.____

46. Of the following explanations about steps in the computation at the right, the one which is LEAST meaningful or accurate is that the
    A.   64 represents 200 x 32
    B.   265 is the result of subtracting 320 from 585
    C.   9 is part of the quotient
    D.   256 symbolizes the subtraction of 32 eight times

$$\begin{array}{r} 218 \\ 32\overline{)6985} \\ 64 \\ \hline 58 \\ 32 \\ \hline 265 \\ 256 \\ \hline 9 \end{array}$$

46.____

47. Assuming that a system of meridians and parallels of latitude like that used on maps of the earth's surface was designed for the moon's surface, the distance covered by a man traveling 1° on the moon as compared to that covered in traveling 1° on the earth would be   47.____

    A. equal
    B. less
    C. greater
    D. sometimes greater and sometimes less

48. 1958 may MOST correctly be expressed in Roman numerals as   48.____

    A. MDCDLVIII   B. CMMLVIII   C. MCMLVIII   D. MCMLIIX

49. If the same positive quantity is added to both the numerator and the denominator of a proper fraction, the value of the new fraction, as compared to that of the original fraction, will be   49.____

    A. greater   B. less
    C. equal   D. either greater or less

50. If the Fahrenheit temperature is 74°, the Centigrade equivalent would be [Use the formula C = 5/9 (F-32)]   50.____

    A. 9 1/9°   B. 23 1/3°   C. 42°   D. 56 2/9°

KEY (CORRECT ANSWERS)

1. A	11. C	21. D	31. A	41. A
2. D	12. A	22. C	32. B	42. C
3. A	13. A	23. C	33. C	43. C
4. B	14. D	24. D	34. C	44. C
5. D	15. A	25. B	35. B	45. D
6. D	16. C	26. D	36. C	46. C
7. C	17. C	27. B	37. C	47. B
8. A	18. B	28. C	38. C	48. C
9. B	19. A	29. C	39. B	49. A
10. C	20. B	30. B	40. C	50. B

SOLUTIONS TO PROBLEMS

1. CORRECT ANSWER: A

    12 (multiplicand)
    ×2 (multiplier)
    24 (product)

2. CORRECT ANSWER: D
   The most efficient way is to divide .32 by 8.
   .125 = .12 1/2 = 12 1/2% = 1/8

   $$1/8 \text{x} \; .32 = .32/8 = 8\overline{)\begin{array}{r} .04 \\ .32 \\ \underline{.32} \end{array}}$$

3. CORRECT ANSWER: A

365 (days in 1 year)	4 (leap-year days)
x 3 (meals)	x 3 (meals)
1095 (meals in 1 year)	12 (leap-year meals)
x 19 (number of years)	

    20,805 (number of meals eaten in 19 years)
    + 12 (number of meals eaten in leap years)
    20,817 (total)

4. CORRECT ANSWER: B

    875 watts
    1100
    300
    2275 ÷ 1000 = 2 11/40 kw. hours
    2 11/40 x 7.5 = .17 (approximately)

5. CORRECT ANSWER: D

    A.   .021% = .00021

    B.   1/4% = 1/400 = $400\overline{)\begin{array}{r} .0025 \\ 1.0000 \end{array}}$

    C.   1.5% = .015 = 15/1000 = 3/200
    D.   225% = 2.25, NOT .225

6. **CORRECT ANSWER: D**
    <u>Suggestions for Series Problems</u>
    1. Find the difference between the numbers (or squares of differences).
    2. In this series, each difference is multiplied by 3 and added to the succeeding number.
        3,5 The difference is 2
            3x2 = 6
            5 + 6 = 11
        5, 11 The difference is 6
            3 x 6 = 18
            11 + 18 = 29
        11, 29 The difference is 18
            3 x 18 = 54
            29 + 54 = 83

7. **CORRECT ANSWER: C**
    Total area = 224 square inches

    ```
      16"
    ×14"
      64
      16
     224 square inches
    ```

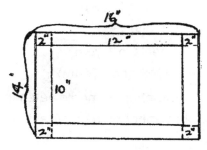

8. **CORRECT ANSWER: A**
    <u>Solution</u>

    Successive discounts
        20%, 30%
    1. Convert to decimals .2, .3
    2. Subtract from 1.0   .8, .7
    3. Multiply .8 x .7 = .56
    4. 1.00 - .56 = .44

    ```
     25.00
    ×  .44
      100
      100
    $11.00
    ```
    ∴ $25 - $11 = $14

    <u>Alternate Solution</u>

    ```
      $25
    ×  .20
    $5.00
    ```

    $25 - 5 = $20.00

    ```
     $20
    ×  .20
    $6.00
    ```

    $20 - $6 = $14 ANSWER

9. **CORRECT ANSWER: B**
    63" = 63/36 yards

    <u>Alternate Solution</u>
    12¢ per yard
    12/36=1/3¢ per inch

    21   .01
    $\dfrac{\cancel{63}}{\cancel{36}} \times \dfrac{\cancel{12}}{} = 21¢$

    3
    63"/1 x 1/3¢ = 63/3 = 21¢

10. **CORRECT ANSWER: C**
    <u>Proportion</u>
    1st mixture
    2nd mixture
    3/4 is half of 1 1/2
    Therefore, half of 4 1/2 is 2 1/4

Cereal	Water
1½ cups	4½ cups
3/4 cups	x cups

11. **CORRECT ANSWER: C**
    The speed of sound is 1100 ft. per second. 88 ft. per second = 60 miles an hour
    1100/88 = indicates the number of times greater than 60 miles an hour is the speed of sound

    $$12\frac{1}{2} \text{ times}$$
    $$88\overline{)1100}$$

    $$\begin{array}{r} 60 \\ \times 12\frac{1}{2} \\ \hline 750 \text{ miles per hour} \end{array}$$

12. **CORRECT ANSWER: A**
    <u>Conversion</u>
    A meter = 39 inches (39.37 inches)
           = 3 1/4 ft. (39/12 = 3 1/4)
    A centimeter = .39 inches
    1 rod = 5 1/2 yards (5.5 yards x 3 = 16.5 feet)
           = 16 1/2 feet
    A rod is approximately 5 meters (See choice (C) which is, therefore, wrong)
    A meter is 100 centimeters (one cm. = .01) 3 1/4 feet = 1 meter or 100 centimeters

    $$1 \text{ ft} = \frac{100}{3\frac{1}{4}} = \frac{100}{1} \div \frac{13}{4} = \frac{100}{1} \times \frac{4}{13} = \frac{400}{13}$$

    $$\begin{array}{r} 30.76 \\ 13\overline{)400.00} \end{array}$$

13. **CORRECT ANSWER: A**
    Let x = 2nd angle
    Let 3x = 1st angle
    Let x + 20° = 3rd angle
    3x + x + x + 20 = 180
         5x + 20 = 180
              5x = 160
                x = 32°

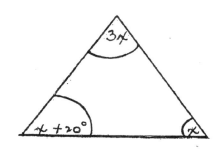

14. CORRECT ANSWER: D

$$\frac{\frac{1}{4}"}{12} = \frac{3\,3/8"}{x}$$

1/4 ÷ 12/1 = 27/8 ÷ x/1

1/4 x 1/12 = 27/8 x 1/x

1/4 = 27/8x

8x = 48 x 27 = 1296

x = 162 inches

= 13 1/2 ft.

15. CORRECT ANSWER: A

Time Belts

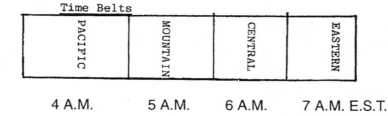

4 A.M.	5 A.M.	6 A.M.	7 A.M. E.S.T.
			8 A.M. D.S.T.

In traveling eastward, we set our clocks forward for each time zone.

Plane left at 1 P.M.

Traveled around clock 12 hours or 13 hours at 2 A.M. Subtract 2 hours difference between Mountain Time and Eastern Standard Time. Subtract another hour for Daylight Savings Time. That is, 13 - 3 = 10 hours.

16. CORRECT ANSWER: C

$$\frac{42.10 \times .0003}{.002} = \frac{42 \times .0003}{.002} \text{ (approximating)}$$

<u>Work</u>

42

$$\frac{\times .0003}{.0126} = \frac{.0126}{.002} = \frac{12.6}{2} = 6.3$$

17. CORRECT ANSWER: C

$1.16	$3.87	$18.06	$25.00
× 3 3/4	× 4 2/3	+4.35	-22.41
$4.35	$18.06	$22.41	$ 2.59

18. CORRECT ANSWER: B

42 x 75 x 1/3 ft (4") = 1050 cu. ft.

$$\times\ 7\frac{1}{2}$$

7875 gallons

19. CORRECT ANSWER: A

$$\frac{24}{360}=\frac{2}{30}=\frac{1}{15}=.06\ 2/3=6\ 2/3\%$$

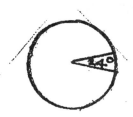

20. CORRECT ANSWER: B

$1.66 total charge
- .62 1st 5 oz
$1.04 charge at 8 cents an oz.

13 oz.
.08)$1.04

13 oz
+5 oz
18 oz.

$$\frac{18}{16}=1\frac{2}{16}=\frac{1}{8}\ \text{lb}$$

8

21. CORRECT ANSWER: D   21._____

Cans	Men	Days	Number of days one man would need to consume the cans
15	7	2	14 days
x	4	7	28 days

x = 2(15) = 30 cans

22. CORRECT ANSWER: C   22._____

$.13
× 30
$3.90
-3.45
$ .45

$$\frac{30}{12}=2\frac{1}{2}\ \text{dozens}$$

$1.38
× 2½
$3.45

23. CORRECT ANSWER: C   23._____
36/4=9

24. CORRECT ANSWER: D 1/3 of ? = 1/2 of 90   24._____
1/3x = 45
x = 3 x 45
= 135

25. CORRECT ANSWER: B   25._____
4/5 = .80
2/3 = .66
7/9 = .78
8/11 = .73
5/8 = .63

26. CORRECT ANSWER: D   26.____

$$
\begin{array}{r}
22\frac{1}{2} \\
\times 4 \\
\hline
80 \\
8 \\
2 \\
\hline
90
\end{array}
$$

Choice (D) $(4 \times 20) + (4 \times 2) + (4 \times 1/2) = 80 + 8 + 2 = 90$ (This is an example of the Distributive Law, which links the operations of addition and multiplication.)

27. CORRECT ANSWER: B   27.____

$$16\frac{1}{2} \div 4 = \frac{16\frac{1}{2}}{4} = 16\frac{1}{2} \times 4/1 = (4 \times 16) + (4 \times \frac{1}{2})$$

28. CORRECT ANSWER: C   28.____

$$\frac{3}{4} = \frac{6}{8}; \frac{3.4}{.2} = \frac{34}{2} = 17$$

29. CORRECT ANSWER: C   29.____

A.	B.	C.
$10 \times 15 = 150$	$2 \times 15 = 30$	$2 \times 15 = 30$
$2 \times 15 = \frac{30}{180}$	$10 \times 15 = \frac{150}{180}$	$10 \times 15 = \frac{150}{180}$

The Distributive Law links the operations of addition and arithmetic.

30. CORRECT ANSWER: B   30.____
<u>Partial Sums</u>

$$
\begin{array}{r}
36 \\
+25 \\
\hline
61
\end{array}
\qquad
\begin{array}{r}
(A)\ 11 \\
+20 \\
\hline
31 \\
+30 \\
\hline
61
\end{array}
\qquad
\begin{array}{r}
(C)\ 11 \\
+30 \\
\hline
41 \\
+20 \\
\hline
61
\end{array}
\qquad
\begin{array}{r}
(D)\ 36 \\
+20 \\
\hline
56 \\
+\ 5 \\
\hline
61
\end{array}
$$

31. CORRECT ANSWER: A   31.____
$100,000 \times 10 = 1,000,000$

32. CORRECT ANSWER: B   32.____

$$12\overline{)256} \quad \substack{21 \text{ quotient}}$$

      12)256   dividend

    24
    16   minuend - partial dividend
    12
     4   partial dividend

36	multiplicand	5	addend
x 45	multiplier	+6	addend
180	partial product	11	sum
144	partial product		
1620	product		

   7,485 minuend
  -2,648 subtrahend
   4,837 remainder (difference)

33. CORRECT ANSWER: C   33.____

$600	$480	$600	$480
x .20	x .20	- 120	- 96
120.00	96.00	$480	$384 approximately

34. CORRECT ANSWER: C   34.____

Cost of one dozen $33.00 $2.50
Selling price of one   x 1 2
   dozen   30.00 $30.00 (sold at close-out sale)
Loss $ 3.00

$$\frac{L}{C} = \frac{\$3}{\$33} = \frac{1}{11} = 9\ 1/11\%$$

35. CORRECT ANSWER: B SOLUTION   35.____

   10:56-A.M.   Add 3 hours, ~~58~~ minutes
   11:00 A.M.   54 minutes
  +3:00 hours   (see 10:56 A.M.)
   2:00 P.M
  + :54 minutes
   2:54 P.M.

36. CORRECT ANSWER: C   36.____

15¢	31¢	$7.33	$20.00
11¢	x3	+ .93	- 8.26
5¢	93¢	$8.26	$11.74
31¢			

37.   CORRECT ANSWER: C

$$
\begin{array}{ll}
\$30.19 & \$150.95 \text{ (amount on \$5000)} \\
\underline{\times\quad 5} & \underline{+\ 15.10} \text{ (amount on \$500)} \\
\$150.95 & \$166.05 \text{ (approximately)}
\end{array}
$$

38.   CORRECT ANSWER: C

1 cup = 8 oz.
1 quart = 4 cups (4 x 8 oz. = 32 oz.)
1 gallon = 32 oz. x 4 = 128 oz.
(1 gallon = 4 qts. or 128 oz.)
1/2 gallon = 64 oz.

$$
\begin{array}{r}
128 \text{ oz.} \\
+\ 64 \text{ oz.} \\
\hline
6\,\overline{)\,192} \\
\hline
32 \text{ cups}
\end{array}
$$

39.   CORRECT ANSWER: B

Cost	=	$36.00	Selling price =	$48.60
10% of cost	=	3.60	Cost =	36.00
Profit	=	9.00	Markup =	$12.60
Selling Price	=	$48.60		

$$
\frac{\text{Markup}}{\text{Cost}} = \frac{\$12.60}{\$36.00} = 35\%
$$

40.   CORRECT ANSWER: C

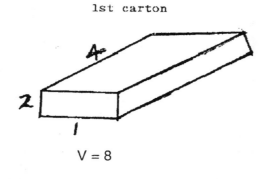
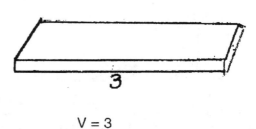

1st carton   2nd carton

V = 8   V = 3

$$
\frac{V1}{V2} = \frac{8}{3}
$$

41. CORRECT ANSWER: A   41._____
     Step (1) Principal = $300
             Interest = $18 in 9 months (9 months = 3/4 year)

             To find annual interest:
                 Let x = annual interest
                 3/4x = 18
                     x = 18 x 4/3
                     x = $24

             To find rate:
                 Let R = rate

                 $R = \dfrac{I}{P} = \dfrac{24 \, \text{interest}}{300 \, \text{principal}} \times 1 \, (\text{year})$

$$\begin{array}{r} .80 \\ 300\overline{)24.00} \\ 24\ 00 \\ \hline 00 \end{array}$$

                 Interest rate = 8%
     Step (2) Principal (?) to be invested at 8% to yield $120
             interest in 6 months:
             6 months = 1/2 year
             Yearly interest = $240 ($120 x 2)

             $P = \dfrac{I}{R}$

             $P = \dfrac{\$240 \ (\text{interest})}{.08 \quad (\text{rate})}$

$$.08\overline{)240} = 8\overline{)24000}^{\ 3000}$$

             P = $3000 (the amount of money that would have to be invested)

42. CORRECT ANSWER: C   42._____
     26 x 10 = $2.60 + .50 = $3.10

43. CORRECT ANSWER: C   43._____
     (approximately) 300 x 1,000 = 300,000

44. CORRECT ANSWER: C   44._____

$C = \pi D$

$C = 22/7 \times 28 = 88"$

1 revolution of wheel covers 88"

1/12 x 5280 x 12/1 = traveling distance in inches

6 x 5280 = 31680 inches

```
        360
   88)31680
      264
      528
      528
```

45. CORRECT ANSWER: D   45._____

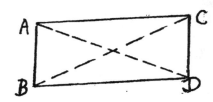

triangle = 180°
parallelogram = 360°

46. CORRECT ANSWER: C   46._____

Division is repeated subtraction

Below is a division *pyramid,* which shows what actually happens when we divide.

```
         8
        10
       200
   32)6945 dividend
      6400
       585  partial dividend
       320
       265  partial dividend
       256
         9  partial dividend
```

32 x100 = 3200
32 x 200= 6400
32 x 10 = 320

47. CORRECT ANSWER: B   47._____
   Diameter of moon = 2000 miles
   Diameter of earth = 8000 miles

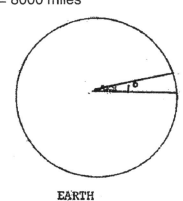

MOON

EARTH

The larger the circle,
the larger the arc.

$$1° \text{ of arc} = \frac{1}{360} \text{ of}$$

circle.

Circumference of earth = 25,000 miles Circumference of moon = 6,200 miles (1/4 of earth)

```
        69+
360)25,000          1° = 69+ miles on the equator (Earth)
    21 6            1° = 17+ miles (Moon)
     3 40
     3 24
       16
```

48. CORRECT ANSWER: C   48._____
   M = 1000
   CM = 900
   L = 50

   $$VIII = \frac{8}{1958}$$

49. CORRECT ANSWER: A   49._____

   $$\frac{2+2}{3+2} = \frac{4}{5} = \frac{12}{15}$$

   $$\frac{2}{3} = \frac{10}{15}$$

50. CORRECT ANSWER: B   50._____

   $$C = \frac{5}{9}(74-32) \qquad C = \frac{5}{9} \times \frac{42}{1} = \frac{70}{3}$$
   $$= \frac{5}{9}(42) \qquad\qquad = 23\ 1/3°$$

ARITHMETICAL REASONING
EXAMINATION SECTION
TEST 1

DIRECTIONS: Each question or incomplete statement is followed by several suggested answers or completions. Select the one that BEST answers the question or completes the statement. *PRINT THE LETTER OF THE CORRECT ANSWER IN THE SPACE AT THE RIGHT.*

1. To check the correctness of the answer to a multiplication example, divide the   1._____

    A. product by the multiplier
    B. multiplier by the product
    C. multiplicand by the multiplier
    D. multiplier by the multiplicand

2. Of the following correct ways to solve .125 x .32, the MOST efficient is to   2._____

    A. write .125 under .32, multiply, point off 5 places
    B. write .32 under .125, multiply, point off 5 places
    C. multiply 125 by 32 and divide by 1000 x 100
    D. divide . 32 by 8

3. If you were to eat each meal in a different restaurant in the city's eating places, assuming   3._____
that you eat three meals a day, it would take you more than 19 years to cover all of the city's eating places.
On the basis of this information, the BEST of the following choices is that the number of restaurants in the city

    A. exceeds 20,500
    B. is closer to 21,000 than 22,000
    C. exceeds 21,000
    D. does not exceed 21,500

4. The cost of electricity for operating an 875 watt toaster, an 1100 watt steam iron, and four   4._____
75 watt lamps, each for one hour, at 7.5 cents per kilowatt hour (1 kilowatt equals 1000 watts) is

    A. 15¢   B. 17¢   C. $1.54   D. $1.71

5. Of the following, the pair that is NOT a set of equivalents is   5._____

    A. .021%, .00021   B. 1/4%, .0025
    C. 1.5%, 3/200   D. 225%, .225

6. Assuming that the series will continue in the same pattern, the NEXT number in the   6._____
series 3, 5, 11, 29, ... is

    A. 41   B. 47   C. 65   D. 83

7. If the total area of a picture measuring 10 inches by 12 inches plus a matting of uniform   7._____
width surrounding the picture is 224 square inches, the width of the matting is _____ inches.

    A. 2   B. 2 4/11   C. 3   D. 4

8. The net price of a $25 item after successive discounts of 20% and 30% is   8._____

    A. $11   B. $12.50   C. $14   D. $19

9. The cost of 63 inches of ribbon at 12¢ per yard is   9._____

    A. $.20   B. $.21   C. $.22   D. $.23

10. If 14 cups of cereal are used with 4 1/2 cups of water, the amount of water needed with 3/4 of a cup of cereal is _____ cups.   10._____

    A. 2   B. 2 1/8   C. 2 1/4   D. 2 1/2

11. Under certain conditions, sound travels at about 1100 ft. per second. If 88 ft. per second is approximately equivalent to 60 miles per hour, the speed of sound, under the above conditions, is, of the following, CLOSEST to _____miles per hour.   11._____

    A. 730   B. 740   C. 750   D. 760

12. Of the following, the MOST NEARLY accurate set of equivalents is   12._____

    A. 1 foot equals 30.48 centimeters
    B. 1 centimeter equals 2.54 inches
    C. 1 rod equals 3.28 meters
    D. 1 meter equals 1.09 feet

13. If one angle of a triangle is three times a second angle and the third angle is 20° more than the second angle, the second angle is   13._____

    A. 32°   B. 34°   C. 40°   D. 50°

14. Assuming that on a blueprint 1/4 inch equals 12 inches, the ACTUAL length, in feet, of a steel bar represented on the blueprint by a line 3 3/8 inches long is   14._____

    A. 3 3/8   B. 6 3/4.   C. 12 1/2   D. 13 1/2

15. A plane leaves Denver, Colorado on June 1st at 1 P.M. Mountain Standard Time and arrives at New York City on June 2nd at 2 A.M. Eastern Daylight Savings Time. The ACTUAL time of flight was _____ hours.   15._____

    A. 10   B. 11   C. 12   D. 13

16. Of the following, the CLOSEST to that of 42.10 x .0003/.002   16._____

    A. .063   B. .63   C. 6.3   D. 63

17. If Mrs. Jones bought 3 3/4 yards of dacron at $1.16 per yard and 4 2/3 yards of velvet at $3.87 per yard, the amount of change she receives from $25 is   17._____

    A. $2.12   B. $2.28   C. $2.59   D. $2.63

18. The water level of a swimming pool 75 feet by 42 feet is to be raised 4 inches. The number of gallons of water needed for this purpose is (1 cubic foot equals 7 1/2 gallons)   18._____

    A. 140   B. 7,875   C. 31,500   D. 94,500

19. The part of the total quantity represented by a 24 degree sector of a circle graph is   19.____

    A. 6 2/3%   B. 12%   C. 13 1/3%   D. 24%

20. If the shipping charges to a certain point are 62 cents for the first 5 oz. and 8 cents for   20.____
each additional ounce, the weight of a package for which the charges are $1.66 is

    A. 13 oz.   B. 1 1/8 lbs.   C. 14 lbs.   D. 1 1/2 lbs.

21. If 15 cans of food are needed for 7 men for 2 days, the number of cans needed for 4 men   21.____
for 7 days is

    A. 15   B. 20   C. 25   D. 30

22. The total saving in purchasing thirty 13¢ ice cream pops for a class party at a reduced   22.____
rate of $1.38 per dozen is

    A. 35¢   B. 40¢   C. 45¢   D. 50¢

23. The quotient for the division of 36 apples among 4 children may be CORRECTLY found   23.____
by thinking _____

    A. 36 ÷ 1/4

                B. $36\overline{)4.0}$

    C. 1/4 of 36   D. 4/36

24. The missing term in the equation 1/3 of ?= 1/2 of 90 is   24.____

    A. 45   B. 30   C. 15   D. 135

25. The fraction CLOSEST to 4/5 is   25.____

    A. 2/3   B. 7/9   C. 8/11   D. 5/8

26. Of the following, the one which may be used CORRECTLY to compute the value of 4 x   26.____
22 1/2 is

    A. (4 x 45) + (4 x 1/2)
    B. (4 x A) + (4 x 2) + (4 x 2)
    C. (1/2 of 4) + (2 x 4) + (2 x 4)
    D. (4 x 20) + (4 x 2) + (4 x 1/2)

27. 16 1/2 ÷ 1/4 may CORRECTLY be expressed as   27.____

    A. (1/4 x 16) + (1/4 x 1/2)   B. (4 x 16) + (4 x 1/2)
                            D. 1/4 times 33/2
    C. $4\overline{)16.5}$

28. In computation, 3/4 may be CORRECTLY transformed into 6/8 for the same reason that   28.____

    A. 7(3+4) = 21 +28   B. 3 apples+5 apples = 8
                             D. 3+4=4+3
    C. $.2\overline{)3.4} = 2\overline{)34}$

29. The mathematical law of distribution is illustrated by all of the following EXCEPT   29._____

A.
$$\begin{array}{r} 15 \\ \times 12 \\ \hline 150 \\ 30 \\ \hline 180 \end{array}$$
B.
$$\begin{array}{r} 15 \\ \times 12 \\ \hline 30 \\ 150 \\ \hline 180 \end{array}$$
C.
$$\begin{array}{r} 15 \\ \times 12 \\ \hline 180 \end{array}$$
D.
$$\begin{array}{r} 15 \\ \times 12 \\ \hline 30 \\ 15 \\ \hline 180 \end{array}$$

30. Of the following series of partial sums which might arise in the addition of 36 and 25, the   30._____
one that is INCORRECT is

A. 11, 31, 61   B. 11, 4, 6, 61
C. 11, 41, 61   D. 36, 56, 61

31. Of the following, the one which equals one million is   31._____

A. ten hundred thousand
B. 10^7
C. 10 x 10 x 10 x 10 x 10 x 10 x 10
D. 1 plus 6 zeroes

32. Of the following groups, the one containing four terms all associated with one algorismic   32._____
process is

A. addend, quotient, dividend, divisor
B. dividend, quotient, divisor, minuend
C. dividend, quotient, addend, minuend
D. multiplicand, product, minuend, addend

33. Depreciation of a certain machine is estimated, for any year, at 20% of its value at the   33._____
beginning of the year. If the machine is purchased for $600, its estimated net value at the
end of two years is CLOSEST to

A. $325   B. $350   C. $375   D. $400

34. Hats are purchased at the rate of $33 per dozen.   34._____
If they are sold at a close-out sale for $2.50 each, the percent loss on the cost price is

A. 3   B. 3 1/3   C. 9 1/11   D. 10

35. The time 3 hours, 58 minutes after 10:56 A.M. _____ P.M.   35._____

A. 4:54   B. 2:54   C. 4:14   D. 2:14

36. Mr. Brown had $20.00 when he took his three children on a bus trip. He spent $7.33 for   36._____
the four tickets and bought each of the children a magazine costing 15¢, a candy bar
costing 11¢, and a 5¢ package of chewing gum. His change from the $20.00 was

A. $12.74   B. $11.43   C. $11.74   D. $12.84

37. The loan value on a life insurance policy at the end of five years is $30.19/ $1000 of   37._____
insurance.
The LARGEST amount, to the nearest dollar, that can be borrowed on a $5500 policy
at the end of five years is

A. $17   B. $151   C. $166   D. $1660

38. Using cups that hold six ounces of milk, the number of cupfuls a person can obtain from 1 1/2 gallons of milk is   38.____

    A. 16   B. 24   C. 32   D. 64

39. A storekeeper purchased an article for $36.   39.____
    In order to include 10% of cost for overhead and to provide $9 of net profit, the markup should be

    A. 25%   B. 35%   C. 37 1/2%   D. 40%

40. A rectangular carton has twice the height, one-third the length, and four times the width   40.____
    of a second carton. The ratio of the volume of the first carton to that of the second carton is

    A. 16:3   B. 2:1   C. 8:3   D. 3:8

41. If $300 is invested at simple interest so as to yield interest income of $18 in 9 months, the   41.____
    amount of money that must be invested at the same rate of interest so as to yield a return of $120 in 6 months is

    A. $3000   B. $3300   C. $2800   D. $2400

42. If a boy has a number of dimes and quarters in his pocket adding up to $3.10, the LARG-   42.____
    EST possible number of dimes he can have is

    A. 16   B. 28   C. 26   D. 21

43. In a number system using the base 10, the value represented by the first digit 3 reading   43.____
    from the left, in the number 82,364,371 is _____ times the value represented by the second digit 3.

    A. 30   B. 100   C. 1,000   D. 10,000

44. The number of revolutions made by a bicycle wheel of 28 inch diameter in traveling 1/2   44.____
    mile is CLOSEST to

    A. 720   B. 180   C. 360   D. 120

45. Of the following, the property which is TRUE of all parallelograms is that the   45.____

    A. diagonals are equal
    B. diagonals meet at right angles
    C. sum of the interior angles is 180°
    D. diagonals bisect each other

46. Of the following explanations about steps in the computation at the right,   46.____
    the one which is LEAST meaningful or accurate is that the
    A. 64 represents 200 x 32
    B. 265 is the result of subtracting 320 from 585
    C. 9 is part of the quotient
    D. 256 symbolizes the subtraction of 32 eight times

$$
\begin{array}{r}
218 \\
32\overline{)6985} \\
64 \\
\overline{58} \\
32 \\
\overline{265} \\
256 \\
\overline{9}
\end{array}
$$

47. Assuming that a system of meridians and parallels of latitude like that used on maps of the earth's surface was designed for the moon's surface, the distance covered by a man traveling 1° on the moon as compared to that covered in traveling 1° on the earth would be

    A. equal
    B. less
    C. greater
    D. sometimes greater and sometimes less

47.____

48. 1958 may MOST correctly be expressed in Roman numerals as

    A. MDCDLVIII   B. CMMLVIII   C. MCMLVIII   D. MCMLIIX

48.____

49. If the same positive quantity is added to both the numerator and the denominator of a proper fraction, the value of the new fraction, as compared to that of the original fraction, will be

    A. greater   B. less
    C. equal   D. either greater or less

49.____

50. If the Fahrenheit temperature is 74°, the Centigrade equivalent would be [Use the formula $C = 5/9 (F-32)$]

    A. 9 1/9°   B. 23 1/3°   C. 42°   D. 56 2/9°

50.____

KEY (CORRECT ANSWERS)

1.	A	11.	C	21.	D	31.	A	41.	A
2.	D	12.	A	22.	C	32.	B	42.	C
3.	A	13.	A	23.	C	33.	C	43.	C
4.	B	14.	D	24.	D	34.	C	44.	C
5.	D	15.	A	25.	B	35.	B	45.	D
6.	D	16.	C	26.	D	36.	C	46.	C
7.	C	17.	C	27.	B	37.	C	47.	B
8.	A	18.	B	28.	C	38.	C	48.	C
9.	B	19.	A	29.	C	39.	B	49.	A
10.	C	20.	B	30.	B	40.	C	50.	B

SOLUTIONS TO PROBLEMS

1. CORRECT ANSWER: A

   12 (multiplicand)
   ×2 (multiplier)
   24 (product)

2. CORRECT ANSWER: D
   The most efficient way is to divide .32 by 8.
   .125 = .12 1/2 = 12 1/2% = 1/8

   $$1/8 \times .32 = .32/8 = 8\overline{)\begin{array}{c}.04 \\ .32 \\ \underline{.32}\end{array}}$$

3. CORRECT ANSWER: A

   365 (days in 1 year)   4 (leap-year days)

   x 3 (meals)   x 3 (meals)

   1095 (meals in 1 year)   12 (leap-year meals)

   x 19 (number of years)

   20,805 (number of meals eaten in 19 years)

   + 12 (number of meals eaten in leap years)

   20,817 (total)

4. CORRECT ANSWER: B

   875 watts
   1100
   300
   2275 ÷ 1000 = 2 11/40 kw. hours
   2 11/40 x 7.5 = .17 (approximately)

5. CORRECT ANSWER: D

   A. .021% = .00021

   B. 1/4% = 1/400 = $400\overline{)\begin{array}{c}.0025 \\ 1.0000\end{array}}$

   C. 1.5% = .015 = 15/1000 = 3/200
   D. 225% = 2.25, NOT .225

6. CORRECT ANSWER: D
   Suggestions for Series Problems
   1. Find the difference between the numbers (or squares of differences).
   2. In this series, each difference is multiplied by 3 and added to the succeeding number.

   3,5 The difference is 2
       3x2 = 6
       5 + 6 = 11
   5, 11 The difference is 6
       3 x 6 = 18
       11 + 18 = 29
   11, 29 The difference is 18
       3 x 18 = 54
       29 + 54 = 83

7. CORRECT ANSWER: C
   Total area = 224 square inches

     16"
   ×14"
     64
   16
   224 square inches

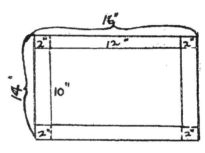

8. CORRECT ANSWER: A
   Solution

   Successive discounts
     20%, 30%
   1. Convert to decimals .2, .3
   2. Subtract from 1.0   .8, .7
   3. Multiply .8 x .7 = .56
   4. 1.00 - .56 = .44

     25.00
   × .44
      100
     100
   $11.00
   ∴ $25 - $11 = $14

   Alternate Solution
       $25
   × .20
    $5.00

   $25 - 5 = $20.00

      $20
   × .20
    $6.00

   $20 - $6 = $14 ANSWER

9. CORRECT ANSWER: B
   63" = 63/36 yards

   Alternate Solution
   12¢ per yard
   12/36=1/3¢ per inch

     21   .01
   $$\frac{\cancel{63}}{\cancel{36}} \times \frac{\cancel{12}}{} = 21¢$$
      3

   63"/1 x 1/3¢ = 63/3 = 21¢

10. CORRECT ANSWER: C
    Proportion
    1st mixture
    2nd mixture
    3/4 is half of 1 1/2
    Therefore, half of 4 1/2 is 2 1/4

Cereal	Water
$1\frac{1}{2}$ cups	$4\frac{1}{2}$ cups
$3/4$ cups	x cups

11. CORRECT ANSWER: C
    The speed of sound is 1100 ft. per second. 88 ft. per second = 60 miles an hour
    1100/88 = indicates the number of times greater than 60 miles an hour is the speed of sound

    $$12\frac{1}{2} \text{ times}$$
    $$88\overline{)1100}$$

    $$60$$
    $$\times 12\frac{1}{2}$$
    $$\overline{750} \text{ miles per hour}$$

12. CORRECT ANSWER: A
    Conversion
    A meter = 39 inches (39.37 inches)
          = 3 1/4 ft. (39/12 = 3 1/4)
    A centimeter = .39 inches
    1 rod = 5 1/2 yards (5.5 yards x 3 = 16.5 feet)
          = 16 1/2 feet
    A rod is approximately 5 meters (See choice (C) which is, therefore, wrong)
    A meter is 100 centimeters (one cm. = .01) 3 1/4 feet = 1 meter or 100 centimeters

    $$1 \text{ ft} = \frac{100}{3\frac{1}{4}} = \frac{100}{1} + \frac{13}{4} = \frac{100}{1} \times \frac{4}{13} = \frac{400}{13}$$

    $$13\overline{)400.00} \quad 30.76$$

13. CORRECT ANSWER: A
    Let x = 2nd angle
    Let 3x = 1st angle
    Let x + 20° = 3rd angle
    3x + x + x + 20 = 180
          5x + 20 = 180
              5x = 160
              x = 32°

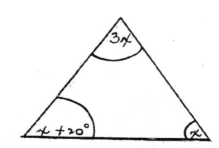

14. CORRECT ANSWER: D

$$\frac{\frac{1}{4}"}{12} = \frac{3\,3/8"}{x}$$

1/4 ÷ 12/1 = 27/8 ÷ x/1
1/4 x 1/12 = 27/8 x 1/x
1/4 = 27/8x
8x = 48 x 27 = 1296
x = 162 inches
= 13 1/2 ft.

15. CORRECT ANSWER: A

Time Belts

PACIFIC	MOUNTAIN	CENTRAL	EASTERN

4 A.M.　　　5 A.M.　　　6 A.M.　　　7 A.M. E.S.T.
　　　　　　　　　　　　　　　　　　8 A.M. D.S.T.

In traveling eastward, we set our clocks forward for each time zone.
Plane left at 1 P.M.
Traveled around clock 12 hours or 13 hours at 2 A.M. Subtract 2 hours difference
between Mountain Time and Eastern Standard Time. Subtract another hour for Daylight
Savings Time. That is, 13 - 3 = 10 hours.

16. CORRECT ANSWER: C

$$\frac{42.10 \times .0003}{.002} = \frac{42 \times .0003}{.002} \text{ (approximating)}$$

Work

$$\begin{array}{c} 42 \\ \times .0003 \\ \hline .0126 \end{array} = \frac{.0126}{.002} = \frac{12.6}{2} = 6.3$$

17. CORRECT ANSWER: C

$1.16	$3.87	$18.06	$25.00
× 3 3/4	× 4 2/3	+4.35	-22.41
$4.35	$18.06	$22.41	$ 2.59

18. CORRECT ANSWER: B

42 x 75 x 1/3 ft (4") = 1050 cu. ft.

$$\times 7\frac{1}{2}$$
7875 gallons

19. CORRECT ANSWER: A

$$\frac{24}{360}=\frac{2}{30}=\frac{1}{15}=.06\ 2/3=6\ 2/3\%$$

20. CORRECT ANSWER: B

$1.66 total charge
- .62 1st 5 oz
$1.04 charge at 8 cents an oz.

13 oz
+5 oz
18 oz.

$$\frac{18}{16}=1\frac{2}{16}=\frac{1}{8}\text{lb}$$

21. CORRECT ANSWER: D

Cans	Men	Days	Number of days one man would need to consume the cans
15	7	2	14 days
x	4	7	28 days

x = 2(15) = 30 cans

22. CORRECT ANSWER: C

$.13
× 30
$3.90
-3.45
$ .45

$$\frac{30}{12}=2\frac{1}{2}\text{ dozens}$$

$1.38
× 2½
$3.45

23. CORRECT ANSWER: C
36/4=9

24. CORRECT ANSWER: D   1/3 of ? = 1/2 of 90
1/3x = 45
x = 3 x 45
= 135

25. CORRECT ANSWER: B
4/5 = .80
2/3 = .66
7/9 = .78
8/11 = .73
5/8 = .63

21.____

22.____

23.____

24.____

25.____

26. CORRECT ANSWER: D   26.____

$$22\frac{1}{2}$$
$$\underline{\times 4}$$
$$80$$
$$8$$
$$\underline{2}$$
$$90$$

Choice (D) (4 x 20) + (4 x 2) + (4 x 1/2) = 80 + 8 + 2 = 90 (This is an example of the Distributive Law, which links the operations of addition and multiplication.)

27. CORRECT ANSWER: B   27.____

$$16\frac{1}{2} \div 4 = \frac{16\frac{1}{2}}{4} = 16\frac{1}{2} \times 4/1 = (4 \times 16) + (4 \times \frac{1}{2})$$

28. CORRECT ANSWER: C   28.____

$$\frac{3}{4} = \frac{6}{8}; \frac{3.4}{.2} = \frac{34}{2} = 17$$

29. CORRECT ANSWER: C   29.____

A.	$10 \times 15 = 150$	B.	$2 \times 15 = 30$	C.	$2 \times 15 = 30$
	$2 \times 15 = \dfrac{30}{180}$		$10 \times 15 = \dfrac{150}{180}$		$10 \times 15 = \dfrac{150}{180}$

The Distributive Law links the operations of addition and arithmetic.

30. CORRECT ANSWER: B   30.____
Partial Sums

	36	(A) 11	(C) 11	(D) 36
	$\underline{+25}$	$\underline{+20}$	$\underline{+30}$	$\underline{+20}$
	61	31	41	56
		$\underline{+30}$	$\underline{+20}$	$\underline{+5}$
		61	61	61

31. CORRECT ANSWER: A   31.____
100,000 x 10 = 1,000,000

32. CORRECT ANSWER: B

$$\begin{array}{r} 21 \\ 12\overline{)256} \end{array}$$ quotient
dividend

$$\begin{array}{r} 24 \\ \overline{16} \end{array}$$ minuend - partial dividend

$$\begin{array}{r} 12 \\ \overline{4} \end{array}$$ partial dividend

36	multiplicand	5	addend
x 45	multiplier	+6	addend
180	partial product	11	sum
144	partial product		
1620	product		

7,485 minuend
-2,648 subtrahend
4,837 remainder (difference)

33. CORRECT ANSWER: C

$600	$480	$600	$480
x .20	x .20	- 120	- 96
120.00	96.00	$480	$384 approximately

34. CORRECT ANSWER: C

Cost of one dozen	$33.00	$2.50
Selling price of one		x 1 2
dozen	30.00	$30.00 (sold at close-out sale)
Loss	$ 3.00	

$$\frac{L}{C} = \frac{\$3}{\$33} = \frac{1}{11} = 9 \, 1/11\%$$

35. CORRECT ANSWER: B <u>SOLUTION</u>

10:56 A.M.   Add 3 hours, 58 minutes
11:00 A.M.   54 minutes
+3:00 hours   (see 10:56 A.M.)
2:00 P.M
+ :54 minutes
2:54 P.M.

36. CORRECT ANSWER: C

15¢	31¢	$7.33	$20.00
11¢	x3	+ .93	- 8.26
5¢	93¢	$8.26	$11.74
31¢			

32._____

33._____

34._____

35._____

36._____

37. CORRECT ANSWER: C

$30.19 $150.95 (amount on $5000)
x   5   + 15.10 (amount on $500)
$150.95 $166.05 (approximately)

38. CORRECT ANSWER: C

1 cup = 8 oz.
1 quart = 4 cups (4 x 8 oz. = 32 oz.)
1 gallon = 32 oz. x 4 = 128 oz.
(1 gallon = 4 qts. or 128 oz.)
1/2 gallon = 64 oz.

```
   128 oz.
 + 64 oz.
6 | 192
   ‾‾‾‾
    32 cups
```

39. CORRECT ANSWER: B

Cost   = $36.00   Selling price = $48.60
10% of cost   =   3.60   Cost   =   36.00
Profit   =   9.00   Markup   = $12.60
Selling Price = $48.60

$$\frac{\text{Markup}}{\text{Cost}} = \frac{\$12.60}{\$36.00} = 35\%$$

40. CORRECT ANSWER: C

1st carton   2nd carton

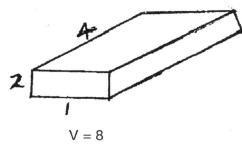   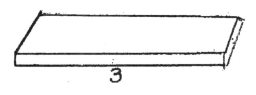

V = 8   V = 3

$$\frac{V1}{V2} = \frac{8}{3}$$

41.　CORRECT ANSWER: A　　　　　　　　　　　　　　　　　　　　　41.____

　　Step (1) Principal = $300
　　　　　　Interest = $18 in 9 months (9 months = 3/4 year)

　　　　　　To find annual interest:
　　　　　　　Let x = annual interest
　　　　　　　3/4x = 18
　　　　　　　　x = 18 x 4/3
　　　　　　　　x = $24

　　　　　　To find rate:
　　　　　　　Let R = rate

$$R=\frac{I}{P}=\frac{24\,\text{interest}}{300\,\text{principal}}\times 1(\text{year})$$

$$\begin{array}{r}.80\\300\overline{)24.00}\\24\ 00\\\hline 00\end{array}$$

　　　　　　Interest rate = 8%

　　Step (2) Principal (?) to be invested at 8% to yield $120
　　　　　　interest in 6 months:
　　　　　　6 months = 1/2 year
　　　　　　Yearly interest = $240 ($120 x 2)

$$P=\frac{I}{R}$$

$$P=\frac{\$240\ (\text{interest})}{.08\ \ \ (\text{rate})}$$

$$.08\overline{)240}=8\overline{)24000}\ \ \ \ \ \overset{3000}{}$$

　　　　　　P = $3000 (the amount of money that would have to be invested)

42.　CORRECT ANSWER: C　　　　　　　　　　　　　　　　　　　　　42.____

　　26 x 10 = $2.60 + .50 = $3.10

43.　CORRECT ANSWER: C　　　　　　　　　　　　　　　　　　　　　43.____

　　(approximately) 300 x 1,000 = 300,000

44. CORRECT ANSWER: C

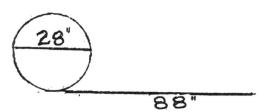

$C = \pi D$
$C = 22/7 \times 28 = 88''$

1 revolution of wheel covers 88"
1/12 x 5280 x 12/1 = traveling distance in inches
6 x 5280 = 31680 inches

```
       360
  88)31680
     264
     ‾528
      528
```

44._____

45. CORRECT ANSWER: D

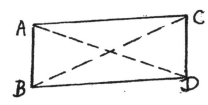
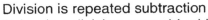

triangle = 180°
parallelogram = 360°

45._____

46. CORRECT ANSWER: C
Division is repeated subtraction
Below is a division *pyramid,* which shows what actually happens when we divide.

```
        8
       10
      200
  32)6945  dividend
     6400
     ‾585  partial dividend
      320
      ‾265  partial dividend
      256
      ‾‾9  partial dividend
```

32 x100 = 3200
32 x 200= 6400
32 x 10 = 320

46._____

47. CORRECT ANSWER: B
Diameter of moon = 2000 miles
Diameter of earth = 8000 miles

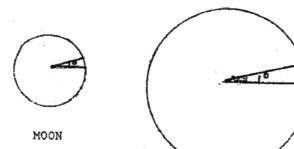

MOON

EARTH

The larger the circle, the larger the arc.

$$1° \text{ of arc} = \frac{1}{360} \text{ of circle.}$$

Circumference of earth = 25,000 miles Circumference of moon = 6,200 miles (1/4 of earth)

$$\begin{array}{r} 69+ \\ 360)\overline{25,000} \\ \underline{21\ 6} \\ 3\ 40 \\ \underline{3\ 24} \\ \overline{16} \end{array}$$

1° = 69+ miles on the equator (Earth)
1° = 17+ miles (Moon)

47._____

48. CORRECT ANSWER: C
M = 1000
CM = 900
L = 50

$$VIII = \frac{8}{1958}$$

48._____

49. CORRECT ANSWER: A

$$\frac{2+2}{3+2} = \frac{4}{5} = \frac{12}{15}$$

$$\frac{2}{3} = \frac{10}{15}$$

49._____

50. CORRECT ANSWER: B

$$C = \frac{5}{9}(74-32)$$
$$= \frac{5}{9}(42)$$

$$C = \frac{5}{9} \times \frac{42}{1} = \frac{70}{3}$$
$$= 23\ 1/3°$$

50._____

INTERPRETING STATISTICAL DATA
GRAPHS, CHARTS AND TABLES

Graphs, charts, and tables help us to visualize and to understand more readily ideas that might otherwise be more difficult to grasp.

The language of pictures is one of the oldest and easiest to understand.

There are several types of graphs.

The _pictograph_ is used to compare numerical quantities. Symbols or pictures are used to represent numbers. Each symbol or picture represents a certain number of the quantities being compared.

The _bar graph_ is employed to emphasize comparisons between numbers. If the graph is constructed of vertical bars, it is called a _vertical bar graph_. A fundamental part of this graph is the scale, which must begin with zero (0). In addition, a title heads this type of graph.

A _horizontal bar graph_ employs horizontal bars. Here, too, the scale begins with zero (0), and there is a title

The _line graph_ shows how a quantity, such as prices, sales, temperature, rises or falls or changes. This type of graph is particularly good for delineating when the quantity is increasing and when it is decreasing. It also strikingly reveals trends or situations.

The _circle graph_ is also used to show comparisons, particularly the relationship between a whole thing and a part of the thing. The whole thing is represented by the circle, which is divided into pieces, called sectors, by the drawing of radii which form central angles. In order to find the number of degrees in the central angle of each sector, the method is to ascertain the fraction of the whole which the sector represents and to multiply by 360°.

Charts and tables also are used to visualize and to concretize facts and figures, to lead to comparisons, and to draw conclusions. Careful reading of the directions given with the charts or tables and of the questions employed in connection therewith, make these visual devices clear and meaningful as the student or candidate learns to be precise and resourceful in his reading and interpretation.

The tests with questions that follow are intended to guide the candidate into the amazing world of graphs, charts, and tables and to point up the importance of the quantitative ability to interpret statistical data.

TEST 1

DIRECTIONS: The following graph represents the national debt of the United States from the year 1991 through the year 2000. From this graph, determine the answers to Questions 1 through 8.

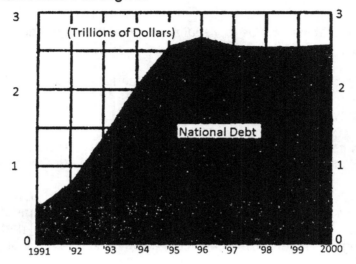

1. How many years are represented by the graph?   1.____

2. In what year was our national debt the smallest?   2.____

3. What was the national debt in 1994?   3.____

4. What was the approximate increase in the national debt from 1993 to 1994?   4.____

5. In what year was our national debt the largest?   5.____

6. In what year did the national debt begin to decrease?   6.____

7. How much greater was the national debt in 2000 than it was in 1991?   7.____

8. In what two consecutive years was the national debt the same?   8i.____

KEY (CORRECT ANSWERS)

1.   10 (1991 through 2000)

2.   1991 (slightly below .50 trillions of dollars as indicated on the graph)

3.   2 trillion dollars (the line graph for the year 1994 touches exactly on the 2 trillion dollar mark)

4.   Approximately .60-.65 trillion dollars (2 trillion dollars in 1994 minus approximately .13 to .14 trillions in 1993)

5.   1996 (approximately .26 trillion dollars)

6.   1996 (the line graph begins to decline starting in this year)

7.   Approximately 5 times greater (national debt in 2000, approximately .25 trillion dollars; national debt in 1991, approximately .50 trillion dollars)

8.   1998, 1999 (the line graph does not change for these years)

TEST 2

DIRECTIONS: The following pictogram represents the number of telephones in use in a certain city. Each complete symbol represents 20,000 telephones.

1970 ☎ ☎ ☎ ☎ ☎ ☎ ☎ ☎ ☎ ☎

1975 ☎ ☎ ☎ ☎ ☎ ☎ ☎ ☎ ♪

1980 ☎ ☎ ☎ ☎ ☎ ☎ ☎ ☎ ☎ ♪

1985 ☎ ☎ ☎ ☎ ☎ ☎ ☎ ☎ ☎ ☎

1990 ☎ ☎ ☎ ☎ ☎ ☎ ☎ ☎ ☎ ☎ ☎ ♪

1. How many telephones were in use in this city in 1985? 1._____

2. How many more telephones were in use in this city in 1985 than in 1975? 2._____

3. Find the percent of increase in the number of telephones in use in 1990 over the number in use in 1970. 3._____

4. If it is estimated that 280,000 telephones will be in use in 1995, how many symbols should be used to picture this on the graph? 4._____

_____

KEY (CORRECT ANSWERS)

1. 220,000 (20,000 × 11 = 220,000)

2. 50,000 (20,000 × 2½)

3. 25% or 25
   (Each symbol = 20,000
   2½ symbols = 50,000
   $\dfrac{50,000}{200,000}$ (1970 has 10 symbols = ¼ or 25%)

4. 14 (280,000 ÷ 20,000)

———

TEST 3

DIRECTIONS: The following graph shows the noon temperature at a certain weather station on seven consecutive days in June.

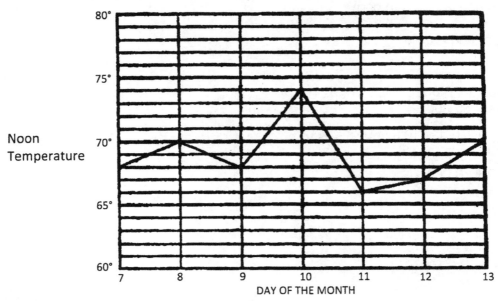

1. On what day was the noon temperature the highest?   1.____

2. For what two consecutive days was the change in noon temperature the least?   2.____

3. For what two consecutive days was the change in noon temperature the greatest?   3.____

4. What was the average noon temperature for the week?   4.____

5. How many degrees warmer was it at noon on June 9 than at noon on June 12?   5.____

KEY (CORRECT ANSWERS)

1. 10th (74°)

2. 11th and the 12th (on these days the temperature rose from 66° to 67°, a change of 1°)

3. The 10th and the 11th (as shown by the steepest line, when the temperature fell from 74° to 66°, a change of 8°)

4. 69° (adding the temperatures from June 7th to June 13th, we get 483; dividing by 7, we find the average to be 69°)

5. 1° (noon temperature, June 9th: 69°; noon temperature, June 12th: 67°)

———————

TEST 4

DIRECTIONS: The following graph shows food expenditures in the United States for each of the years 1970 to 1990, inclusive.

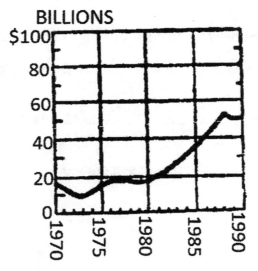

1.   During what year were expenditures for food the lowest?   1._____

2.   During what year were expenditures for food the highest?   2._____

3.   Approximately how many billions of dollars were spent for food in 1990?   3._____

4.   In what year did expenditures for food first reach 40 billion?   4._____

5.   During which one of these five-year periods (1970-75, 1975-80, 1980-85,   5._____
     1985-1990) did expenditures for food remain about the same?

KEY (CORRECT ANSWERS)

1. 1973 (low point of about 8 billion dollars in this year)

2. 1988 (high point of about 52 billion dollars in this year

3. 50 (approximately 50 billion dollars)

4. 1986 (graph crosses the 40 billion dollar line in this year)

5. 1975-80 (graph line relatively stable for this period)

———————

TEST 5

DIRECTIONS: In a recent year, a large industrial concern used each dollar of its sales income as shown in the following graph.

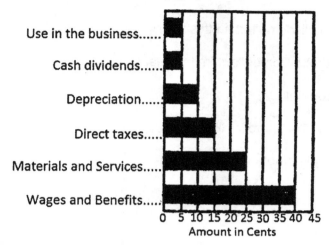

Use in the business......
Cash dividends......
Depreciation......
Direct taxes.....
Materials and Services.....
Wages and Benefits.....

0   5 10 15 20 25 30 35 40 45
Amount in Cents

1. How many cents of each dollar of sales income did the company use to pay wages and benefits?   1.____

2. How many more cents out of each sales dollar was spent on wages and benefits than on materials and services?   2.____

3. What was the total number of cents out of each sales dollar that the company set aside for depreciation and for use in the business?   3.____

4. The amount the company paid in direct taxes was how many times the amount it paid in cash dividends?   4.____

5. What percent of each sales dollar was paid in cash dividends?   5.____

KEY (CORRECT ANSWERS)

1. 40 (the bottom bar which represents wages and benefits, reaches the 40-cent line.

2. 15 (40, representing wages and benefits, minus 25, representing materials and services)

3. 15 (0, representing depreciation, plus 5, representing use in the business)

4. 3 (15 represents direct taxes and 5 represents cash dividends, a ratio of 3 to 1

5. $5 \left(\frac{5}{100}\right) = 5\%$

TEST 6

DIRECTIONS: The following circle graph shows how the wage earners in a certain city earned their living in a recent year. The number of degrees required for each angle is given on the graph.

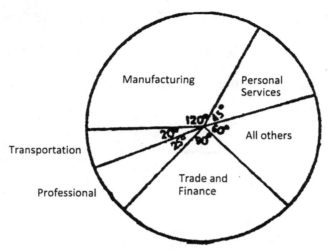

1. Using the number of degrees shown on this graph, find the fractional part of the graph that represents the number of wage earners earning their living in each of the following:

    a. Trade and finance
    b. Personal services
    c. Manufacturing

1.____

2. How many times as many persons worked in the area of trade and finance as in the area of personal services?

2.____

3. If there were 180,000 wage earners in the city that year, how many persons were engaged in transportation?

3.____

KEY (CORRECT ANSWERS)

1. ¼ ($\frac{90°}{360°}$ = ¼)

2. ⅛ ($\frac{80°}{360°}$ = ⅛)

3. ⅓ ($\frac{120°}{360°}$ = ⅓)

4. 2 ($\frac{90°}{45°}$ = 2)

5. 10,000 ($\frac{20°}{360°}$ × 180,000)

———————

TEST 7

DIRECTIONS: The following graph shows the relation between car speed and tire wear. The graph appeared in a magazine advertisement.

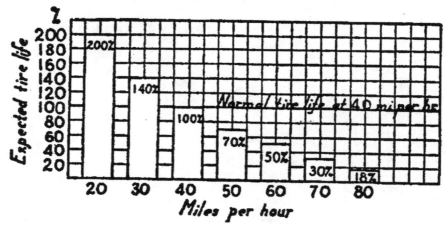

1. At what speed is the normal life of a tire determined?   1._____

2. The life of a tire on a car driven at 20 miles per hour is how many times greater than the life of a tire on a car driven at 40 miles per hour?   2._____

3. What car speed will result in tires lasting only half of their normal tire life?   3._____

4. If a car is driven at 30 miles per hour, what percent more than normal tire life may be expected?   4._____

5. If a car is driven at 70 miles per hour, what percent less than normal tire life may be expected?   5._____

KEY (CORRECT ANSWERS)

1. 40 miles per hour (as stated in the graph proper)

2. 2 (at 20 miles per hour: expected tire life, 200%; at 40 miles per hour: expected tire life, 100%)

3. 60 miles per hour (as indicated on the graph)

4. 40% (as stated in the graph. 140% or 40% more than normal tire life (100%)

5. 70% (at 70 miles per hour: expected tire life, 30%; this is 70% less than normal tire life (100%)

TEST 8

DIRECTIONS: The following graphs were published by the federal government to show where the tax dollar comes from and where it goes.

WHERE THE TAX DOLLAR
COMES FROM

Corporation income taxes
Borrowing
Excise taxes
Customs & other taxes
Individual income taxes

WHERE THE TAX DOLLAR
GOES

Cost of national security
Costs fixed by law
Cost of other government operations

1. What percent of the federal tax dollar was spent on national security?

1.____

2. What percent more money was obtained from individual income taxes than from corporation income taxes?

2.____

3. How many dollars, of every million dollars collected in taxes, were obtained from excise taxes?

3.____

4. List the four sources of income whose total approximately equals the amount spent for national security?

4.____

KEY (CORRECT ANSWERS)

1. 68% ($\frac{68}{100}$ = 68%)

2. 12% (43 − 31 = 12d on each dollar or 12%)

3. 160,000 (1,000,000 × .16 = 180,000)

4. Borrowing, excise taxes, customs, and other taxes, individual income taxes
    (.04 + .16 + .06 + .43 = .69 (cost of national security, .68))

———————

TEST 9

DIRECTIONS: A savings bank in a large city published the following graph for its depositors. use the graph to answer Questions 1 through 4.

HOW YOUR SAVINGS WORK FOR YOU

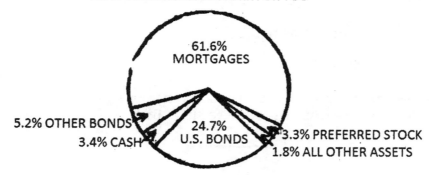

1.   In what way is approximately one-fourth of the bank's assets invested?   1.____

2.   Which fraction is nearest to the bank's total investment in mortgages: ½, ¾, ⁵/₈?   2.____

3.   The bank's total assets are $162,575,800. Of this total, what amount is kept in cash?   3.____

4.   Approximately how many times as much money is invested in United States Bonds as in other bonds?   4.____

KEY (CORRECT ANSWERS)

1. U.S Bonds (24.7%)

2. $^5/_8$ (61.6% is close to 62.5% or $^5/_8$)

3. $5,527,577.20 (162,575,800 × 3.4% or .034)

4. 5 (approximately 25% - 5 ÷ approximately 5%)

———————

TEST 10

DIRECTIONS: The following graph appeared in a publication.

GROWTH IN MOTOR VEHICLE REGISTRATION
FROM 1950—1995

MOTOR VEHICLES
REGISTERED IN
MILLIONS

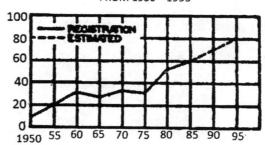

1. Approximately how many motor vehicles were registered in 1985?

1.____

2. Approximately how many times as many motor vehicles were registered in 1985 as in 1955?

2.____

3. According to the estimate made on this graph, how many more motor vehicles will be registered in 1995 than in 1985?

3.____

4. What percent of increase in registration is expected between 1985 and 1995?

4.____

KEY (CORRECT ANSWERS)

1. 60 million (as indicated on the graph as registered)

2. 3 (60 ÷ 20)

3. 20 million (80 million – 60 million)

4. $33\frac{1}{3}$ ($\frac{29\text{ million}}{60\text{ million}} = \frac{1}{3} = 33\frac{1}{3}\%$)

———

TEST 11

DIRECTIONS: Questions 1 through 5 are based on the following graphs. On the line at the right of each of these statements or questions, write the letter preceding the word or expression that BEST completes the statement or answers the question.

WHAT WE SEND LATIN AMERICA AS A PERCENT OF OUR TOTAL EXPORTS

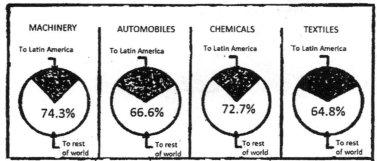

WHAT LATIN AMERICA SENDS US AS A PERCENT OF OUR TOTAL IMPORTS

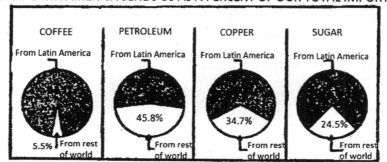

1. The GREATEST export of the United States to Latin America is   1.____
   A. automobiles   B. chemicals   C. machinery   D. textiles

2. Latin America's GREATEST export to the United States is   2.____
   A. coffee   B. sugar   C. copper   D. petroleum

3. Products exported by the United States to Latin America are CHIEFLY   3.____
   A. agricultural   B. manufactured
   C. mineral   D. forest

4. As compared with Latin America's export trade to the United States, the export   4.____
   trade of the United States to Latin America is
   A. greater   B. a little less
   C. about the same   D. much less

5. Which statement concerning the foreign trade of the United States is TRUE?   5.____
   A. Most of our chemical exports go to areas other than Latin America.
   B. Most of our automobile exports go to Latin America.
   C. Most of our petroleum imports come from areas other than Latin America.
   D. All of our coffee imports come from Latin America.

KEY (CORRECT ANSWERS)

1. D
2. A
3. B
4. D
5. A

TEST 12

DIRECTIONS: Last winter in a certain school, Grades 2, 3, 4, 5, and 6 decided to get together supplies to send to needy children in other parts of the world. The total amount collected was 720 pounds.

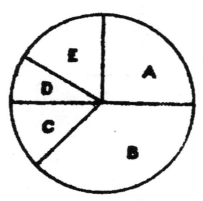

1. The above table shows the number of pounds collected by each grade.
    Complete the table by writing for each grade the letter that indicates on the
    graph the fractional part of the total that was collected by that grade.
    a. Grade 2: 180 pounds =
    b. Grade 3: 90 pounds =
    c. Grade 4: 120 pounds =
    d. Grade 5: 60 pounds =
    e. Grade 6: 270 pounds =

    1a.____
    1b.____
    1c.____
    1d.____
    1e.____

2. How many degrees are there in each section of the circle, A, B, C, D, and E?

    2A.____
    2B.____
    2C.____
    2D.____
    2E.____

KEY (CORRECT ANSWERS)

1.   a.   180 pounds – A (second largest angle in the circle)
     b.   90 pounds – C (fourth largest angle in the circle)
     c.   120 pounds – E (third largest angle in the circle)
     d.   60 pounds – D (smallest angle in the circle
     e.   270 pounds – B (the largest angle in the circle)

2. $A = 90° \left(\frac{180}{720} \approx \frac{1}{4}\right)$

   $B = 135° \left(\frac{270}{720} \approx \frac{3}{8}\right)$

   $C = 45° \left(\frac{90}{720} \approx \frac{1}{8}\right)$

   $D = 30° \left(\frac{60}{720} \approx \frac{1}{12}\right)$

   $E = 60° \left(\frac{120}{720} \approx \frac{1}{6}\right)$

————

TEST 13

DIRECTIONS: The following pictograph shows the growth in production of a shoe company for the period 2008-2014. (Each symbol represents 20,000 pairs of shoes.)

1. How many times as many shoes were produced in 2013 as in 2008?   1._____

2. How many pairs of shoes were produced in 2012?   2._____

3. How many more shoes were produced in 2014 than in 2013?   3._____

KEY (CORRECT ANSWERS)

1.   10 (10 to 1)

2.   120,000 (6 × 20,000)

3.   50,000 (2½ × 20,000)

———

———

EXAMINATION SECTION
TEST 1

DIRECTIONS: Each question or incomplete statement is followed by two suggested answers or completions. Select A or B, or C if the two figures have the same value, as the BEST answer that completes the statement or completes the statement. *PRINT THE LETTER OF THE CORRECT ANSWER IN THE SPACE AT THE RIGHT.*

1.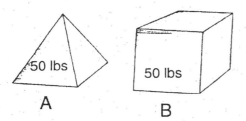

With which windlass can a man raise the heavier weight?

1.____

2.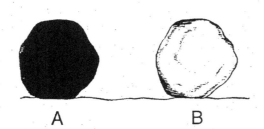

Which of these solid blocks will be the harder to tip over?

2.____

3.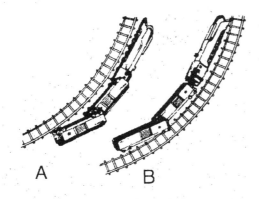

Which rock will get hotter in the sun?

3.____

4.

Which of these is the more likely picture of a train wreck?

4.____

211

5.

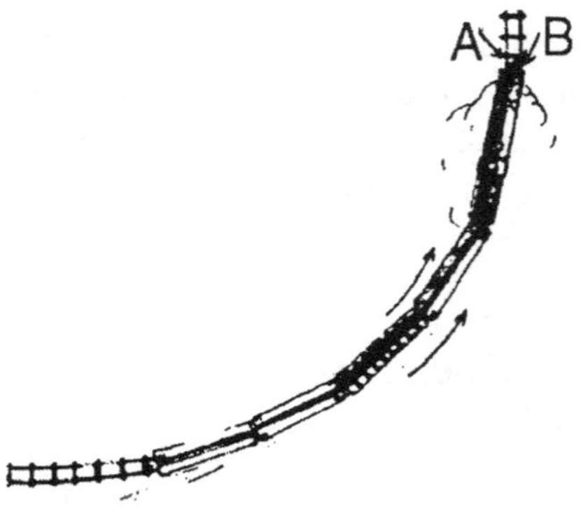

If the track is exactly level, on which rail does more pressure come?

5.____

6.

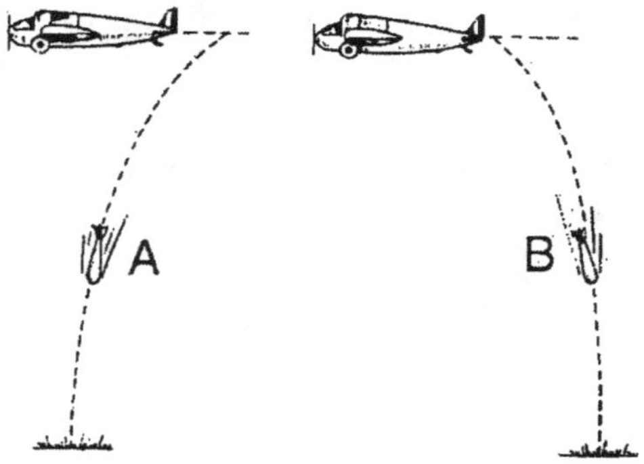

Which picture shows the way a bomb falls from a moving airplane if there is no wind?

6.____

7.

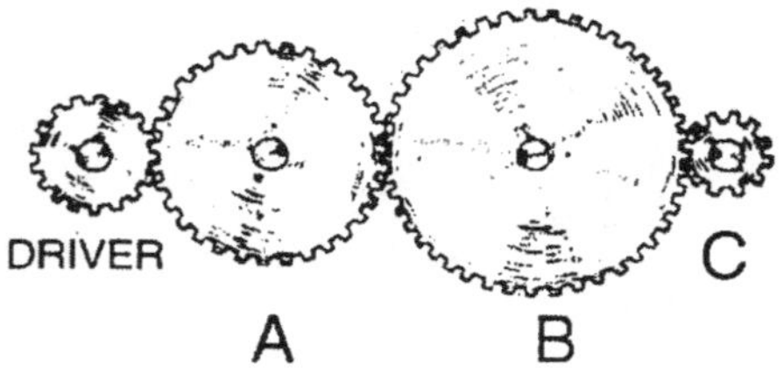

Indicate a gear which turn the same direction as the driver.

7.____

8.

If there are no clouds, on which night will you be able to see more stars?

8.____

9.

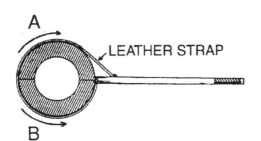

This wrench can be used to turn the pipe in direction:

9.____

10.

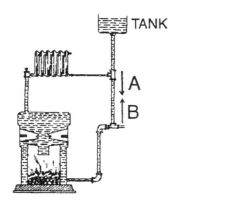

In which direction does the water in the right-hand pipe go?

10.____

11.

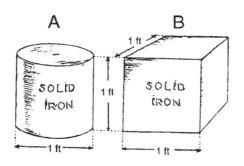

Which weighs more?

11.____

12.

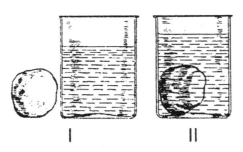

If the rock and tank of water together in picture I weigh 100 pounds, what will they weigh in picture II?

12.____

13.

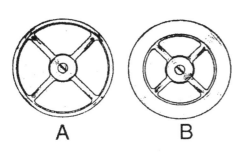

Which steel wheel will keep going longer after the power has been shut off?

13.____

14.

The top of the wheel *X* will go

    A.   steadily to the right

    B.   steadily to the left

    C.   by jerks to the left

14.____

15.

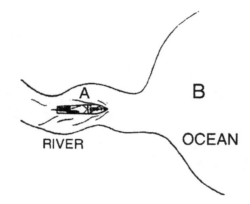

At which point will the boat be lower in the water?

15.____

16.

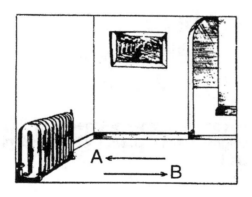

Which arrow shows the way the air will move along the floor when the radiator is turned on?

16.____

17.

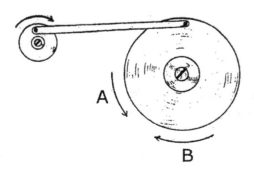

When the little wheel turns around, the big wheel will

    A.   turn in direction A

    B.   turn in direction B

    C.   move back and forth

17.____

18.

50 WATT BULB   100 WATT BULB

A   B

Which boy gets more light on the pages of his book?

18.____

19.

A   B

Milk   Cream

1 QUART   1 QUART

Which weighs more?

19.____

20.

A   B

Which of these wires offers more resistance to the passage of an electric current?

20.____

21.

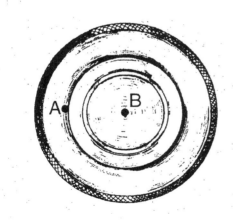

Which spot on the wheel travels faster?

21.____

22.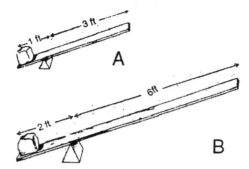

With which arrangement can a man lift the heavier weight?

22.____

23.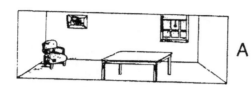

Which room has more of an echo?

23.____

24.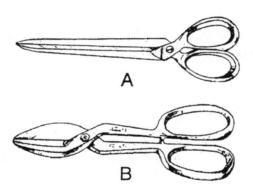

Which would be the BETTER shears for cutting metal?

24.____

KEY (CORRECT ANSWERS)

1.	A		11.	B
2.	A		12.	C
3.	A		13.	B
4.	A		14.	C
5.	B		15.	A
6.	A		16.	A
7.	B		17.	C
8.	B		18.	A
9.	A		19.	A
10.	A		20.	A

21.	B
22.	B
23.	A
24.	B

———

NONVERBAL REASONING

DIRECTIONS: In each question, there are five drawings (A-E presented from left to right). One drawing does NOT belong with the other four. You are to decide which drawing does NOT belong and PRINT THE LETTER of that drawing on your answer sheet.

EXAMPLES

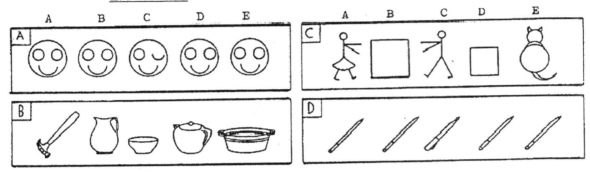

EXAMPLE A:
    C does NOT belong because the eye is incomplete.

EXAMPLE B:
    A does not belong because it is a hammer and the rest are objects relating to food.

EXAMPLE C:
    E does not belong because while there are 2 each of the straight stick figures and squares, there is only one cat made of circular strokes.

EXAMPLE D:
    C does not belong because it is thicker than the other pens, has a clip on its cap and it is a fountain pen while the rest are ballpoint pens.

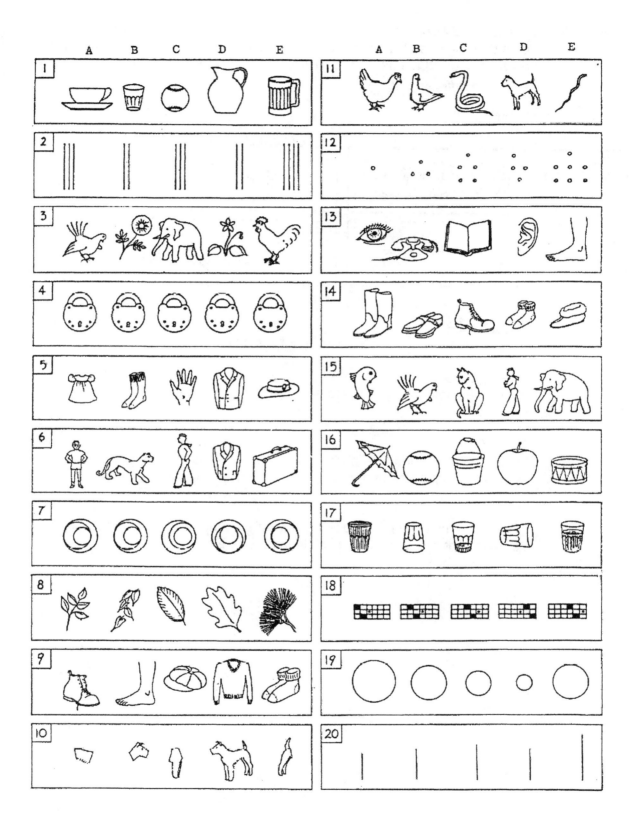

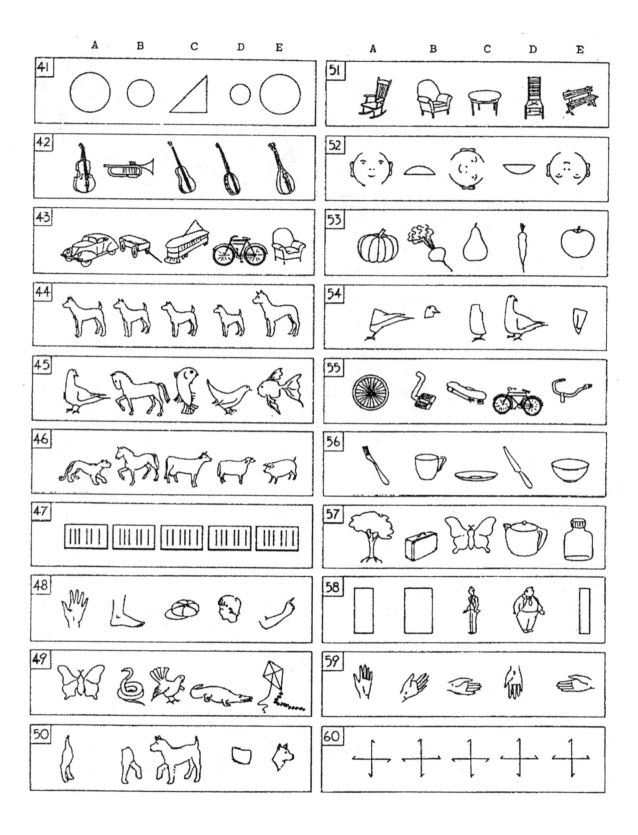

KEY (CORRECT ANSWERS)

1.	C	16.	D	31.	E	46.	A
2.	E	17.	D	32.	B	47.	C
3.	C	18.	D	33.	A	48.	C
4.	C	19.	E	34.	D	49.	E
5.	C	20.	D	35.	C	50.	C
6.	B	21.	C	36.	C	51.	C
7.	C	22.	E	37.	D	52.	C
8.	E	23.	C	38.	A	53.	A
9.	B	24.	C	39.	D	54.	D
10.	D	25.	C	40.	B	55.	D
11.	D	26.	B	41.	C	56.	C
12.	D	27.	D	42.	B	57.	A
13.	E	28.	A	43.	E	58.	A
14.	D	29.	A	44.	E	59.	B
15.	D	30.	D	45.	B	60.	D

_____

ABSTRACT REASONING
SPATIAL RELATIONS/TWO DIMENSIONS

COMMENTARY

Since intelligence exists in many forms or phases and the theory of differential aptitudes is now firmly established in testing, other manifestations and measurements of intelligence than verbal or purely arithmetical must be identified and measured.

The spatial relations test, including that phase designated as spatial perception, involves and measures the ability to solve problems, drawn up in the form of outlines or pictures, which are concerned with the shapes of objects or the interrelationship of their parts. While, concededly, little is known about the nature and scope of this aptitude, it appears that this ability is required in science, mathematics, engineering, and drawing courses and curricula. Accordingly, tests of spatial perception involving the reconstruction of two-dimensional patterns, are presented in this section.

It is to be noted that the relationships expressed in spatial tests are geometric, definitive, and exact. Keeping these basic characteristics in mind, the applicant is to proceed to solve the spatial perception problems in his own way. There is no set method of solving these problems. The examinee may find that there are different methods for different types of spatial problems. Therefore, the BEST way to prepare for this type of test is to *TAKE* and study the work-practice problems in two-dimensional patterns provided in this section.

———

ABSTRACT REASONING
SPATIAL RELATIONS/TWO DIMENSIONS

The tests of spatial relations that follow consist of items which involve the visualization of two dimensions.

Each of the items of these tests consists of a line of figures -- a complete figure on the left and four lettered alternatives of component parts on the right, only one of which can be fitted together exactly to form the complete figure on the left.

The candidate is then required to select that choice of component parts which could be fitted together to form the complete figure given at the left.

SAMPLE QUESTIONS AND EXPLANATIONS

DIRECTIONS: The items in this part constitute a test of spatial relations involving two dimensions. Each item consists of a line of figures. The first figure is the complete figure. This is followed by four lettered choices of component parts, only one of which can be fitted together exactly to form the first (complete) figure.
Rules to be followed:
1. The lettered choice of component parts selected as the answer must have the same number of parts as the first (complete) figure.
2. The parts must fit exactly.
3. The parts may be turned around but may not be turned over.

1.

The correct answer is D. When the two parts of D are completely closed, they form the complete figure on the left.

2.

The correct answer is B. When the two parts of B are reversed in position, they form the complete figure on the left.

TEST 1

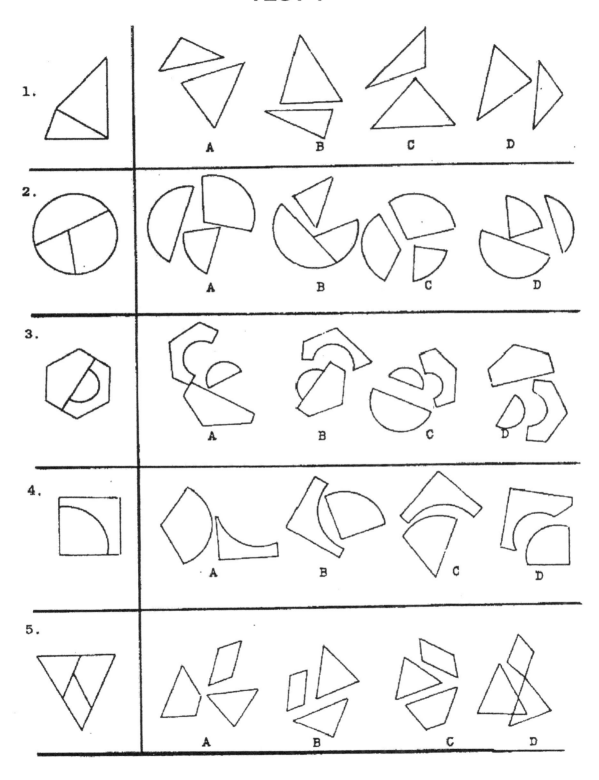

1.
A B C D

2.
A B C D

3.
A B C D

4.
A B C D

5.
A B C D

KEY (CORRECT ANSWERS)

1. B
2. A
3. D
4. B
5. C

TEST 2

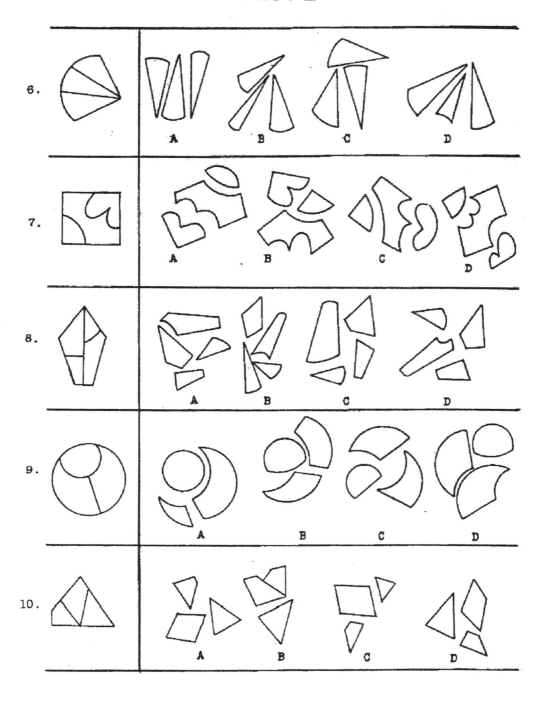

6.

    A   B   C   D

7.

    A   B   C   D

8.

    A   B   C   D

9.

    A   B   C   D

10.

    A   B   C   D

KEY (CORRECT ANSWERS)

6. C
7. B
8. A
9. D
10. B

———

TEST 3

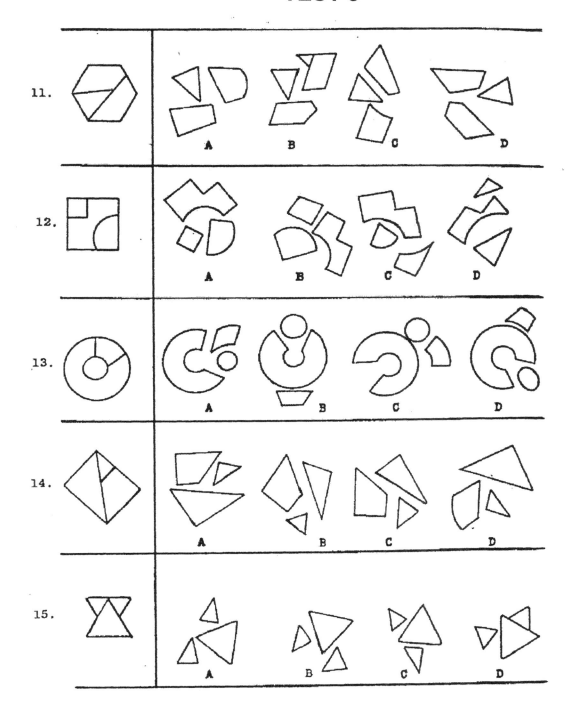

KEY (CORRECT ANSWERS)

11. D
12. A
13. C
14. A
15. D

———

TEST 4

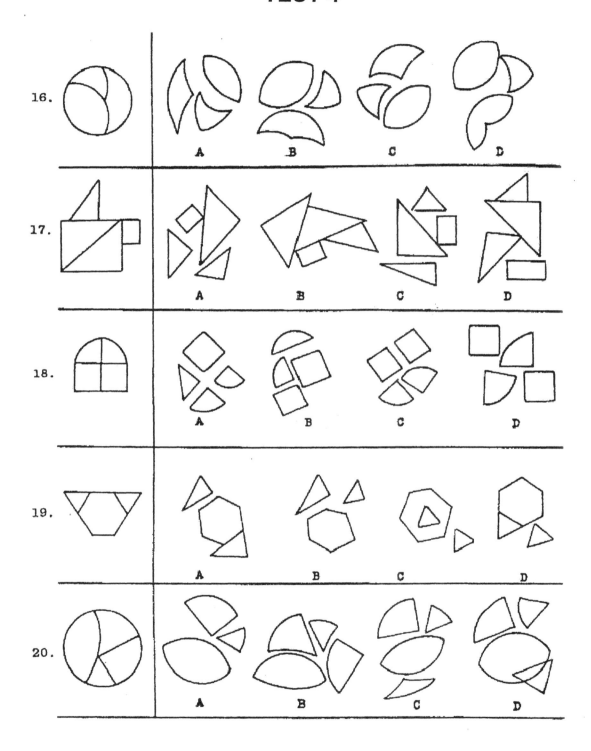

KEY (CORRECT ANSWERS)

16. B
17. B
18. C
19. D
20. B

TEST 5

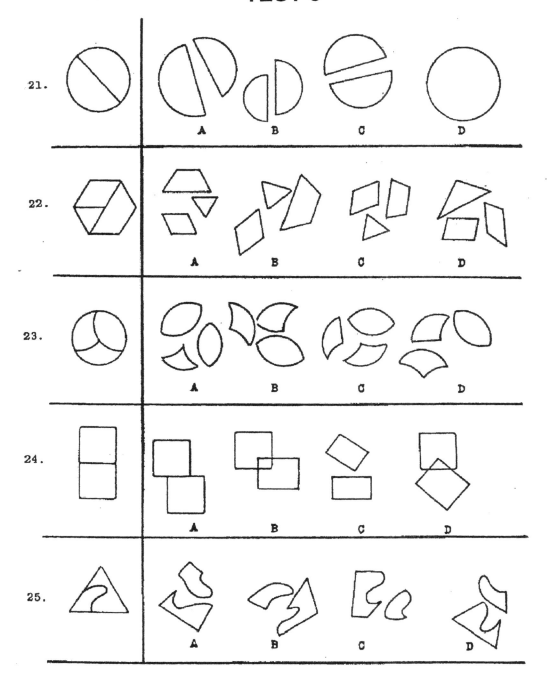

KEY (CORRECT ANSWERS)

21. C
22. B
23. B
24. A
25. D

———

NUMBER SERIES PROBLEMS
COMMENTARY

Number series problems constitute an important means for measuring quantitative ability on the part of applicants for beginning and trainee positions as well as for regular, mid-level, and senior level positions.

In this method, numerical reasoning forms the primary technic for measuring mathematic-cal ability.

This test measures your ability to think with numbers instead of words.

In each problem, you are given a series of numbers that are changing according to a rule - followed by five sets of 2 numbers each. Your problem is to figure out a rule that would make one of the five sets the next two numbers in the series.

The problems do not use hard arithmetic. The task is merely to see how the numbers are related to each other. The sample questions will explain several types in detail so that you may become familiar with what you have to do.

HINTS FOR ANSWERING NUMBER SERIES QUESTIONS

1. Do the ones that are easier for you *first.* Then go back and work on the others. Enough time is allowed for you to do all the questions, provided you don't stay too long on the ones you have trouble answering.
2. Sound out the series to yourself. You may hear the rule: 2468 10 12 14 ... What are the next two numbers?
3. Look at the series carefully. You may see the rule: 9294969... What are the next two numbers?
4. If you can't hear it or see it, you may have to figure it out by writing down how the numbers are changing: 6 8 16 18 26 28 36 ... What are the next two numbers?

   6^{+2} 8^{+8} 16^{+2} 18^{+8} 26^{+2} 28^{+8} 36.... What are the next two numbers if this is +2 +8? 36 + 2 = 38 + 8 = 46 or 38 46. You would mark the letter of the answer that goes with 38 46.
5. If none of the answers given fits the rule you have figured out, try again. Try to figure out a rule that makes one of the five answers a correct one.
6. Don't spend too much time on any one question. Skip it and come back. A fresh look sometimes helps.

———

SAMPLE QUESTIONS

DIRECTIONS: In each of the questions in this test, there is at the top a series of numbers which follow some definite order and, below, five sets of two numbers each. You are to look at the numbers in the series at the top and find out what order they follow. Then decide what the next two numbers in that series would be if the same order were continued. Next find these two numbers in one of the sets below. *PRINT THE LETTER OF THE CORRECT ANSWER IN THE SPACE AT THE RIGHT.*

1. 1 2 3 4 5 6 7 .....   1.____

    A. 1 2   B. 5 6   C. 8 9   D. 4 5   E. 7 8

    How are these numbers changing? The numbers in this series are increasing by 1 or the rule is "add 1." If you apply this rule to the series, what would the next two numbers be? 7+1=8+1=9.
    Therefore, the CORRECT answer is 8 and 9, and you would select C. 8 9 as your answer.

2. 15 14 13 12 11 10 9 ....   2.____

    A. 2 1   B. 17 16   C. 8 9   D. 8 7   E. 9 8

    The numbers in this series are decreasing by 1 or the rule is "subtract 1." If you apply that rule, what would the next two numbers be? 9-1=8-1=7. The CORRECT answer is 8 and 7, and you would select D. 8 7 as your answer.

3. 20 20 21 21 22 22 23 ....   3.____

    A. 23 23   B. 23 24   C. 19 19   D. 22 23   E. 21 22

    In this series each number is repeated and then increased by 1. The rule is "repeat , add 1. repeat, add 1, etc." The series would be $20^{+0}20^{+1}21^{+0}21^{+1}22^{+0}22^{+1}23^{+0}23^{+1}24$. The CORRECT answer is 23 and 24, and you should have selected B. 23 24 as your answer.

4. 17 3 17 4 17 5 17 ....   4.____

    A. 6 17   B. 6 7   C. 17 6   D. 5 6   E. 17 7

    If you can't find a single rule for all the numbers in a series, see if there are really two series in the problem. This series is the number 17 separated by numbers increasing by 1, starting with 3. If the series were continued for two more numbers, it would read 17 3 17 4 17 5 17 6 17. The CORRECT answer is 6 and 17, and you should have selected A. 6 17 for question 4.

5. 1 2 4 5 7 8 10 ....   5.____

    A. 11 12   B. 12 14   C. 10 13   D. 12 13   E. 11 13

    The rule in this series is not easy to see until you actually set down how the numbers are changing: $I^{+1}2^{+2}4^{+1}5^{+2}7^{+1}8^{+2}10$. The numbers in this series are increasing first by 1 (that is, plus 1) and then by 2 (that is, plus 2). If the series were continued for two more numbers, it would read: 1 2 4 5 7 8 10 (plus 1) which is 11 (plus 2) which is 13. Therefore, the CORRECT answer is 11 and 13, and you should have selected E. 11 13 for question 5.

NOW READ AND WORK SAMPLE QUESTIONS 6 THROUGH 10 AND MARK FOUR ANSWERS IN THE SPACE PROVIDED AT THE RIGHT.

6. 21 21 20 20 19 19 18 ....
    A. 18 18   B. 18 17   C. 17 18   D. 17 17   E. 18 19   6.____

7. 1 22 1 23 1 24 1 ....
    A. 2 61   B. 25 26   C. 2 51   D. 1 26   E. 1 25   7.____

8. 1 20 3 19 5 18 7 ....
    A. 8 9   B. 8 17   C. 17 10   D. 17 9   E. 9 18   8.____

9. 4 7 10 13 16 19 22 ...
    A. 23 26   B. 25 27   C. 25 26   D. 25 28   E. 24 27   9.____

10. 30 2 28 4 26 6 24 ....
    A. 23 9   B. 26 8   C. 8 9   D. 26 22   E. 8 22   10.____

EXPLANATIONS FOR QUESTIONS 6 THROUGH 10.

6. Each number in the series repeats itself and then decreases by 1 or minus 1; 21 (repeat) 21 (minus 1) which makes 20 (repeat) 20 (minus 1) which makes 19 (repeat) 19 (minus 1) which makes 18 (repeat) ? (minus 1) ? The CORRECT answer is B.
7. The number 1 is separated by numbers which begin with 22 and increase by 1; 1 22 1 (increase 22 by 1) which makes 23 1 (increase 23 by 1) which makes 24 1 (increase 24 by 1) which makes ? The CORRECT answer is C.
8. This is best explained by two alternating series - one series starts with 1 and increases by 2 or plus 2; the other series starts with 20 and decreases by 1 or minus 1. The CORRECT answer is D.

1↑3↑5↑7↑?

9. This series of numbers increases by 3 (plus 3) beginning with the first number - 4 (plus 3) 7 (plus 3) 10 (plus 3) 13 (plus 3) 16 (plus 3) 19 (plus 3) 22 (plus 3) ? The CORRECT answer is D.
10. Look for two alternating series - one series starts with 30 and decreases by 2 (minus 2); the other series starts with 2 and increases by 2 (plus 2). The CORRECT answer is E.

30↑28↑26↑24↑?
2   4   6   7

KEY (CORRECT ANSWERS)

1.	C	6.	B
2.	D	7.	C
3.	B	8.	D
4.	A	9.	D
5.	E	10.	E

NUMBER SERIES PROBLEMS
EXAMINATION SECTION
TEST 1

DIRECTIONS : In each of the questions in this test, there is at the top a series of numbers which follow some definite order and, below, five sets of two numbers each. You are to look at the numbers in the series at the top and find out what order they follow. Then decide what the next two numbers in that series would be if the same order were continued. Next find these two numbers in one of the sets below. *PRINT THE LETTER OF THE CORRECT ANSWER IN THE SPACE AT THE RIGHT.*

1. 5 6 20 7 8 19 9 ....   1.____
   - A. 10 18
   - B. 18 17
   - C. 10 17
   - D. 18 19
   - E. 10 11

2. 9 10 1 11 12 2 13 ....   2.____
   - A. 2 14
   - B. 3 14
   - C. 14 3
   - D. 14 15
   - E. 14 1

3. 4 6 9 11 14 16 19 ....   3.____
   - A. 21 24
   - B. 22 25
   - C. 20 22
   - D. 21 23
   - E. 22 24

4. 8 8 1 10 10 3 12 ....   4.____
   - A. 13 13
   - B. 12 5
   - C. 12 4
   - D. 13 5
   - E. 4 12

5. 14 1 2 15 3 4 16 ....   5.____
   - A. 5 16
   - B. 6 7
   - C. 5 17
   - D. 5 6
   - E. 17 5

6. 10 12 50 15 17 50 20 ....   6.____
   - A. 50 21
   - B. 21 50
   - C. 50 22
   - D. 22 50
   - E. 22 24

7. 1 2 3 50 4 5 6 51 7 8 ....   7.____
   - A. 9 10
   - B. 9 52
   - C. 51 10
   - D. 10 52
   - E. 10 50

8. 20 21 23 24 27 28 32 33 38 39 ....   8.____
   - A. 45 46
   - B. 45 52
   - C. 44 45
   - D. 44 49
   - E. 40 46

9. 17 15 21 18 10 16 19 ....   9.____
   - A. 20 5
   - B. 5 11
   - C. 11 11
   - D. 11 20
   - E. 15 14

10. 12 16 10 14 8 12 6 ....   10.____
    - A. 10 14
    - B. 10 8
    - C. 10 4
    - D. 4 10
    - E. 4 2

KEY (CORRECT ANSWERS)

1.	A	6.	D
2.	C	7.	B
3.	A	8.	A
4.	B	9.	B
5.	D	10.	C

TEST 2

DIRECTIONS : In each of the questions in this test, there is at the top a series of numbers which follow some definite order and, below, five sets of two numbers each. You are to look at the numbers in the series at the top and find out what order they follow. Then decide what the next two numbers in that series would be if the same order were continued. Next find these two numbers in one of the sets below. *PRINT THE LETTER OF THE CORRECT ANSWER IN THE SPACE AT THE RIGHT.*

1. 10 11 12 10 11 12 10 ....   1.____
    A. 10 13   B. 12 10   C. 11 10   D. 11 12   E. 10 12

2. 4 6 7 4 6 7 4   2.____
    A. .6 7   B. 4 7   C. 7 6   D. 7 4   E. 6 8

3. 7 7 3 7 7 4 7 ....   3.____
    A. 4 5   B. 4 7   C. 5 7   D. 7 5   E. 7 7

4. 3 4 10 5 6 10 7 ....   4.____
    A. 10 8   B. 9 8   C. 8 14   D. 8 9   E. 8 10

5. 6 6 7 7 8 8 9 ....   5.____
    A. 10 11   B. 10 10   C. 9 10   D. 9 9   E. 10 9

6. 3 8 9 4 9 10 5 ....   6.____
    A. 6 10   B. 10 11   C. 9 10   D. 11 6   E. 10 6

7. 2 4 3 6 4 8 5 ....   7.____
    A. 6 10   B. 10 7   C. 10 6   D. 9 6   E. 6 7

8. 11 5 9 7 7 9 5 ....   8.____
    A. 11 3   B. 7 9   C. 7 11   D. 9 7   E. 3 7

9. 12 10 8 8 6 4 4 ....   9.____
    A. 2 2   B. 6 4   C. 6 2   D. 4 6   E. 2 0

10. 20 22 22 19 21 21 18 ....   10.____
    A. 22 22   B. 19 19   C. 20 20   D. 20 17   E. 19 17

KEY (CORRECT ANSWERS)

1. D	6. B
2. A	7. C
3. D	8. A
4. E	9. E
5. C	10. C

TEST 3

DIRECTIONS : In each of the questions in this test, there is at the top a series of numbers which follow some definite order and, below, five sets of two numbers each. You are to look at the numbers in the series at the top and find out what order they follow. Then decide what the next two numbers in that series would be if the same order were continued. Next find these two numbers in one of the sets below. *PRINT THE LETTER OF THE CORRECT ANSWER IN THE SPACE AT THE RIGHT.*

1. 5 7 6 10 7 13 8 ....   1.____
    A. 16 9   B.   16 10   C.   9 15   D.   10 15   E.   15 9

2. 13 10 11 15 12 13 17 ....   2.____
    A. 18 14   B.   18 15   C.   15 16   D.   14 15   E.   15 18

3. 30 27 24 21 18 15 12 ....   3.____
    A. 9 3   B.   9 6   C.   6 3   D.   12 9   E.   8 5

4. 3 7 10 5 8 10 7 ....   4.____
    A. 10 11   B.   10 5   C.   10 9   D.   10 10   E.   9 10

5. 12 4 13 6 14 8 15 ....   5.____
    A. 10 17   B.   17 10   C.   10 12   D.   16 10   E.   10 16

6. 21 8 18 20 7 17 19 ....   6.____
    A. 16 18   B.   18. 6   C.   6 16   D.   5 15   E.   6 18

7. 14 16 16 18 20 20 22 ....   7.____
    A. 22 24   B.   26 28   C.   24 26   D.   24 24   E.   24 28

8. 5 6 8 9 12 13 17 ....   8.____
    A. 18 23   B.   13 18   C.   18 22   D.   23 24   E.   18 19

9. 1 3 5 5 2 4 6 6 3....   9.____
    A. 74   B.   55   C.   13   D.   57   E.   77

10. 12 24 15 25 18 26 21 ....   10.____
    A. 27 22   B.   24 22   C.   29 24   D.   27 27   E.   27 24

KEY (CORRECT ANSWERS)

1.	A	6.	C
2.	D	7.	D
3.	B	8.	A
4.	E	9.	D
5.	E	10.	E

TEST 4

DIRECTIONS : In each of the questions in this test, there is at the top a series of numbers which follow some definite order and, below, five sets of two numbers each. You are to look at the numbers in the series at the top and find out what order they follow. Then decide what the next two numbers in that series would be if the same order were continued. Next find these two numbers in one of the sets below. *PRINT THE LETTER OF THE CORRECT ANSWER IN THE SPACE AT THE RIGHT.*

1. 8 9 9 8 10 10 8 ....   1.____
    A. 11 8   B. 8 13   C. 8 11   D. 11 11   E. 8 8

2. 10 10 11 11 12 12 13 ....   2.____
    A. 15 15   B. 13 13   C. 14 14   D. 13 14   E. 14 15

3. 6 6 10 6 6 12 6 ....   3.____
    A. 6 14   B. 13 6   C. 14 6   D. 6 13   E. 6 6

4. 17 11 5 16 10 4 15 ....   4.____
    A. 13 9   B. 13 11   C. 8 5   D. 9 5   E. 9 3

5. 1 3 2 4 3 5 4 ....   5.____
    A. 6 8   B. 5 6   C. 6 5   D. 3 4   E. 3 5

6. 11 11 10 12 12 11 13 ....   6.____
    A. 12 14   B. 14 12   C. 14 14   D. 13 14   E. 13 12

7. 18 5 6 18 7 8 18 ....   7.____
    A. 9 9   B. 9 10   C. 18 9   D. 8 9   E. 18 7

8. 7 8 9 13 10 11 12 14 13 14 ....   8.____
    A. 15 16   B. 13 15   C. 14 15   D. 15 15   E. 13 14

9. 5 7 30 9 11 30 13 ....   9.____
    A. 15 16   B. 15 17   C. 14 17   D. 15 30   E. 30 17

10. 5 7 11 13 17 19 23 ....   10.____
    A. 27 29   B. 25 29   C. 25 27   D. 27 31   E. 29 31

KEY (CORRECT ANSWERS)

1.	D		6.	E
2.	D		7.	B
3.	A		8.	D
4.	E		9.	D
5.	C		10.	B

TEST 5

DIRECTIONS : In each of the questions in this test, there is at the top a series of numbers which follow some definite order and, below, five sets of two numbers each. You are to look at the numbers in the series at the top and find out what order they follow. Then decide what the next two numbers in that series would be if the same order were continued. Next find these two numbers in one of the sets below. *PRINT THE LETTER OF THE CORRECT ANSWER IN THE SPACE AT THE RIGHT.*

1. 9 15 10 17 12 19 15 21 19....

    A. 23 24   B. 25 23   C. 17 23   D. 23 31   E. 21 24   1.____

2. 34 37 30 33 26 29 22 ....

    A. 17 8   B. 18 11   C. 25 28   D. 25 20   E. 25 18   2.____

3. 10 16 12 14 14 12 16 ....

    A. 14 12   B. 10 18   C. 10 14   D. 14 18   E. 14 16   3.____

4. 11 12 18 11 13 19 11 14 ....

    A. 18 11   B. 16 11   C. 20 11   D. 11 21   E. 17 11   4.____

5. 20 9 8 19 10 9 18 11 10 ....

    A. 19 11   B. 17 10   C. 19 12   D. 17 12   E. 19 10   5.____

6. 28 27 26 31 30 29 34 ....

    A. 36 32   B. 32 31   C. 33 32   D. 33 36   E. 35 36   6.____

7. 10 16 14 20 18 24 22 ....

    A. 28 32   B. 27 26   C. 28 26   D. 26 28   E. 27 28   7.____

8. 9 9 7 8 7 7 9 10 5 ....

    A. 5 11   B. 11 12   C. 5 9   D. 9 11   E. 5 5   8.____

9. 5 7 11 17 10 12 16 22 15 17 ....

    A. 27 26   B. 19 23   C. 19 27   D. 21 23   E. 21 27   9.____

10. 12 19 13 20 14 21 15 ....

    A. 16 17   B. 22 16   C. 16 22   D. 15 22   E. 15 16   10.____

KEY (CORRECT ANSWERS)

6.	A	11.	C
7.	E	12.	C
8.	B	13.	A
9.	C	14.	E
10.	D	15.	B

TEST 6

DIRECTIONS : In each of the questions in this test, there is at the top a series of numbers which follow some definite order and, below, five sets of two numbers each. You are to look at the numbers in the series at the top and find out what order they follow. Then decide what the next two numbers in that series would be if the same order were continued. Next find these two numbers in one of the sets below. *PRINT THE LETTER OF THE CORRECT ANSWER IN THE SPACE AT THE RIGHT.*

1. 13 12 8 11 10 8 9 ....   1.____
    A. 8 7   B. 6 8   C. 8 6   D. 8 8   E. 7 8

2. 13 18 13 17 13 16 13 ....   2.____
    A. 15 13   B. 13 14   C. 13 15   D. 14 15   E. 15 14

3. 13 13 10 12 12 10 11 ....   3.____
    A. 10 10   B. 10 9   C. 11 9   D. 9 11   E. 11 10

4. 6 5 4 6 5 4 6....   4.____
    A. 4 6   B. 6 4   C. 5 4   D. 5 6   E. 4 5

5. 10 10 9 8 8 7 6 ....   5.____
    A. 5 5   B. 5 4   C. 6 5   D. 6 4   E. 5 3

6. 20 16 18 14 16 12 14 ....   6.____
    A. 16 12   B. 10 12   C. 16 18   D. 12 12   E. 12 10

7. 7 12 8 11 9 10 10 ....   7.____
    A. 11 9   B. 9 8   C. 9 11   D. 10 11   E. 9 10

8. 13 13 12 15 15 14 17 ....   8.____
    A. 17 16   B. 14 17   C. 16 19   D. 19 19   E. 16 16

9. 19 18 12 17 16 13 15 ....   9.____
    A. 16 12   B. 14 14   C. 12 14   D. 14 12   E. 12 16

10. 7 15 12 8 16 13 9 ....   10.____
    A. 17 14   B. 17 10   C. 14 10   D. 14 17   E. 10 14

KEY (CORRECT ANSWERS)

1.	D		6.	B
2.	A		7.	C
3.	E		8.	A
4.	C		9.	B
5.	C		10.	A

TEST 7

DIRECTIONS : In each of the questions in this test, there is at the top a series of numbers which follow some definite order and, below, five sets of two numbers each. You are to look at the numbers in the series at the top and find out what order they follow. Then decide what the next two numbers in that series would be if the same order were continued. Next find these two numbers in one of the sets below. *PRINT THE LETTER OF THE CORRECT ANSWER IN THE SPACE AT THE RIGHT.*

1. 18 15 6 16 14 6 14 ....   1.____
   A. 12 6   B. 14 13   C. 6 12   D. 13 12   E. 13 6

2. 6 6 5 8 8 7 10 10 ....   2.____
   A. 8 12   B. 9 12   C. 12 12   D. 12 9   E. 9 9

3. 17 20 23 26 29 32 35 ....   3.____
   A. 37 40   B. 41 44   C. 38 41   D. 38 42   E. 36 39

4. 15 5 7 16 9 11 17 ....   4.____
   A. 18 13   B. 15 17   C. 12 19   D. 13 15   E. 12 13

5. 19 17 16 16 13 15 10 ....   5.____
   A. 14 7   B. 12 9   C. 14 9   D. 7 12   E. 10 14

6. 11 1 16 10 6 21 9 ....   6.____
   A. 12 26   B. 26 8   C. 11 26   D. 11 8   E. 8 11

7. 21 21 19 17 17 15 13 ....   7.____
   A. 11 11   B. 13 11   C. 11 9   D. 9 7   E. 13 13

8. 23 22 20 19 16 15 11 ....   8.____
   A. 6 5   B. 10 9   C. 6 1   D. 10 6   E. 10 5

9. 17 10 16 9 14 8 11 ....   9.____
   A. 7 11   B. 7 7   C. 10 4   D. 4 10   E. 7 4

10. 11 9 14 12 17 15 20 18 23 ....   10.____
   A. 21 24   B. 26 21   C. 21 26   D. 24 27   E. 26 29

KEY (CORRECT ANSWERS)

1.	E	6.	C
2.	B	7.	B
3.	C	8.	E
4.	D	9.	B
5.	A	10.	C

TEST 8

DIRECTIONS : In each of the questions in this test, there is at the top a series of numbers which follow some definite order and, below, five sets of two numbers each. You are to look at the numbers in the series at the top and find out what order they follow. Then decide what the next two numbers in that series would be if the same order were continued. Next find these two numbers in one of the sets below. *PRINT THE LETTER OF THE CORRECT ANSWER IN THE SPACE AT THE RIGHT.*

1. 13 4 5 13 6 7 13 ....   1._____

   A. 13 8   B. 8 13   C. 8 9   D. 8 8   E. 7 8

2. 10 10 9 11 11 10 12 ....   2._____

   A. 13 14   B. 12 11   C. 13 13   D. 12 12   E. 12 13

3. 6 6 8 10 10 12 14 ....   3._____

   A. 14 14   B. 14 16   C. 16 16   D. 12 14   E. 10 10

4. 8 1 9 3 10 5 11 ....   4._____

   A. 7 12   B. 6 12   C. 12 6   D. 7 8   E. 6 7

5. 30 11 24 12 19 14 15 17 12 21 10 ....   5._____

   A. 23 8   B. 25 8   C. 26 9   D. 24 9   E. 25 9

6. 24 30 29 22 28 27 19 26 25 15 24 ....   6._____

   A. 14 23   B. 19 18   C. 23 22   D. 25 11   E. 23 10

7. 7 5 9 7 11 9 13 ....   7._____

   A. 11 14   B. 10 15   C. 11 15   D. 12 14   E. 10 14

8. 9 10 11 7 8 9 5 ....   8._____

   A. 6 7   B. 7 8   C. 5 6   D. 6 4   E. 7 5

9. 8 9 10 10 9 10 11 11 10 11 12 ....   9._____

   A. 11 12   B. 12 10   C. 11 11   D. 12 11   E. 11 13

10. 5 6 8 9 12 13 17 18 23 24 ....   10._____

    A. 30 31   B. 25 31   C. 29 30   D. 25 30   E. 30 37

KEY (CORRECT ANSWERS)

1.	C	6.	E
2.	B	7.	C
3.	B	8.	A
4.	A	9.	D
5.	C	10.	A

TEST 9

DIRECTIONS : In each of the questions in this test, there is at the top a series of numbers which follow some definite order and, below, five sets of two numbers each. You are to look at the numbers in the series at the top and find out what order they follow. Then decide what the next two numbers in that series would be if the same order were continued. Next find these two numbers in one of the sets below. *PRINT THE LETTER OF THE CORRECT ANSWER IN THE SPACE AT THE RIGHT.*

1. 8 9 10 8 9 10 8 ....   1._____
   A. 89   B. 910   C. 98   D. 108   E. 810

2. 3 4 4 3 5 5 3....   2._____
   A. 33   B. 63   C. 36   D. 66   E. 6 7

3. 7 7 3 7 7 4 7....   3._____
   A. 77   B. 78   C. 57   D. 87   E. 75

4. 18 18 19 20 20 21 22 ....   4._____
   A. 22 23   B. 23 24   C. 23 23   D. 22 22   E. 21 22

5. 2 6 10 3 7 11 4 ....   5._____
   A. 12 16   B. 5 9   C. 8 5   D. 12 5   E. 8 12

6. 11 8 15 12 19 16 23 ....   6._____
   A. 27 20   B. 24 20   C. 27 24   D. 20 24   E. 20 27

7. 16 8 15 9 14 10 13 ....   7._____
   A. 12 11   B. 13 12   C. 11 13   D. 11 12   E. 11 14

8. 4 5 13 6 7 12 8 .0...   8._____
   A. 9 11   B. 13 9   C. 9 13   D. 11 9   E. 11 10

9. 3 8 4 9 5 10 6 11 7....   9._____
   A. 7 11   B. 7 8   C. 11 8   D. 12 7   E. 12 8

10. 18 14 19 17 20 20 21 ....   10._____
    A. 22 24   B. 14 19   C. 24 21   D. 21 23   E. 23 22

KEY (CORRECT ANSWERS)

1.	B		6.	E
2.	D		7.	D
3.	E		8.	A
4.	A		1.	E
5.	E		2.	E